Hoe, Heaven, and Hell

Hoe, Heaven, and Hell

MY BOYHOOD IN RURAL NEW MEXICO

❖ ❖ ❖

Nasario García

FOREWORD BY MARC SIMMONS

UNIVERSITY OF NEW MEXICO PRESS • ALBUQUERQUE

LIBRARY OF CONGRESS CATALOGING-IN-PUBLICATION DATA
García, Nasario.
Hoe, heaven, and hell : my boyhood in rural New Mexico / Nasario García ;
foreword by Marc Simmons.
pages cm
Includes bibliographical references.
ISBN 978-0-8263-5565-2 (pbk. : alk. paper) — ISBN 978-0-8263-5566-9 (electronic)
1. García, Nasario—Childhood and youth. 2. New Mexico—Biography.
I. Title.
PQ7079.2.G35Z46 2015
868'.64—dc23
[B]
2014021675

COVER PHOTOGRAPH: Nasario García on his horse Bayito, c. 1944. Ojo del Padre.
All photos courtesy of the author unless otherwise noted.
DESIGNED BY Lila Sanchez
COMPOSED IN Minion; display type is Meridien and Optima

In Memoriam

In honor of my

paternal grandparents,

Teodoro and Emilia Padilla García;

my beloved parents;

and all former Río Puerco Valley residents.

Que en paz descansen.

The deep furrows of yesterday are today's graves of memories.

—NASARIO GARCÍA

En este mundo no hay nada mejor que ser uno de buen corazón.
On this earth there is nothing better than to have a kind heart.

—AGAPITA LÓPEZ-GARCÍA
(Nasario García's mother)

Contents

Foreword

We are fortunate that New Mexico's leading folklorist, Nasario García, has poured several years of effort into the writing of this autobiographical account of his early years growing up in the remote valley of the Río Puerco. The author has a keen memory for small details of daily life in a rural community, where many customs and practices from the distant past survived into the mid-twentieth century.

Born in 1936, García spent his childhood in a simple two-room adobe house outside the village of Ojo del Padre (later renamed Guadalupe). He watched his hardworking parents struggle to wrest a living from the land, farming and raising livestock. By 1945 changing times and environmental hardships obliged the Garcías and neighboring families to pull up stakes and retreat eastward to Albuquerque and its satellite towns on the Río Grande, where wage labor could be had. The abandoned towns and farms of the Río Puerco fell into ruin, to be inhabited by vagrant ghosts.

For the boy Nasario, who began his childhood education in a one-room schoolhouse, his delivery into the modern world would open undreamed-of opportunities in higher education. In time he received his BA and MA degrees in Spanish and Portuguese at the University of New Mexico. After advanced studies at the University of Granada, Spain, he received his PhD in nineteenth-century Spanish literature from the University of Pittsburgh.

There followed a busy career as a professor and lecturer in this country and abroad. With the passage of years, Nasario García increasingly turned his attention toward writing, with a focus upon New Mexico's distinctive Spanish language and culture. Both, as he has lamented, are on the point of being lost by the younger generations of Hispanos.

Specifically, he has warned, "The linguistic and cultural treasures our ancestors have bequeathed to us since colonial days are slowly being eroded by apathy, technological intrusion, and assimilation into the Anglo culture."

García himself has not surrendered to the trend, for among the more than twenty books he has thus far published, the majority are collections of folkways he obtained from the lips of old-timers. As an author he has provided English translations, resulting in bilingual editions.

Nothing in García's previous output, however, can rival in either size or scope his new volume, *Hoe, Heaven, and Hell: My Boyhood in Rural New Mexico*. Drawing upon his own experiences as well as the memories of the *viejitos*, old-timers, in his valley, including his own parents and paternal grandparents (all of them now deceased), he has faithfully resurrected the flesh and bones, verbally at least, of the old lifestyle that once existed along the Río Puerco. Further, his memoir is presented in a skilled narrative that avoids any hint of pretension or tediousness.

Altogether *Hoe, Heaven, and Hell* offers a wealth of information and at the same time is a delight to read, at least for those who have some curiosity concerning the parameters of New Mexico's Hispanic heritage, one of America's great cultural treasures.

MARC SIMMONS, HISTORIAN

Acknowledgments

Seeing one's work come to fruition can oftentimes be a long and arduous process, but a collective effort has been made by a core of dedicated professionals at the University of New Mexico Press, in particular W. Clark Whitehorn, editor-in-chief; Katherine White, marketing and sales manager; Lauren Consuelo Tussing, publicist; and Lila Sanchez, designer. I tip my hat to each one of them. Last but not least, a special word of gratitude goes to the copyeditor, Diana Rico, for a superb job of editing the manuscript.

Introduction

Hoe, Heaven, and Hell: My Boyhood in Rural New Mexico is a genuine effort at recapturing my boyhood during the 1940s in Ojo del Padre (called Guadalupe in more modern times), where I spent the formative years of my life with my parents and siblings on my paternal grandparents' ranch. Ojo del Padre, today a ghost town whose adobe buildings are crumbling and, sadly, melting into the ground, is situated in the Río Puerco Valley southeast of Chaco Canyon.

My memoir takes the reader back to a bygone era replete with an assortment of thrilling, joyful, and sad recollections that may seem more than a trifle anachronistic to most of us in this modern age of dizzying technological frenzy.

A handful of New Mexican Hispanics have authored excellent biographies. Today two or three of these works with rural or semirural settings are considered classics, but the authors, who hailed from moderate to well-to-do families, described life from the top down. Conversely, I want readers to identify with my childhood by looking at it from the bottom up. In that way, they can learn what life was actually like seventy years ago for kids like me, whose richness stemmed more from a unified family and customs and traditions than it did from material goods.

Following my parents' marriage on June 17, 1935, my father, who was the youngest of six siblings, built a home next to his parents' dwelling. Like most Río Puercoans, my parents were poor and uneducated, but they were a proud and hardworking couple who did not dwell on their economic state or seek pity. Doing so would have been ignoble and counter to their pride. Evidence of self-respect meant, among other things, never failing to put food on the dinner table for their children and themselves.

Ranch life could be challenging because of the uncertainty people faced in eking out an existence from the land they loved and nurtured. Ominous droughts and adverse, changeable weather conditions in spring and summer at times hung over farmers' heads like a dark halo. Even women true to their abiding faith invoked the santos, religious statues, pleading to them for much-needed rain to soak the arid fields and thus rescue crops from total devastation. The often-meager yield of corn, a mainstay in every household, posed a threat to the farmers' continued existence, as well as to the animals they raised for consumption.

All things considered, not only did people cling to hope, but they also did not stand on ceremony waiting for a handout, because there was no such thing. Either you fended for yourself, or you and your family suffered the consequences. But let us be clear on at least one point: people were resilient, and they learned how to cope regardless of the challenges that confronted them.

As a young boy, I wondered whether the world beyond my village and my grandparents' rancho was similar to or different from mine. I would even ponder and question in my mind many aspects of our being, with no suitable answers at hand because we as kids were to be seen and not heard. Yet children espoused and practiced—as I did—the customs and folkways of our forefathers and foremothers. At times such undefined human qualities as personal *respeto y honor*, dignity and honor, both culturally charged terms, were our guiding beacons in the treatment of *el prójimo*, one's fellow man.

We emulated our parents and grandparents and extolled their enduring principles in exercising good moral judgment.

These days, as I reflect upon my childhood, I do so with certain reverence and nostalgia. At the same time, the cultural upbringing and values my parents instilled in my siblings and me in Ojo del Padre remain a constant part of my persona to this day. Unless a person is apathetic about the past, he or she can ill afford to toss those values out the kitchen door as though they were dirty dishwater.

The accounts in *Hoe, Heaven, and Hell* are testimony to the bare realities of an all-but-forgotten life and the world I was raised in. It is the life of a child who grew up with dirt under his fingernails (but never at the dinner table, for Mom would not allow that), a trademark of hard work and determination to survive at times against seemingly insurmountable odds.

But it is also the life of a happy child who grew up roaming the landscape on horseback, caring for animals—especially my rabbits and horses—and working in the cornfields. Shooting marbles, flying homemade kites, mending my own socks, and, yes, even learning how to embroider dish-towels alongside my mother were part of my upbringing.

From my heart and soul in the hinterland to the printed page, I have striven to portray my childhood years as I experienced them and to the best of my recollection. Such an affirmation is a tribute to my beloved parents. My mother's affection, altruism, and happy-go-lucky personality resonate implicitly and explicitly throughout every page of my remembrances. My father, on the other hand, tips the scales, so to speak, for he was the consummate perfectionist ("*Haz las cosas al revés y las haces otra vez. Haste makes waste,*" he used to say), self-disciplined, honest, exceedingly intelligent, and hardworking, just like my mother.

In the main, their spirit is what inspired me to put together *Hoe, Heaven, and Hell.* This work is a tribute to them that I now wish to share with readers who may have an interest in learning what life was like—but is no more—seventy years ago in rural Hispanic communities like mine.

NASARIO GARCÍA
SANTA FE, NEW MEXICO

Nasario P. García, author's father, with prominent butte in the background, 1984.

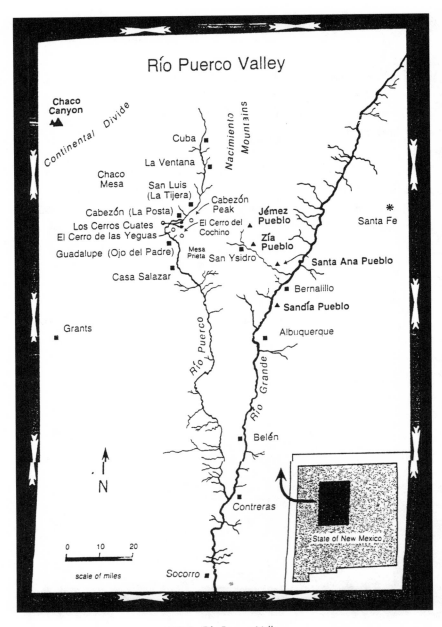

MAP 1. Río Puerco Valley.

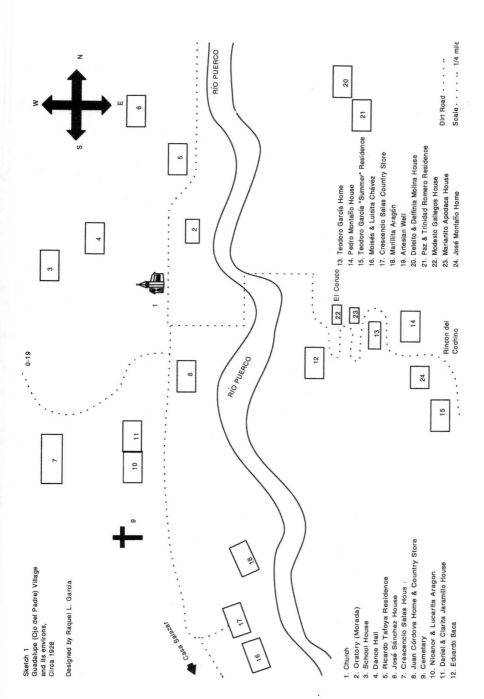

Sketch 1
Guadalupe (Ojo del Padre) Village
and its environs,
Circa 1928

Designed by Raquel L. Garcia

1. Church
2. Oratory (Morada)
3. School House
4. Dance Hall
5. Ricardo Tafoya Residence
6. José Sánchez House
7. Crescencio Salas House
8. Juan Córdova Home & Country Store
9. Cemetary
10. Nicanor & Lucarita Aragon
11. Daniel & Clarita Jaramillo House
12. Eduardo Baca

13. Teodoro García Home
14. Pedro Montaño House
15. Teodoro García "Summer" Residence
16. Moisés & Luisita Chávez
17. Crescencio Salas Country Store
18. Mar!ilita Aragón
19. Artesian Well
20. Deleito & Delfinia Molina House
21. Paz & Trinidad Romero Residence
22. Modesto Gallegos House
23. Marianito Apodaca House
24. José Montaño Home

El Coruco

Rincon del Cochino

Casa Salazar

RÍO PUERCO

Dirt Road · · · · · · ··
Scale · · · · · ·· 1/4 mile

MAP 2. Ojo del Padre (Guadalupe) village. Sketch by Raquel L. García.

Butte adjacent to the Río Puerco and near author's boyhood home, 1984.

1

My *Placita*

Setting the Stage

SURROUNDED BY BUTTES AND hills on all sides except to the east, where the Río Puerco meanders a scant one hundred yards away, today my *placita* of Ojo del Padre, also known as Guadalupe (see introduction), once the pride and joy of every Guadalupano, lies in somber ruins (see map 2). Like her neighboring villages of Cabezón (La Posta), San Luis (La Tijera), and Casa Salazar up and down the Río Puerco Valley, Ojo del Padre is emblematic of a glorious past etched only in historical treatises or the minds of those people who are still alive.

The foregoing communities fell victim to a chain of natural and man-made disasters. They include the fencing and loss of the Ojo del Espíritu Santo Grant; unreasonable government land-use regulations imposed on the farmer-rancher; the indiscriminate slaughtering of cattle by federal *rinches*, rangers; and soil erosion, poverty, and droughts.

With astronomical odds against every family, including my own parents, the allure of the Big City—Albuquerque and its outlying settlements—beckoned them. Within time people had no recourse but to tuck their pride under their shoes and abandon their beloved villages in search of new and elusive dreams. None would ever return to their former homes except for periodic visits, wondering if they could have done something differently to seal a more propitious fate.

The history of Ojo del Padre dates back to the 1760s and is deeply rooted in the Río Puerco Valley's past. According to some old-timers, my village

1

(also known in historical documents as Guadalupe de los García) earned its name after a priest inadvertently stumbled upon an *ojito*, spring, which to this day miraculously still oozes water from the ground near the epicenter of the once proud community. This natural spring at one time was the main water source for Ojo del Padre residents and for those like my family whose homes were scattered along the Río Puerco, away from the village.

Back in the eighteenth century the Navajos roamed and ruled the region until Governor Tomás Vélez Cachupín approved several land grants that opened the gates to two settlements. The first one was short-lived because of the tenuous relationship between Navajos and the recent Hispano settlers. The second settlement, which lasted almost a century, came one hundred years later—around 1860 or 1870. The Navajo Reservation was established in 1868, helping stabilize relationships between Hispanics and Navajos. Then again, sporadic Navajo incursions still continued to disrupt life until they petered out toward the end of the nineteenth century.

Such pronouncements are based on oral testimony from old-timers like my paternal grandmother, who migrated when she was a little girl from Corrales, northwest of Albuquerque, to the Río Puerco Valley during the 1890s with relatives of hers.

In examining the 1880 census, it is patently clear that by then Ojo del Padre, Casa Salazar, Cabezón, and San Luis (see map 1) were well established. At that time my village boasted a population of 161 inhabitants. That same census shows that Ojo del Padre and Casa Salazar, a few miles to the south, together numbered 361 residents, whereas in 1910, when they were listed jointly, their total population still stood at 357.

On the basis of the foregoing data, we can surmise that populations in the respective villages remained pretty much unchanged between 1880 and 1910 and shortly thereafter. With the advent of World War I, what began to change were the demographics. Healthy young men, most of them illiterate, were drafted and whisked off to fight in Europe. Some died abroad, while others were fortunate to come back alive, though disabled. They refused to return to ranch life. This triggered the beginning of an exodus that intensified little by little, until by the late 1950s it signaled the death knell of the four communities mentioned above, including my beloved placita of Ojo del Padre.

These days land in my valley is peppered with ghost towns and dilapi-dated homes that straddle the Río Puerco. They command little attention, let alone large monetary value, in comparison to other, less arid parts of New Mexico where water is not a scarce commodity.

A few heirs whose properties remain in their families continue to visit the Río Puerco Valley on weekends or during holidays. On occasion the curious or wayward tourist can be seen driving aimlessly on a winding dirt road, not knowing where he or she will end up. Treasure seekers with an insatiable appetite for buried treasures have ransacked abandoned homes or dug up dirt kitchen floors, as happened to my grandparents' dwelling, but their cravings have produced nothing.

My village proper as I was growing up in the early 1940s consisted of several families. Among them were the Salas, Aragón, Romero, Valdez, Sánchez, Tafoya, and Jaramillo households. The population, varying in ages, hovered, I would guesstimate, around fifty to sixty-five inhabitants.

The layout of Ojo del Padre during my childhood and a few years before I was born (see map 2) was quite traditional and typical of many Hispanic vil-lages of northern New Mexico. The church where I made my First Holy Communion, named for our local patroness, La Virgen de Guadalupe (Our Lady of Guadalupe), occupied center stage. The school, the dance hall, the oratory or *morada*—a praying refuge for the Penitentes, a Roman Catholic brotherhood, during Holy Week—the general store, the local post office, and private adobe dwellings acted as a supporting cast. Each entity, individually and collectively, hugged, cuddled, and offered the church sustenance and protection year-round, like a mother caring for her newborn child.

The mayordomos, usually a husband and wife team, both respected and active members of the community, served as caretakers of the church for at least one year and sometimes longer. Among other things, they were responsible for collecting *diezmos y primicias*, tithes and first fruits, offer-ing food and lodging to the visiting priest, overseeing year-round religious functions and activities, plus ensuring the physical upkeep of the church.

Every summer without fail a group of women from the placita banded together to mud plaster the church. They were considered the master mud plasterers and consequently played a vital role in caring for the exterior as well the inside condition of the church. Some women were *entronas*, tough enough to climb the ladder or the *burros*, scaffolds, to tackle the task at hand. The job of whitewashing the walls inside the church also fell on the women's shoulders, but that did not occur as often as mud plastering, perhaps every two years, since the elements were kinder to the church's interior. Keeping the white walls sparkling had a cosmetic purpose, but it also conveyed tidiness and local pride.

Though not exactly a perfunctory contribution in mud plastering, the men's role was to some degree much limited to hauling dirt, mixing it with water and straw, and plastering the upper portions of the church walls. They also repaired roof leaks in the spring, when the winter snow melted, or during the summers' monsoon seasons. Additionally, men helped to paint and repair windows and door frames.

Whether a family dwelled in the placita proper or in one of the outlying areas, as mine did, it was duty bound to support the tenets of the Roman Catholic Church. Upholding its religious precepts while raising children was second nature to every parent and grandparent. Some people were more religious than others, of course, but, overall, women in most cases were the spiritual leaders and standard bearers of family faith.

The Virgen de Guadalupe Church was central to everything that transpired in my village, be it religious or secular. From baptisms, weddings, First Holy Communions, events honoring the patron saint, and Lent to popular festivities like Saint John's Day, all revolved around the church. Barring inclement weather or the priest falling ill, Mass was celebrated once a month and for virtually every special occasion, whereupon the entire Ojo del Padre population descended on the placita to honor and participate in the respective celebrations. The church indeed was the magnet that drew people together, whether in moments of joy or of sadness.

And whenever people congregated, just about everyone seemed to refer to each other as *primo*, cousin, even if they weren't related by blood. This gesture of *primorazgo*, as it were, not only underscored unparalleled camaraderie among villagers, but it also symbolized the hallmark of unity that often transcended the community. The primorazgo phenomenon, as I call it, was far-reaching and profound.

My immediate family, along with my paternal grandparents and an aunt and uncle and their children, belonged to the Ojo del Padre community, even though our homes were located about two miles away. Collectively, the three families made up our own miniature village, but our loyalty to our placita was unequivocal.

My paternal grandfather, Teodoro José García, whom we grandchildren called Lolo, migrated to the Río Puerco Valley in the 1880s. He was about eight years old at the time. A brother named Ramón and his sister Paula accompanied their parents, Juan and Juliana. The entire family moved there from Algodones, approximately twenty miles north of Albuquerque, where my grandfather was born.

Juan, my grandfather's father, who was blind and unable to fend for the family, was granted a 160-acre tract of land for him and his family under the Homestead Act of 1862. At the age of fourteen or sixteen (circa 1886–1888), my grandfather began to help his mother, Juliana, support the family. At that time he started working as a cow wrangler for John Miller, a cattle rancher in Casa Salazar who also owned a country store. Following John Miller's death, my grandfather worked for José Miller, the son, and the Miller family, until 1899 or 1900, when my grandfather's father died. My grandfather's mother had passed away a few years previously. His association with the Millers lasted ten to fifteen years.

In his job with the Millers, my grandfather kept half of his monthly earnings of fifteen dollars; the rest went to his mother to buy groceries and other household necessities. Nevertheless, he was able to save enough money to marry my grandmother, Emilia Padilla, whose family had migrated to the Río Puerco Valley in the 1890s. Lale, as we called her, was joined in matrimony to my grandfather in Casa Salazar on December 10, 1898. She was perhaps thirteen and certainly no older than fifteen. He was twenty-six. According to an aunt of mine, they spent their wedding night in a corral with his horses (no honeymoon!).

By virtue of hard work, diligence, and careful planning, they gradually acquired property, raised a family, and built a life for themselves. Shortly after their marriage, circa 1900, my grandparents purchased their first tract of land in Rincón del Cochino, north of Casa Salazar. Located about four to five miles east of my village, it straddled the Río Puerco and consisted of a strip about a half mile long and fifty yards wide adjacent to the property where I would start school in a one-room schoolhouse in 1943. There they built their first home, had their first offspring, farmed, and raised various animals for domestic consumption and use on the farm.

In 1918 and again in 1931, my grandparents bettered their lot and purchased additional properties. These landholdings were about two miles east of Ojo del Padre, where my father was born and where I grew up. Today these properties belong to different family members, who acquired them as part of the estate settlement following my grandparents' deaths in 1972.

By 1918 my grandfather became a freighter for Richard Heller—don Ricardo Heller, as he was called—a respected merchant and rancher born in Prague, Czechoslovakia, who ran the Heller Trading Post in Cabezón. There my grandfather would hitch up a team of four, sometimes six, horses to wagons loaded with wool or cowhides and drive them to Albuquerque. Moreover, by inviting my grandfather to participate in the *partido* system, Ricardo Heller helped him raise enough cattle that my grandparents were ultimately able to become self-sufficient.

At one time they owned some one hundred head of cattle, a number of horses, goats, and chickens, and countless hogs—the latter thanks to my grandmother, who, like my grandfather, was an industrious person. Overall they were better off than most farmers in the Río Puerco Valley.

Time passed and the family grew. My father was the youngest of six siblings. He had two older brothers, Ramón and Antonio, and three older sisters, Julianita, Petrita, and Teodorita. Julianita and Petrita died young in Ojo del Padre, but the rest passed away in old age in Albuquerque, including my father, the last survivor of the siblings, who died in 2001 at eighty-eight.

My parents constructed an adobe home in the Río Puerco Valley in 1935, the year they were married. Our casita, or small house, was built on my grandparents' land next to their home. The modest house consisted of two moderately sized rooms: the kitchen and a bedroom. The flat roof, which seemed to leak whenever it rained hard, required periodic repairs. Until that happened, empty coffee cans and buckets were strewn throughout the house to catch the dripping water. In the winter, a wood-burning stove in the kitchen provided heat for both that room and our bedroom. From the kitchen window facing north, I could see the famous Cabezón Peak every day as we sat down to eat our meals.

Like in every household in our valley, there were no modern amenities. We had no running water or indoor plumbing; an *escusao*, outhouse, was the order of the day.* Of course, there was no electricity, either. A dim kerosene lamp was our only source of light at night; striking a match to get around in the middle of the night to fetch a glass of water or to use *el bacín*, the chamber pot, was in no way atypical in Río Puerco Valley households.

Both my grandparents as well as my parents shared the *horno*, adobe oven, situated between their home and ours. This was especially true during Holy Week and at Christmas, when baking bread and *molletes*, sweet rolls, was a tradition among the two households. The adobe oven was also used other times throughout the year for less traditional occasions, such as preparing *chicos*, the dehydrated corn used in pinto beans for added flavor.

Traditions aside, as time marched on, Río Puerco Valley families found themselves between a rock and a hard spot. Putting food on the table became more and more difficult because of droughts and meager crops, and they lacked money to buy clothing and other personal necessities. This stark reality opened their eyes, on the one hand, but at the same time it forced them to close the doors to their homes and abandon their beloved valley, never to return again to stay.

My own parents, too, saw the writing on the wall. Virtually penniless, with nothing more than the clothing on their backs, an old car, plus five children to feed and to clothe, they took us out of the Río Puerco Valley during the summer of 1945 to join many of our Río Puerco compatriots in Albuquerque in search of a better life. The future that awaited my father, mother, four siblings, and me in the so-called Duke City was as uncertain as it was gloomy, but that's a story for another day. Despite our move, we kept one foot in our former ranch home, where we continued to spend summers and countless weekends for an indeterminate number of years.

On those occasions we visited my grandfather, who disliked the city and therefore clung tenaciously to a rural way of life. In 1958, in old age and in poor health, he was one of the last residents to bid goodbye to Ojo del Padre.

....

* In standard Spanish, *escusado*. Henceforth, Spanish words in this work that deviate from the standard lexicon in pronunciation and spelling (e.g., the local *volvites* versus the standard *volviste*) are treated as indigenous to the Río Puerco Valley, although they may also be heard in other parts of the Spanish-speaking world.

He joined my grandmother in Albuquerque (she loved the city), where they had bought a second home in 1912 in Santa Barbara (Martíneztown). They died in Albuquerque in 1972 within two weeks of each other—she passed away on August 26, when she was eighty-seven or eighty-nine years old; he died September 12, at the age of one hundred. They were just one year shy of celebrating their seventy-fifth wedding anniversary.

Toward the end of their lives, their Río Puerco Valley properties were rendered next to worthless because of a lack of water. As a result, my grandparents died virtually poor, a saga that sadly could be replicated manyfold among former valley residents whom I interviewed for several of my books on oral history and folklore (see bibliography).

Fate sometimes can indeed be cruel and nonredemptive to those who worked hard all their lives with almost nothing to show in their golden years except pride and the memories of the good old days.

Following the death of my paternal grandparents and the subsequent settling of their estate, their landholdings were divided among their off-spring, including my father. At that time my parents' house, which was next to my grandparents' home, reverted back to my father's only surviving sister.

From then on our little casita was destined to melt into the earth because of neglect. Today the only physical evidence of my childhood home are the forlorn wooden doors and window frames that rest next to a pile of dirt, all that is left of the crumbled old adobe walls that my father and grandfather built with their bare hands.

Nevertheless, my childhood memories are indelibly lodged in the fateful abode dwelling where my parents embarked on a long marriage and started a family. My father, at twenty-two considered an "old" man back in 1935, married my mother when she was the tender age of fifteen. They were both born in September: he on September 10, 1912, and she, September 5, 1919.

As a child (I was the oldest of four boys and four girls), I spent my formative years in the Río Puerco Valley. At that time my father was away from Monday to Friday working for the Civilian Conservation Corps (CCC) camps of the Great Depression while Mom stayed home, took care of me and my siblings, and tended to farm chores. On weekends my father came home and assumed some of the farm tasks so that Mom could bake and prepare enough food to last him the whole week at the CCC camp at Rito de Semilla. This camp was located south of the village of Cuba before one turned off of old Route 44 (now U.S. Highway 550) leading to the Río Puerco Valley.

As a child you think only of eating, playing, and sleeping, but still there are certain things that you don't forget very easily. Love between your parents is a case in point. Through all the tough work and hardships of the Great Depression and the period subsequent to it, I witnessed an unbreakable bond between my mom and dad that brought a glow to my heart and a great sense of pride and tranquillity. To this day I reflect on and marvel at their affectionate relationship.

But beyond their wonderful love and partnership, nothing could have been more soothing and conducive to my upbringing than the topography that surrounded me in my native valley. The landscape was enticing, beautiful, mystical, and challenging to my imagination.

What unfolded before my eyes conjured up a multitude of stunning images that transformed imposing, dark blue volcanic plugs like Cabezón Peak, eons old, into friendly monsters and the Mesa Prieta into a large loaf of blue-corn bread. The Rincón del Cochino, a canyon with a cavernous mouth where hogs once roamed like javelinas, reminded me of a large frog prepared to swallow its insect prey. But there was nothing more impressive than the inimitable butte a stone's throw from my little casita. The butte, a favorite place from which hawks spied, hoping to whisk off one of Mom's baby chicks, resembled a genuine replica of one of Grandma Lale's golden loaves of bread or Christmas molletes baked in our adobe oven.

And of course the Río Puerco Valley panorama would not be complete without a word or two about the imposing Río Puerco itself. A tributary of the Río Grande, it bore a resemblance to a slithering snake constantly on the prowl as it meandered downstream from its headwaters in the Nacimiento Mountains north of Cuba. Heavy rainstorms during July and August, the rainy season, made the rushing waters sound like a roaring bull. To me, as I peered down from atop the Río Puerco's embankment near my house, the giant walls of rushing waters at the head of the current resembled those grooves on Mom's washboard magnified a thousandfold.

These images and countless others came to me endlessly; they livened up the landscape if I dared to fantasize. For me as a child there was no better entertainment than the topography, because it was real and nonintrusive. The connection between the landscape and me came without any strings attached, for it was not only intimate and redolent, the scenery was also magical. It was mine to savor.

These attributes, along with my mother's joyful outlook on life and my father's pragmatism, provided a beautiful balance to my childhood in the Río Puerco Valley. The foregoing dichotomy palpitates and can be seen stamped on every single page in *Hoe, Heaven, and Hell: My Boyhood in Rural New Mexico.*

2

A Broken Window

I SUDDENLY FELT A slight tugging at my feet, but I knew that it wasn't my dog, Chopo, who liked to nip playfully at my ankles whenever he chased after me outside the house. Mom allowed him inside only during the winter, provided it was very cold. This was early spring, however.

The next thing I heard was Mom's gentle voice. "*Anda, hijito, ¡levántate!* Up, up, my dear son! Your dad's coming home today. We've got lots to do."

Of course her words were music to my ears. This meant one thing—it was the day Dad came home for the weekend after being away all week long at the CCC camp in Rito de Semilla. The government job he had during the Great Depression was hard work. He and his coworkers constructed roads, engaged in flood and soil erosion control, put up fences, and built lagoons to trap water for livestock.

Mom knew it was Friday, even though there was no *almanaque*, calendar, on the kitchen wall, where most ranch families kept at least one. Besides, it didn't matter whether we had a calendar or not because Mom, as I would learn later on when I started school, couldn't read or write in Spanish, her native tongue, much less in English. Through some magic or personal system, she knew or kept track of the days of the week. Fridays for her and me were a cause for celebration. And Dad's presence, plus the fact that he was the bearer of good tidings, was the foremost reason.

Friday was also when Mom seemed to pack all of her week's energy into one day. Amid the hustle and bustle of activity that beckoned both of us, she sang one song after another as if to say, "*¡Qué alegría!* What joy!" Her singing took center stage while she tidied up the house, swept and washed floors, and cooked and baked. After all, Dad was coming home, and Mom and I rejoiced. My little brother was just a tot, three years old. I was five.

Somehow I got the impression, and maybe it was not altogether an illusion on my part, that Mom invariably started her repertoire of songs with "Cielito lindo," a popular Mexican song whose words she had memorized from listening to the battery-operated radio that Dad bought her.

Cielito lindo	Beautiful Little Sky
¡Ay, ay, ay, ay!	Oh, oh, oh, oh!
Canta y no llores,	Sing and don't cry,
porque cantando se alegran	because singing makes the
cielito lindo	hearts happy,
los corazones.	my beautiful little sky.
De la Sierra Morena	From the Sierra Morena,
cielito lindo,	my beautiful little sky,
vienen bajando	is descending
un par de ojitos negros,	a pair of little black eyes,
cielito lindo	my beautiful little sky,
de contrabando.*	by way of contraband.

Her beautiful voice echoed as if to bounce off the nearby butte that protected us from the westerly winds during *febrero loco*, crazy February, or *marzo aigriento*, windy March. Her melodies floated into the air, ricocheted east across the sagebrush, and faded into the nearby foothill where the cornfields would soon come alive. This was April, a more tranquil and cheerful time of the year, to be sure. Springtime was in the air, and Mom's happy songs were testimony to the start of a new season.

I was no less excited than Mom. I especially looked forward to Dad's homecomings because week after week he brought me a small brown bag of hard candy. He routinely stopped at don Ricardo Heller's Trading Post in Cabezón, a village about five miles north of our home. Besides candy for me, he would also buy a small gift for Mom. Sometimes he even splurged

---

*   Words to the song that I memorized as a child are still with me today.

and bought her an article of clothing. My little brother was too young to appreciate any kind of a present, so I shared a piece or two of candy with him. He liked that. Sharing is something Mom taught my siblings and me from the time we were toddlers.

In the meantime, the clock was ticking away—but only in a manner of speaking, because we didn't own a clock. The one that Mom used to have landed on the floor and broke after my Angora cat knocked it off the dresser. Clock or not, it was the sun or our stomachs that invariably told us the time of day, depending on the season or whether it was overcast or not.

Later on, a cousin of mine and I worked for don Cresencio weeding his cornfields and pumpkin patches across the Río Puerco from where we lived. It was then that I saved enough money to replace my mom's clock. I ordered a Westclox through J. C. Penney's catalog. That's how I learned to tell time, something my mother knew and taught me before I even started first grade in a one-room schoolhouse (see chapter 14).

Mom kept a pile of wood she had chopped near the adobe oven not far from our house and close to my paternal grandparents' home. I had been carting wood from that pile to the bin next to the stove. As I unloaded my armful of wood, Mom hollered at me through the bedroom window.

"And don't forget the *palitos*, kindling, so you can light the stove fire tomorrow morning when you get up."

I made one more trip and came back in with kindling. No sooner had I dumped it into a wooden crate than Mom said to me, "We have to go catch a chicken for supper."

One of Dad's favorite dishes, and mine, too, was *arroz con pollo*, chicken and rice, which Mom prepared bimonthly in a red clay pot that an Indian woman from Jémez Pueblo had given her on one of our trips there. We went to trade some of our homegrown crops for their fruit and chile, because these were not readily available in our valley. Mom was an excellent cook, and she enjoyed preparing meals for Dad. Chicken and rice was only one of her specialties. On weekends she tried to fix Dad dishes that she knew he enjoyed, since he and the other CCC campers had to cook and fend for themselves throughout the week.

Mom and I headed for the chicken coop to catch a chicken. She carefully opened the gate so that the chickens wouldn't rush out, above all the rooster, who liked to roam about in the corral or barn area. I scrambled helter-skelter trying to capture one of the chickens and dove for one, but it flew off. Upon seeing my repeated fruitless attempts, Mom said to me, "Not the chicken with the red and black feathers, hijito; that's the one that's been laying all the eggs. Try to catch the white one. That one has been stingy."

I wondered how she knew which chickens laid eggs and which ones didn't, but this was no time to ask questions. Now my sights were on the snow-white target. After a couple of futile attempts, I managed to pounce on the feathery bird as it fluttered on the ground, trying to elude my little hands. I grabbed its legs to secure my catch as the chicken cackled. I must have scared the dickens out of the poor fowl when I landed on top of her. If chickens had teeth, it probably would have bitten me.

As I stood up, Mom burst out laughing. "Look at you! Look at your face!"

"What? What?" I asked, feeling something cool and damp.

"You've got gray caca on your face." She then walked over, wrested the hen from me, and rubbed its feathers up against my face to remove my newly acquired makeup. I wasn't sure if I wanted to enter a chicken coop again any time soon.

From the chicken coop Mom and I headed for the woodpile. There she had a special chunk of juniper wood. That's where the fowl's fate would be sealed. She told me to hold the chicken firmly by its legs with its neck resting on the log, a new experience for me. Before Mom performed her act, she asked me to close my eyes. This scared me to death. Everything was pitch-black with streaks of yellow and pink running across the darkness of my eyelids. All of a sudden I heard a swift whack. "Now you may open your eyes."

I was so shocked at what I saw that I let go of the chicken. As I did, the headless bird began jumping aimlessly and twirling hither and thither, like a whip snake. I had never seen anything like it before. Once over the initial shock, I actually found this quite funny. Even Mom laughed after she caught the poor errant chicken that was destined for the red clay pot.

Out of the blue I began to feel queasy. My mouth turned a trifle watery. Strange and warm saliva rolled off my tongue. Mom noticed that something wasn't right. I must have turned as white as *cuajada*, homemade yogurt.

"What's wrong, hijito? Are you sick? You're as pale as this white chicken," she observed with a puzzled look on her face.

"The rolling head, the rolling head" was all I could utter.

"*Mira, hijito, pa vivir hay que morir,*" she said, as though I was to understand what she meant. "*¿Me entiendes? La gallina muere pa que nosotros ténganos algo que comer*"—words I sort of understood, but I left it at that.

The next thing we had to do was to defeather the chicken, quite a challenge, to say the least. Plucking out each feather was no easier than the time Dad had pulled porcupine quills from my dog Chopo's nose with a pair of pliers following a fight with the prickly beast. The secret was to dip the chicken in warm water to soften the skin, so it would not tear when one pulled the feathers. Feather by feather, the job was accomplished.

The hen was now ready to be cut up before it went into the clay pot. The chicken and rice would be ready in a few hours, just in time for Dad's arrival. By then the sun would begin to disappear behind the San Mateo Mountains.

"Keep your eyes open for your dad's car. It will be coming up the hill any moment now," Mom hollered from the kitchen.

I usually sat on the wooden doorsteps to the kitchen and looked down the hill as I waited for him, anxious to put my little hands on the brown bag of candy. Although I had no real sense of time, waiting seemed like an eternity, but suddenly I heard the roar of a motor as the car approached Grandpa's corral, leaving a trail of dust behind. I ran inside the kitchen to tell Mom. As she and I came out (she was holding my little brother Beltrán by the hand), Dad drove up and parked in front of the house.

Dad got out of the car. "*¿Cómo estás, hija?* How are you, dear?" Never one to show much outward emotion, he gave Mom a slight tap on her left shoulder with his right hand, as if to say, "I'm glad to be home," or "It's good to see you." He gave my little brother a small pinch on his left cheek and then tapped me on the head. I knew better than to ask where my candy was, because I had to wait till supper. The candy was my dessert.

Dad didn't have much to unload, only his dirty clothes, a few empty mason jars in which Mom had packed cooked food for him to heat up at his camping quarters, and an empty twenty-pound lard tin can he used to carry Mom's homemade *galletas*, biscuits. I helped take the jars inside the house.

"Are you hungry, *viejo*?" The latter was a term of endearment.

"Yes, yes," he answered as he washed his hands in a pan of water Mom kept on a tiny blue wooden table in the kitchen next to the wood bin. "*Estoy con la tripa clara.* I'm famished," he quipped with a slight smile.

The kitchen was small, with only the bare necessities, but adequate for a small family like ours. Besides a woodstove, there were an average-size eating table and three chairs. One of them was used as a makeshift high chair for my little brother and me. A *trastero*, cupboard, and a little wooden barrel for our drinking water, draped in burlap during the summer to keep the water cool, complemented the rest of the furnishings. A *jumate*, tin dipper, hung from a nail on one side of the barrel.

Home cooking was a welcome relief for Dad; a sparkle came to Mom's eyes as she watched him eat with gusto. Waiting hand and foot on Dad was Mom's way of showing her love for him, because hugging and kissing were deemed taboo and not something I saw out in the open between them, either in public or at home. Any show of affection was strictly private. That was also true of other married couples in my valley.

Supper was now ready. The modest yet scrumptious meal that decked the table consisted of the following dishes:

chicken and rice (main entrée)
boiled dried peas (side vegetable)
red chile (a staple)
papas molidas (mashed potatoes)
brel (sheepherder's bread)
bizcochitos (cinnamon and anise cookies)
coffee (Hills Bros.)
natillas (Spanish custard pudding)

Dad sat at the head of the table with his back to the only window in the kitchen; from where I sat Cabezón Peak was in the background. I was at the opposite end in a chair that Mom used as a high chair. She placed a wooden crate on top and a homemade cushion for comfort. She sat me on it. Next she pushed me so that my legs fit snugly under the table. I was ready to join my dad.

My mom tended to my little brother as she sat in her chair and chatted with Dad about his job. He in turn asked about household and ranch chores while he ate. Because there were only two complete place settings, Dad ate using one and I used Mom's.

I kept an eye on Dad's plate to see how much longer he had to go before he got to the dessert. I had already eaten—perhaps "gobbled" is a better word—my chicken and rice and was now playing with the peas on my plate, trying to spear them one at a time with Mom's fork, which I held in my right hand like a pitchfork. All I could do was to wait for Mom to serve Dad his dessert. My little bag of candy usually followed . . . except today. From a brown bag Mom pulled out a small red and gray tin toy pistol.

"Look, hijito!" she exclaimed. "Look at what your dad brought you!" And she handed me the pistol.

No doubt looking a trifle befuddled, if not disappointed, I gave the pistol a quick glance and countered by saying, "Where's my candy? I want my candy."

"Listen," my dad said, "don Ricardo didn't have any candy this time. He sold it all."

The last word had barely left Dad's mouth when I flung my toy pistol at him. He ducked to one side, and the errant missile shattered the window behind him. As I heard the tinkling of glass hitting the floor, I pouted and looked at the broken window. Suddenly a whole new magical world opened before my eyes.

In the distance loomed Cabezón Peak, the father of countless volcanic plugs that populated the Río Puerco region. I was awestruck with its size and splendor. My perception of the stark beauty framed in azure within the window frame of our kitchen was intuitive more than anything else I could have expressed at that given moment. Like one of my grandmother's home-made quilts, the colorful panorama that embraced the famous landmark stretched—reached out, in fact—and touched my casita and my own soul.

"Look, hijito. Sometimes things just don't work out the way you want them to. Since don Ricardo didn't have any candy, your dad brought you something else instead. Don't you think that was nice of him?"

When I heard Mom's words, the thought of the little brown paper bag full of candy vanished from my mind for another week. After all, I now had a new toy to play with.

3

Respect, Obedience, and Morality

LIKE RELIGION, THE FOUNDATION for respect, obedience, and morality was established at home with one's parents. Unlike religious training, however, the chief responsibility for which rested for the most part with the mother, the teaching of respect and moral conscience—the sense of right and wrong—fell primarily, albeit not exclusively, on the father's shoulders.

Being the head of the family, it was incumbent upon him not to abrogate his role as a respectful husband and honorable father. In his absence, including through death, the eldest son became the protector of the family in collaboration with the mother. To maintain a strong hold on the family's integrity and honor was paramount.

Any deviation from these precepts or social norms could tarnish the father's as well as the entire family's reputation, whether culpability stemmed from the sons and daughters or even the parents themselves. Regardless of any serious wrongdoing, a black mark on the family in many cases could outlive the family itself. Nothing was worse than a social stigma. For example, it was taboo and frowned upon if a daughter gave birth to a child out of wedlock or if a son fathered a child before marriage. Therefore, respect, obedience, and morality were of prevailing importance in any Hispanic household.

For me as a young boy, these three attributes, regardless of the meaning, interpretation, or nuance affixed to each one, were the same in all the other households that I was privy to observe. The burden of teaching respect and obedience without doubt rested with my father, whereas morality, particularly as it concerned daughters, weighed more on my mother.

Somehow morality in terms of social behavior was viewed, if not judged, more from a religious perspective; hence, the mother's role was pivotal.

The fundamental question as to what constituted respect and who decided on its boundaries was not the father's or mother's decision alone. Three people in my village—as was no doubt true in most Hispanic villages—epitomized respect: the priest, the local teacher, and an elder statesman or stateswoman known for their leadership in the community.

The priest, for better or for worse, commanded the utmost respect among local citizens. Any misdeeds on his part, if they existed, he kept locked up in the closet, although rumblings of misbehavior were not uncommon. After all, any community that did not indulge in *mitote*, gossip, was not worth its salt. As conservative as people were, they were also open-minded, giving the priest the benefit of the doubt, no matter if he imbibed too much or whatever rumors unrelated to his religious role might run rampant.

Being the spiritual leader and God's shepherd carried a lot of weight, something we children were indoctrinated with from the time we learned our first prayer. An outward manifestation of respect came once a month when the priest visited our village. Following the celebration of Mass, he stood at the entrance to the church and bid adieu to his parishioners, many of whom genuflected before him or kissed his right hand or both. People addressed him as Father So-and-So, for he was the head, or father, of the people in his parish.

But his role transcended that of just priest. Aside from spiritual guidance, people sought his advice and assistance in personal matters. In that sense he served as counselor or psychologist to the person in need of moral support and personal understanding. Trust and respect were mutually inclusive and never doubted by either party. The priest was the consummate example of reverence and confidence.

The teacher, unlike the priest, generated respect and obedience because of his or her position as the purveyor of knowledge and truth. Being a *mestro/a (maestro/a),* or master of your craft, meant nobody surpassed the educator when it concerned educating the children in the community. In the eyes of parents, the teacher could do no wrong. Moreover, the teacher had unparalleled discretion in classroom discipline if students misbehaved or were disrespectful. If one dared to go home and complain about the teacher to his parents, the father would ask what punishment was meted out, and he in turn would double it without questioning the teacher's authority or reprimand.

If there's anything kids like me learned fast, it was not to seek sympathy at home for being disciplined in school. And back in my elementary school days at the ranch, corporal punishment—such as spanking with a ruler or being forced to stand in a corner of the classroom facing the wall—was fair game for unruly students.

Aside from the priest and teacher, in the community there was customarily an older person of either gender—by and large a male—whose respectable reputation over time had risen among the villagers. The general population, from the oldest to the youngest, revered that person. People spoke of wisdom as the trademark of a well-regarded man or woman in one's village, given that commanding respect was more honorable than demanding it. They were the pillars that stood head and shoulders above their peers. Everyone with rare exception recognized and paid homage to them without questioning their integrity or stature, qualities that at times transcended their village.

While the three shining examples of truthfulness were important— namely, respect, obedience, and morality—in the final analysis they mattered little unless being respectful was emphasized and taught at home, something that started even before you began to crawl on all fours. On occasion the mother uttered words or commands; other times a mere glance from the father conveyed approval or disapproval of one's actions, above all if other people were present.

I was the oldest of eight children, so in a sense I was the family guinea pig regarding discipline and upbringing. What my parents learned from their parents no doubt influenced them in teaching my brothers, sisters, and me to be upright and respectful citizens. Being the first child was not always easy, because in my mind it posed certain contradictions, especially after other siblings came along.

First of all, I was to be the paragon of good behavior, but at the same time I was spoiled. A prime example of how I was indulged is the large amounts of hard candy my father bought me, and that I ate, which resulted in my developing a multiplicity of cavities and toothaches at the age of five. Yet as I got older, and being a male to boot, I was expected to set a positive example in social decorum for my siblings. It was a balancing act that I learned to juggle thanks to my mother's kindness, on the one hand, and my father's strictness, on the other.

"*Cría cuervos y te sacarán los ojos.* Whatever you do to your parents, your children will do to you" was one of my mother's favorite *dichos*, or folk sayings. In other words, your children will one day treat you the way you treated your parents. Years later I learned to appreciate the wisdom embedded in her words. The message of expecting no more or no less from your offspring than what you indoctrinated them with became crystal clear.

Folk sayings were a subtle yet powerful way of meting out advice without having to beat you over the head or between the eyes to make you understand what constituted proper behavior. Those gems of wisdom handed down throughout the ages were popular in my family. Listening to my father invoke a folk saying at the drop of a hat reminded me of Sancho Panza, don Quixote's sidekick. Whenever my father noticed our disapproval of something he said or did to us children, he was blunt in reminding us that to be lax meant facing dire consequences. "*No hay que criar uno cuervos pa que te saquen los ojos.* One must not raise crows so they can pluck out your eyes." More to the point, don't expect angels if you raise devils. But his words of advice—or warning—needed no explanation. We got the message.

Intuition, something most children possessed, was a great gift in helping you to understand what your parents meant without asking them to decipher each word. To intuit also meant reading between words, syllables, and even vowels. Having a feeling for the advice at hand was analogous to peeling the leaves off of an artichoke to get to the heart of it. With time you came to understand what your parents or grandparents meant to convey to their children and grandchildren. I once overheard my father say, "*El que no hace aprecio a consejos, se queda lejos.*" In other words, he who doesn't heed advice shall lag far behind.

Lecturing and scolding did occur whenever my parents' concern for the future well-being of their children as decent citizens in the community was at stake. Invoking the Ten Commandments as guidance was not unheard of, even with a bit of humor or disbelief. To be told that if you stole something, you'd grow a *corcovita*, small hunchback, was a trifle unreal, even for small children like me. But we would not dare take a chance on testing whether it was true.

Also, whenever visitors came to someone's house, children were to be seen and not heard. Most guests, depending on how formal the host and hostess were, generally sat in the *sala de recibo*, receiving room (today's living room), or in the kitchen if they were intimate friends.

We only had two rooms—the bedroom and the kitchen—so friends who visited my parents sat at the kitchen table. Even if our family home had had a formal receiving room, close friends customarily would have ended up in the kitchen (see chapter 4). This was the place of refuge, as you might say, where good conversation and salacious gossip took place—and where curious children like me longed to be. Eavesdropping was not out of the question, provided we could get away with it.

Of course, once visitors arrived and made themselves at home, I yearned to sit in a corner of the kitchen, pretending to be engaged in my own private world, playing with a toy or whatever, while the grownups engaged in so-called adult talk. If the conversation revolved around normal, everyday things, the temptation to butt in with your own two cents now and then was irresistible, but Mom kept a vigilant eye on me. If she sensed that I wanted to say something, she would make eye contact and nod her head to one side, signaling me to scoot. I would go outside and play. No questions asked.

Many times I was expected to leave the room soon after visitors arrived. As a rule, for a child to sit and listen to adult conversations was not permitted, but you also were to stay out of sight. Otherwise, you were looked upon as an *encimoso*, a pest.

Most parents and grandparents, mine included, hardly ever criticized you in front of people. That was deemed undignified and tacky, but once guests left your house or the family got home from church or wherever, your ears were bound to ring from a good tongue-lashing. If the misconduct was not terribly serious, Mom usually meted out the scolding; or else, Dad was the bearer of an unforgettable reprimand. Throughout it all, corporal punishment was hardly ever in the cards. Idle threats, yes. As a rule, a good verbal lashing sufficed.

If children were present at the dinner table, most grown-ups exercised discretion in what they discussed, but there were times when kids for them became invisible objects and hence they engaged in adult chatter. My ears would perk up like a donkey's, and quickly my mom would signal me to finish eating and to leave the kitchen without much ado.

I always wondered, what did they talk about? From time to time, I would leave the kitchen, enter our bedroom, and hide under the bed so I could eavesdrop. Most of the time, I was disappointed at what I overheard. What they discussed were common, everyday kinds of things related to farm matters.

My maternal grandmother, whom I referred to as Grandma Cinda (for Lucinda), and my step-grandfather, Antonio (we called him Uncle Antonio), lived in Bernalillo, north of Albuquerque. They visited us from time to time. Her conversations were more of the heart-to-heart variety, both in tone and substance, compared to other discussions I heard. Besides, she would involve me in the exchange, and I therefore did not have to leave the kitchen. She was wonderful! She would share fascinating stories with me about witchcraft, buried treasures, and the ubiquitous disobedient son.*

I also learned from her some new cultural tidbits about respect. For example, during one of her visits to our ranch, she asked me for a drink of water. The first mistake I made, thanks to my mom's watchful eye, was to grab the dipper hanging from a nail on the small wooden water barrel. Only my family and I drank from the dipper. Guests, including relatives, were to drink from a glass or a cup from the cupboard. Once I filled Grandma's glass with water using the dipper, I gave it to her, at which point I had to cross my arms until she finished drinking the water. If she asked

----

* See *Rattling Chains and Other Stories for Children / Ruido de cadenas y otros cuentos para niños* and *Grandma's Santo on Its Head: Stories of Days Gone By in Hispanic Villages of New Mexico / El santo patas arriba de mi abuelita: Cuentos de días gloriosos en pueblitos hispanos de Nuevo México.* Consult bibliography for more complete listings.

for another glass, I had to repeat the formal procedure. After she drank the last swallow, she would say, "*Gracias, hijito.*"

The crossing of one's arms while an elder drank water is but one example of a repertoire of cultural practices and gestures that were customary among Hispanic families. As a result, hardly anyone noticed these cultural niceties unless a guest hailed from the city (e.g., Albuquerque) or the person came from a different culture, which tended to pique people's curiosity more than anything else.

My mother taught me, from the time I was a young boy, to be obedient and never to lose my sense of respect or affection for people. To her way of thinking, it was easier to become cynical than to be altruistic and compassionate. "It's better to give of yourself," she would say to my brothers and sisters and me, "than to expect something free from others." Her words ring loud and clear to this day.

4

The Venerable Kitchen

I CAN STATE WITHOUT hesitation that no Hispanic worth his or her salt disputes the fact that the kitchen traditionally has been our most venerable room, however large or small the home. The kitchen has enjoyed, currently enjoys, and will continue to enjoy its moments of jubilation, despair, and disappointment, provided a modicum of cultural traditions is maintained among Hispanics in rural New Mexico or in enclaves of the inner city.

Regardless of the occasion, formal or informal, family, friends, neighbors, and guests of all ages invariably gravitate to the kitchen. It's a magnet that draws people; it's a cultural phenomenon that defies a clear-cut explanation as to why this happens. But the attraction of the kitchen, whether in preparing meals, eating and drinking, or washing dishes, is undeniable.

In looking across time and space, I see that the kitchen at home while I was growing up in Ojo del Padre was no different. The hub of activity was the kitchen. For the most part I have very fond memories of a variety of things that transpired in Mom's kitchen.

And it was her kitchen or domain—let us make no mistake about it—with my father, my siblings, and me acting as supporting characters. Mom made no pronouncements or demands. We understood the unspoken arrangement and therefore respected it. She was the one who kept matters under control and the prime mover and shaker of activities that took place in the kitchen, day in and day out. Everything from cooking, eating, scrubbing floors, discussing family problems, playing games, and entertaining socially to special occasions like Baptism or First Holy Communion revolved around her.

25

My brothers and sisters and I were also taught—and we learned—other things in the kitchen. My father's indoctrination about obedience, morality, responsibility, and hard work (see chapter 3) can be traced to Mom's kitchen.

It was here, too, where each of us learned from her how to sew, mend our socks, and embroider. Gender barriers were nonexistent in my family. Mom made sure of that. She left that notion at the doorsteps of those with more chauvinistic tendencies. She did not believe in pigeonholing boys in one niche and girls in another. Washing dirty dishes and cooking, for example, were transcendental tasks and went beyond a feminine world and female hands. In retrospect, Mom was prudent—and practical—because, knowingly or not, she taught us to fend for ourselves without relying solely on her and my father.

Through fun and games we also learned to entertain ourselves. Playing cards, building objects with matchsticks, or listening to Mom and Dad share stories with us—especially my father, who could mesmerize us with his witchcraft tales—is how we spent many pleasant evenings before going to bed. Idle gossip admittedly crept in from time to time in our conversations, but nothing caustic or demeaning, because my parents didn't allow malicious gossip at the kitchen table or anywhere else.

Whatever came to light in the kitchen, and whatever knowledge my siblings and I gained from our parents, was a tribute to Mom's grace and assurance of interdependence, as well as to Dad's moral rectitude. They strove to make sure we comprehended what constituted being a good and decent human being. And these salient attributes stemmed from Mom's lovable nature and the venerable kitchen she established for the whole family to enjoy.

With the harsh and oftentimes brutally cold winter months of January and February, families took pleasure, as we did, in wintertime seclusion. It was a more tranquil time of the year, when we weren't confronted with an array of farm and ranch chores. Families huddled inside their homes as the frigid temperatures dipped, the snowcapped foothills and gigantic dark blue peaks nearby adding to the beauty of the landscape. As the sun disappeared behind the high point of the San Mateo Mountains (today called Mount Taylor) and the full moon loomed over the Mesa Prieta to the east, my parents, siblings, and I gathered around the warm wood-burning stove in the kitchen.

But sitting around twiddling one's thumbs was not part of the picture. One of the things that Mom did during the winter months, starting with me, the eldest, was to teach her children how to sew, mend clothing, and embroider. In my household, as mentioned earlier, there were no gender barriers decreeing that boys were boys and girls were girls. Mom would have no separation of the sexes as far as domestic chores were concerned.

Despite our getting pricked fingers endless times—with droplets of blood as prima facie evidence—Mom taught us to mend our clothing instead of always relying on her. Darning torn clothes was the rule, not the exception. Similarly, buying a new pair of pants every time you wore a hole in the old ones was out of the question. There was nothing shameful in my community about wearing knee patches or having the seat of your pants repaired with mismatched patches. (Today patched pants cost an arm and a leg at brand-name clothing stores.)

The very first thing Mom taught me was how to mend holes in my socks. The primary casualties were the heels or toes, but the challenge was made easier because of human ingenuity. With a beer bottle in hand—it came from Dad's beer-brewing arsenal and was the perfect fit—Mom showed me how to drape the sock over the fat end of the bottle so that the hole showed up. Once you did that, you ran the thread and needle going back and forth until you closed the hole. It was tricky, but the bottle facilitated the mending process. Otherwise, trying to patch up a hole in a sock without the bottle for me as a little boy would have been both daunting and frustrating. A bottle in mending socks was a boy's best friend.

If a bottle wasn't available because they were all full with Dad's home-made beer, an ear of ripened corn or a corncob also worked well, but either was a tad thornier because the surface was not smooth.

Other mending jobs were more difficult than socks, but with time, I was able to undertake them, albeit with mixed results. For example, cutting out patches from old Levi's to use for knee patches was relatively easy. The difficulty was sewing them on, although the stitching at times was made easier by my using a mason jar that Mom had for canning because it fit the contour of the knee perfectly.

The author's childhood home, built in 1935.

Something much more complicated was turning a worn-out shirt's collar inside out. First you had to use a razor blade to carefully cut the fine
threads. Any slip of the razor could slice the collar and thus ruin it, something that occurred to me on more than one occasion. Luckily, they were
not Dad's dress shirts. Mom as a rule mended his shirt collars. Repairing
the collars extended the life of the shirt twofold.

One thing that I enjoyed thoroughly was sewing buttons on shirts. It
was fun. And the main reason I found the undertaking pleasant is because
I enjoyed trying to run the needle from the bottom—from the inside of the
shirt—up through the two, three, or four buttonholes. The one aspect of
replacing buttons that I found entertaining was the different button colors
and sizes. If you lost a button or two while out on the range or in the fields
and you couldn't match it either in size or in color, you simply replaced it
with whatever Mom had available in a can of buttons that she collected.
Over time the variety of button sizes and colors gave my shirts an entirely
new glow. Needless to say, my shirts were colorful. Again, nobody made
fun of you. On the contrary, kids liked my multihued buttons because they
made my shirts stand out.

An equally fun thing that Mom taught me and that I sincerely delighted
in was embroidery. Numerous times I had sat at the dinner table in the

evening or during Mom and Dad's weekend conversations while she em-
broidered. She went about her embroidery in such a matter-of-fact way
that her demeanor left me wondering if she was even enjoying it, let alone
paying attention to Dad. I learned later on as she began to teach me that
embroidering for her was relaxing and therapeutic at the end of a hard
day's work. Embroidery was on the same plane as her cooking, which she
thoroughly took pleasure in—and she was good at both of them.

"Would you like to learn how to embroider?" she asked me kiddingly
one early evening after she and I finished doing the dishes. "As you know,
embroidery is not only for mothers, grandmothers, and daughters. Boys
should also learn how to embroider, so I'm going to teach you."

"Fine," I responded somewhat sheepishly, since Grandma Cinda in
Bernalillo had already taught me a little bit about stitch embroidery. Her
attitude about boys' versus girls' chores and responsibilities squared pretty
much with Mom's feelings. For my grandma, there were also no gender
barriers. Spreading the work around the house, whether inside or outside,
was a matter of fairness and obligation. Doubtless, Mom espoused and
emulated Grandma's philosophy.

"Okay, here's what we're going to do," Mom said to me. "We'll start
from the beginning. By that I mean, we'll lay out on the table everything
that we need for embroidery," and she meticulously proceeded to exhibit
each item one by one:

cotton or linen fabric
embroidery hoops (wood and metal)
regular eye needles made of chrome
silk thread in different colors
straight pins
thimbles
transfer (hot iron) patterns

The first thing she did was to put a cast iron on the stove for stamping
the hot iron pattern on the clean white cotton cloth that was destined to
be a dishtowel. While the iron was getting hot, Mom carefully cut out
two patterns from a thin transfer sheet of paper with blue ink: the first
one read *Lunes*, Monday, and the second pattern bore a rose. She was also

cautious to cut away any unwanted blue marks before transferring the pattern, because once she applied the hot iron to the cloth they could not be removed.

The next step was to secure the pattern on the fabric by using straight pins, with the letters or design facedown. Once that was done, Mom moistened her index finger and then touched it to the iron. Somehow she could tell by the hissing sound if the iron was too hot or not hot enough. When the iron was ready, she applied it to the pattern, moving it back and forth, evenly and slowly, for a few seconds. To ensure that the design had taken, she played peekaboo by raising one edge of the pattern. If the design was dark and not faint, the hot iron transfer was a success.

Mom then lifted the pattern up, and, like magic, there were the blue letters that spelled Monday in Spanish. They appeared right below the rose that was stamped on the left-hand corner of the dishtowel. The next task was to decide on the thread to begin the stitching with.

"Hijito, choose the thread, but you may want to pick a different color thread for each letter instead of having them all the same color."

"You mean like the different colors of buttons that I sewed on my shirt?"

"That's the idea!" She smiled.

Choosing a color for the first letter was easy enough, since my favorite color was—and still is—blue. The remaining colors were a bit more difficult, but given that there were only six or eight colors in total, I chose them on the basis of animals and things around the house and farm: orange, red, green, and brown. The rose would be all in red with a green stem. It would be reminiscent of the *rosa de Castilla,* a favorite red rose of Mom's that grew in the wild. (The only wild red rose I've ever seen was in Numancia, Spain.)

"Are you ready?" she asked, although I didn't have to answer, since she saw that I had lined each braid of colored thread facing the respective letters.

Each braid of thread, held together with a shiny gold or silver paper ring in the middle, had three or four strands, so I needed to separate one thread from the other strands before threading it through the needle. I had done this a number of times with regular sewing thread from a spool. The embroidery thread was different; it was silky and slippery but striking in color.

For me the real test in embroidery was about to begin: Would I show an artistic bent? Could I adroitly and simultaneously balance the various implements while stitching? Mom handed me two metal hoops, one slightly larger than the other. She draped the cloth with the patterns over the small hoop and then clipped the larger one on top, leaving the cloth nicely stretched and snug.

I was now ready to begin my stitching. I placed the double hoops on my lap—just as Mom did, because she was working on her own embroidery—and held them with my left hand, leaving my right one free to do the embroidering. With the right hand under the cloth, I ran the needle in and pulled it back through, repeating the back-and-forth process several times. The more times I did it, the easier it became. I finally had the letter *L* cross-stitched, even if it was a tad crooked. The bottom portion of the letter was in a droopy posture, making the *L* look more like a broken chair than a letter. Mom was not concerned.

"That's the way you learn," she said, reassuring me about my first experience in cross-stitching. "Besides, it's better to bend than crack, don't you think?" she added with a smile.

"I guess so," I muttered, somewhat unhappy with my results.

"You'll get better. You'll see," she commented as I proceeded with the letter *U*, which I found easier, perhaps because it looked like one of Grandpa's horseshoes.

By the time I finished all the letters and started the red rose a few nights later, I had gained more confidence. My letters were no longer as crooked. I was more and more satisfied with the progress as I tackled each letter. Mom was also very pleased with me. Her words of reassurance made me feel good.

"Are you ready for your next word?" Mom asked. "On Monday evening, after your father has returned to work, you can do Wednesday, *Miércoles*, a very important day."

"*Amá*, why is it important?"

"Because you were born on a Wednesday, which is good!"

"And why is it good?"

"My, but you're full of questions tonight. Because it's smack in the middle of the week, and that gives balance to your character. Do you understand?"

"I guess so."

"You'll see one of these days when you get older. Anyway, by the time you finish all the days of the week, you'll have seven dish towels."

"Wow! That's lots of towels."

"Yes. You'll be an expert by then," she added, when suddenly I heard a knock on the kitchen screen door.

It was Grandma Lale from next door. She was all wrapped up in Grandpa's *borreguera*, sheepherder's jacket. She had come over to borrow some coffee for Grandpa's breakfast the next morning.

"Hijito, tomorrow evening I'll have some fresh bizcochitos. Why don't you come over after supper?"

"But Dad will be home tomorrow and . . ."

"That's okay, hijito," interrupted Mom. "You can go."

"*¡Híjole!* And will you tell me one of your witch stories, Grandma?" I asked without hesitation.

"Yes, if you promise not to eat all the bizcochitos!" she replied with a wry smile as she grabbed her little mason jar of coffee beans and left. She would grind them in Grandpa's coffee grinder.

"Okay, on to bed," Mom said. "It's getting late. Remember, your father will be home tomorrow, so we have a busy day ahead of us." And she joined me at my bedside for my bedtime prayer.

If tomorrow was a busy day, today had been an eventful one. After all, I had learned to embroider, something very few boys could do, including my cousins. Not that I wanted to flaunt my undertaking, lest they start accusing me of wearing skirts—or being a *jotito*, effeminate boy. Even one's cousins could be cruel.

I often heard the folk saying "Like father, like son," but now I could add my own adage, "Like mother, like son," to the repertoire of adages the elders employed. I was proud of mine.

Witchcraft, Beliefs, and Superstitions

I GOT UP EARLY the next morning after my embroidering experience and walked down the hill to Grandpa Lolo's corral, where he kept his milk cow locked up overnight. He called her Ninfa. During the day he would turn Ninfa loose in a small meadow nearby after we milked her.

Today was my turn to milk the affable cow that supplied us milk virtually year-round. In Grandpa's book, she was special. With a *cubeta*, tin bucket, in hand, I arrived at the corral, climbed over the wooden gate, and sauntered to the *potrero*, a small, confined section of the corral where Ninfa was eating (cows were always chewing on something). Then I heard her lowing.

That struck me as strange, but I didn't give the mooing much thought until I sat on the ground to milk Ninfa. That's when I spotted, a few feet away, the largest dark brown snake I had ever seen. I remained quiet, sort of in a trance, but stunned. The snake did not make a noise like rattlesnakes do, except for a kind of rustling sound when it moved stealthily on top of the hay that was scattered on the ground. I debated for a split second whether I should run back up the hill to tell Mom about this creature or not, but as I watched the snake slowly move away, I decided I would go ahead and milk the cow instead of having to come back later.

Once I finished, I walked back up the hill at a fast pace, trying not to spill the milk, although by the time I got home my right hand and pant leg were all splashed with the sticky substance, which is what Mom noticed right away.

"Hijito, is there any milk left in the bucket? Look at your pant leg. It's dark blue from the milk."

Without paying much attention to what she said, I proceeded to tell her about the big, fat snake.

"Amá, I saw the largest round snake I have ever seen!"

"What color was it?" she asked rather calmly.

"It was brown and round like a *morcilla*, blood sausage," I responded, my voice trembling and increasing in loudness by several decibels.

"Boy, that had to be a pretty big snake if it looked like a morcilla! Are you sure your eyes didn't deceive you?" Mom asked, as if to doubt my word.

"No, no, no," I countered in rapid-fire fashion. "I saw it, I saw it!" I added, reasserting my pronouncement. "What do you think it was?"

"It was probably a *mamona*," Mom answered matter-of-factly.*

"And what's a mamona?"

"A mamona is a snake that gets under the cow's udder, reaches up, and sucks the milk from the one of its tits. Trouble is, once a mamona does that, the cow's udder is forever dried up and the cow will produce no more milk."

"¡Híjole! Wow! That could have happened this morning."

"That right. But the cow probably sensed danger and even mooed and scared the snake away."

"Funny you should say that, because as I approached the corral, I did hear the cow mooing."

"You see, hijito, cows aren't as stupid as people make them out to be," Mom added. "Okay, skim the milk foam for your coffee and take some of the milk to your grandma so she and Grandpa Lolo can have some for their oatmeal."

When I got there, I couldn't resist repeating to Grandma Lale my encounter with the mamona. As it happened, she had her own stories about the milk-sucking snake. But it was too early in the morning for such stories, so I would have to wait for another day. Besides, as it turned out, devoid of all the embellishment that generally accompanied these types of stories, she basically agreed with what Mom had told me about the strange snake called the mamona.

As a young boy, I was probably one of the luckiest children when the

---

*   See *The Talking Lizard: New Mexico's Magic and Mystery.*

time came to hearing stories of all types—especially those pertaining to witchcraft and superstitions.* Having two grandmas who were fantastic storytellers—especially my maternal grandmother, a folk healer in Bernalillo, where I was born—was a godsend. In fact, judging from the kids I knew in my valley, including my own cousins who lived nearby, I was indeed fortunate.

Of course, my parents weren't chopped liver, either, especially my shy father, who seemed to be in his element when recounting his personal run-ins with phantasms and ghostly apparitions on the open range before and after he and Mom were married. His tales were captivating and full of zing.

But when it concerned stories of witchcraft and superstitions, Grandma Lale at the ranch, more than Dad or Grandpa Lolo, was the star. Countless times I listened to her tales that varied in breadth and scope; her subjects ranged from witches, spooky animals, and balls of fire to things magical, depending on the time of the year. The winter months were special because Grandpa would invite my cousins and me to eat his *rositas de maíz*, popcorn, which he had harvested especially for these tête-à-têtes. It was then that we'd huddle around my grandparents' potbellied stove to listen to Grandma Lale's enchanting stories.

Other times I heard her tales by sheer happenstance or when she and I were alone, which is what I liked. Her one-on-one narratives were filled with more joie de vivre than when she recounted them in a family gathering. Perhaps the difference rested in tone and delivery rather than in spontaneity. Or it could be that with me alone she had a captive audience.

One of my favorite stories concerned a man named don Benito from our village of Ojo del Padre. His night escapades were legendary. He was a violinist. The story has it that many times he would go play at dances in Casa Salazar, a few miles to the south along the Río Puerco. He always rode a donkey, although some people claim that following a dance he would be too drunk to ride. Regardless, he and his beast were inseparable. There were also disputes regarding whether he was a good musician or not.

....

* See *Brujerías: Stories of Witchcraft and the Supernatural in the American Southwest and Beyond.*

He had his detractors, to be sure, but he was reputed to be an affable old fellow. And as long as he could make sounds with his violin, people danced until the wee hours of the morning. That is all that mattered.

Between Casa Salazar and Ojo del Padre there's a place called El Puertecito; it is situated right across the Río Puerco from where my family and I lived. As a young boy, my cousins and I were forever warned never to climb atop the so-called Mesa Encantada, adjacent to El Puertecito. The mesa was believed to be enchanted, presumably inhabited by witches and other supernatural creatures. In passing through El Puertecito, one came upon El Arroyo de la Tapia (*tapia* means "wall," in reference to a natural lava-type wall connected to a smaller butte next to the Mesa Encantada), which was also reputedly renowned for its ghostly apparitions in the dead of night.

According to Grandma Lale, it was at El Arroyo de la Tapia where don Benito was riding his donkey as he headed home from Casa Salazar, perhaps even a bit tipsy, since musicians back then always had their shots of corn liquor or moonshine. Whether it was a figment of his imagination or not, something or someone jumped on the donkey's rump. Don Benito kept asking, "Who are you? What are you?" As he looked over his shoulder, he could see an object seated behind him. At that point, frightened and scared out of his wits, he spurred his donkey. When he got home the only thing he could utter to his daughters were the words "*La Ñeca, la Ñeca*. The Doll, the Doll," and he fainted on the kitchen floor. The next morning, all their father could recall was something about a doll, but the family could never determine what he really saw.

There were scores of stories about El Arroyo de la Tapia and its immediate environs, and don Benito figured prominently among them, but nobody who had a run-in with the doll could render an adequate description of it. The closest people came was to say it was a babe in arms who had teeth and talked. These details, of course, added to the aura and drama, since infants don't talk or have teeth.

I never heard my grandma proclaim with any certitude who or what the doll was either; nor, to my knowledge, was the mystery ever solved, which led to the speculation among some individuals that the so-called doll was purely something don Benito had hallucinated, since he enjoyed his good shots of liquor. Other people were more inclined to suggest that the doll was the devil in disguise.

Colorful characters like don Benito conjured up stories in our valley, at times involving the same personages, but portrayed with embellishments of sorts, all of which helped to keep the tales alive from village to village and generation to generation.

Grandma's magical words, tone, and buildup of suspense are what gave her narratives pizzazz. Once you heard one of her gripping stories, you were bound to remember both the highlights and the low points. Certain episodes were destined to remain embedded in your psyche. That is why I can still recall vividly some of her descriptive accounts.

Though not rampant in the Río Puerco Valley per se, tales of the supernatural—featuring elements like magical donkeys, witches, enchanted mesas, bewitchment, and evil spirits—were the norm and a great source of entertainment for youngsters like me. Many times the paranormal could occur right in your own backyard, as you might say.

I recollect clearly to this day how Grandpa Lolo's kerosene lantern would light up in the kitchen whenever he was away visiting my grandma at their Albuquerque home in Martíneztown, where she spent part of the year. The first time I saw the kitchen lit up, I must have been about five years old. I ran inside and told my mother. Her reaction was more or less predictable.

"Your Grandpa must be home from Albuquerque" was her response, with a slightly puzzled look on her face. "Why don't you go take a peek through the kitchen window to see if he's back?"

I did as Mom told me, but upon approaching the window, the light began to flicker, and then it went out. Since Grandpa had a cot in the kitchen, where he slept in Grandma's absence instead of their bedroom, I thought maybe he had gone to bed. Still, the minute I started to walk away and headed for home next door, the light came back on. I turned back, but once again the light went out as I came close to Grandpa's house. By now I felt more than a bit queasy, not knowing what to make of the on-again, off-again kerosene lantern, so I double stepped home and told Mom about it.

"Oh, hijito. It's your imagination. You're just seeing things. That happens when you're a small boy. Think nothing of it. Why don't you go to bed? Tomorrow's another day."

Still a trifle uneasy and unable to resist temptation, I said to Mom, "Why don't you go look for yourself? I bet you'll see the same light."

"Well, now. And what if I don't see it? What do we do then?"

"You will, because I think there's some kind of a spirit in Grandpa's kitchen. It may not be an evil spirit, but it's a spirit all right. Count on it," I said with an air of cocky assuredness.

No sooner said than done, Mom came back in the house, seemingly startled. "You're right, hijito! The light was on when I went outside, but it went out as I got close to the kitchen window."

The following day Grandpa came home from Albuquerque, and the first thing Mom and I mentioned to him was the light in his kitchen.

"Oh, it's nothing to worry about," he assured us. "A long time ago, when I was building this house, I accidentally knocked out my two front gold teeth with one of the beams. But I never found them. People have told me about seeing the kitchen light on when I've been away, thinking that it's my gold teeth. You see, people believe in buried treasures where there's gold in a home, because a light will shine at night when the owners are away."

"Do you believe that, Grandpa?" I asked him, expecting a firm yes or no answer.

"Perhaps, but it's not something I worry about. Out here in the country-side all that hocus-pocus stuff comes and goes. It's like La Llorona. Some people liken her to a witch who can inflict harm on you, but that's not true. The Wailing Woman is not a witch. She's just an unfortunate soul who drowned her children, and her punishment is searching fruitlessly for them at night wherever there are rivers, arroyos, or ditches with running water."

Mom sat passively without uttering a word while Grandpa and I carried on a conversation. Mom was always amused at my inquisitiveness, but the simple fact is that I was fascinated with anything pertaining to the supernatural. I wondered silently how these things could happen. I sought answers.

Even my father, who was somewhat shy, left me spellbound with his stories. How can I ever forget one cold night in February while the wind blew to high heaven? He spoke unabashedly but with a sense of anxiety of an encounter he had had with a *bulto*, a ghostly apparition, at a lagoon called Laguna Número Dos, where many ranchers from Ojo del Padre, Cabezón, and San Luis watered their livestock.

"It was past midnight when a community dance ended in San Luis a few miles from my parents' home. I was still a young man on my way home. Not far from San Luis, there was a lagoon. Sensing that my horse was thirsty, I sidetracked a bit from the dirt road so the horse could drink some water. As I loosened the reins and tied them around the saddle horn, my horse took two or three steps forward, until the water reached the stirrups. The night was quite silent. All I could hear was the horse gulping water.

"At that given moment I raised my arms in the air to stretch, and I looked across the lagoon. Lo and behold, what I saw was none other than a bulto, a black object walking on water across the lagoon. I watched and watched. I was awestruck. The ghost or whatever it was never made a sound. There was not even a splash to the water. That was the strange thing about the scene. As the bulto came closer, almost at the edge of the water and near my horse and me, it disappeared underwater. Even the horse perked up his ears. I wondered what it was. I still do to this day."

"Were you scared, Dad?"

"I wouldn't say I was scared. I was transfixed more than anything else because I had never experienced anything like that before."

"What did you do after the bulto went away?"

"Ah, that's the scary part. That's when I started to shake, like when a sudden blast of cold chills penetrates and grips your body. So I spurred my horse to a fast trot until I got home."

"How old were you then?"

"That's before I married your mom. I was probably around eighteen years old."

"Did you tell Grandpa and Grandma about it?"

"No. I didn't want to worry them. Later on I did tell your grandpa about the incident."

"Okay, hijito," said my mom, who had been listening intently to Dad's story, also for the first time. "On to bed. It's getting late."

Places like the Laguna Número Dos and stories like that of the ghostly apparition were not unique near my village or the outlying areas when I was growing up. Between my village and my home there was El Coruco (the Bedbug), legendary for its rattling chains, but any racket occurred only at night.* The deafening noise presumably came from witches in the area who inhabited abandoned homes. Parents warned their children to be on their toes when returning on horseback, for example, from a community dance.

Not far from my home, some five to seven hundred feet away, were some mounds we were told point-blank not to go near because of the *escupiones*, spitting lizards. If you got too close, they could spit on you; their spittle was supposedly poisonous, and you could die. Needless to say, we stayed away, although at times my Cousin J. and I would dare to ride our horses close to the lizards' mounds to see what they looked like. Unlike regular lizards, the so-called spitters were beautifully clad in yellow and green. It was tempting to dismount from our horses to observe them more closely, but our bravery had its limits; we were fearful that we might die if one of those poisonous creatures spat on us.

Aside from stories, I, like many other kids, grew up with a litany of beliefs, *creencias*, or superstitions. A number of these beliefs or superstitions, I took to heart; they constituted an essential part of my upbringing. Most of the superstitions I learned or inherited from my parents and grandparents on both sides of the family. Others came from members of my extended family as well as old-timers in my village of Ojo del Padre.

A popular superstition was the following: "Don't leave hairs in the washbasin, lest they turn into snakes." While I no longer believe the foregoing, I still do not leave hairs in the sink. In this day and age perhaps it's to prevent having to call the plumber to unplug a stopped-up system more than anything else.

When I reached puberty, I became less inclined to put stock in many superstitions. Nevertheless, as an adult I still adhere to some of them, but it's due more to an unbreakable habit than to a self-avowed conviction per se. For example, my paternal grandfather taught me to wash my face with cold water in the morning if I wished to live a long life. Where or from whom he adopted this notion is beyond me, but to this day I practice

* See *Rattling Chains and Other Stories for Children / Ruido de cadenas y otros cuentos para niños*.

what he said. Perhaps there is at least a modicum of truth in his words. After all, he died at the ripe old age of one hundred.

The superstitions that follow comprise some, not all, of those I grew up with in the Río Puerco Valley. Although they are listed in alphabetical order, I recalled them in random order.

1. *Haz la señal de la cruz cuando pases por la iglesia o te toca mala suerte.*
   Make the sign of the cross when going past the church, or bad luck will come to you.

2. *Lávate la cara todas las mañanas con agua fría y vives una larga vida.*
   Wash your face with cold water every morning, and you'll live a long life.

3. *No comas carne de marrano pa' la cena o vas a oyer los marranos en la cama toa la noche.*
   Don't eat pork for supper, or you'll hear pigs oink in bed all night long.

4. *No dejes cabellos en la bandeja o se vuelven víboras.*
   Don't leave hairs in the washbasin, or they'll turn into snakes.

5. *No juegues con lumbre o fósforos antes de acostarte o te vas a mear en la cama.*
   Don't play with fire or matches before bedtime, or you'll wet the bed.

6. *No le hagas cosquillas al niño en la planta de los pies o se le acaba el resuello.*
   Don't tickle the bottom of the baby's feet, or he'll lose his breath.

7. *Nunca mires la hostia en la misa o te castiga Dios.*
   Never look at the host during Mass, or God will punish you.

8. *Quítate el sombrero cuando pases por la iglesia o Dios te castiga.*
   Be sure to take off your hat when passing by the church, or God will punish you.

9. *Si jallas fruta alderedor de la casa, no te la comas porque alguien te quiere hacer mal.*
   If you find fruit around the house, don't eat it, because someone is trying to bewitch you.

10. *Si le pegas a tu padre, se te va secar el brazo (la mano).*
    If you strike your father, your arm (hand) will shrivel up.

11. *Si quieres pescarte una bruja, voltéate la camiseta al revés.*
    If you wish to catch a witch, turn your T-shirt inside out.

12. *Si se está lavando la cara el gato es porque viene gente.*
    If a cat is washing his face, people are coming to visit.
13. *Si te sale un bulto, ponle las cruces y se desaparece.*
    If a ghost appears before you, make a cross [using the thumb and index finger of your right hand], utter the words, *Póngote las cruces*, and it will disappear.
14. *Si una persona mira a una criatura (un niño) muncho, le puede hacer ojo.*
    If a person admires a baby (a child) too much, it can become the victim of the evil eye.

In retrospect, I can see that many superstitions passed on from the elders to young people were intended as moral compasses or gauges to ensure that their children and grandchildren walked a straight line. Doing so thus spared the families embarrassments in their respective communities.

Inherent in countless superstitions or beliefs was the fear factor—for example, when a son was told by the mother or grandmother that if he should strike his father in a moment of uncontrolled rage, not only would his arm shrivel up, but in some cases the earth would swallow him up to his waist. This was the condition in which he would then be destined to roam the four corners of the earth as punishment from God for his transgression. In fact, ballads have been written about the Disobedient Son, highlighting his sinful acts and the consequences he must endure for the rest of his days.

There was even a popular ballad that my mother used to sing at the ranch about Rosita Alvírez, who went to a dance against her mother's wishes. After a young man asked beautiful Rosita to dance, she refused his offer. He warned her not to rebuff him, but she ignored him. Unable to withstand being slighted, coupled with the public humiliation, the young man took out a pistol and killed her.

As the above-mentioned ballad attests, daughters and granddaughters were not spared from being forewarned about the price they could pay for being disobedient. This point was brought home by the mother or grandmother more than anyone else. As stated in chapter 3, the stigma of a young girl bearing a child out of wedlock could be devastating, not to mention the dishonor heaped upon the family. An episode of this type could reverberate in her community and beyond for a long time to come.

The primary responsibility of keeping matters of this type in check fell squarely on the mother and grandmother's shoulders (the fathers and grandfathers counseled the boys), but the fear factor also entered the picture. The girl oftentimes was told that an illegitimate child could be born with physical deformities or with a short tail, reminiscent of the devil. Such pronouncements coming from parents and grandparents injected more than a modicum of dread in boys as well as girls.

For any young man or woman who viewed those seemingly far-fetched admonishments with skepticism, the elders were quick to cite specific cases to drive their point home. Most of the time warnings and advice were adhered to, but in some cases a boy or girl's behavior yielded to human frailty or carnal temptation.

The world of witchcraft, superstitions, and the supernatural is vast and virtually boundless. The few stories and superstitions that I have alluded to in this chapter are merely the tip of the iceberg, but I trust that they convey in a vivid and convincing way the fundamental importance of the role ghostly apparitions, magic, and the paranormal played during my childhood. It was indeed a fascinating, spellbinding, and in many cases creepy world that kept me entertained during the cold winter months secluded in my casita until spring greeted us. For my grandfather, an avid reader of *The Old Farmer's Almanac* (see chapter 18), spring symbolized life and hope.

6

Dad

Master Kite Builder

ONE TIME, WHILE MY family and I were in Bernalillo visiting Grandma Cinda, I saw an object in the sky. It kept moving up and down and sideways near the ditch where my uncle Ben fished for frogs next door to Grandma Cinda. Upon closer examination, I noticed that the object had a long tail. I was fascinated. At first glance it struck me as magical. How could this thing fly without wings . . . and by itself? As I gazed about I saw a little boy about my age; he looked like he was pulling on something. My fascination did not diminish one iota.

Unable to contain my curiosity, I ran inside Grandma's house. She and my parents and my step-grandfather, whom we called Uncle Antonio, were seated around the kitchen table talking and drinking coffee. I didn't want to interrupt their conversation, but I was eager to ask her a question. She took notice of my unexpected presence and what must have been an uncharacteristic look on my face. (Grandmas have a knack for detecting such things.)

"What's wrong, hijito? You're panting. Why were you running?" she asked.

"Cinda, there's something in the sky! And it has like a tail. Do you know what it is?"

"Ah, yes, that's probably Patricio, your cousin. He's flying a *papalote*. He does that in March, when the winds blow."

"He's flying a what?" I queried.

"A papalote, a kite."

"Boy, I sure would like to have one."

"We'll make one when we get home," my father interjected.

"And how are we going to do that?" I added.

"Just wait. You'll see."

The flying kite was a novelty to me. I knew birds could fly because they had wings, and chickens, too, sort of (for very short distances), but I wondered how something like a kite could get up in the air without wings. I could hardly wait for Dad to make me one. That night I barely slept thinking about my cousin Patricio's kite. I even dreamed about a kite high up in the sky.

The next day after breakfast we left for the ranch. As soon as we got home, I began pestering Dad about the papalote, a word that was familiar to me and made more sense than *kite* because *papalote* was also used to refer to a windmill at Grandpa Lolo's Ojo de Esquipula, Esquipula Spring (as we locals pronounced it, not "Esquípulas," as in Nuestro Señor de Esquípulas). As it turned out, there was some relationship between a kite and a windmill. The kite, as I was to learn later, needed wind to fly, and the windmill, wind to be propelled.

That afternoon before supper, Dad stopped by where I was chopping wood. He had been tending to some of the livestock in the corral.

"Listen, when you're done we'll go down to the river to cut some *jaras*, twigs, for your kite."

I knew something about jaras. These were slender red twigs that the teacher kept in a corner near her desk at school to swat the boys' bottoms in case they misbehaved. They came from a huge bush with a pink bloom and could be found in arroyos or at the riverbed of the Río Puerco where water settled after a runoff or a rainfall.

When Dad and I walked down to the river, he knew exactly where to go and the size of twigs that he needed. First, he cut one rod measuring about thirty inches in length and a second one about twenty inches long. The longer one would run up and down the middle of the kite, and the shorter twig ran horizontally, forming a cross where the two intersected. He also cut two additional ones measuring fifteen inches each for the upper part of the kite, which formed a triangle (see kite diagram below).

Cutting the twigs with the sharp pocketknife that Dad carried with him at all times was a snap. According to him, the willowy twigs were ideal for making a kite because they were strong, pliable, light, and thin. Their thinness had some bearing on the weight of the kite and made it easier to fly.

Once back at the ranch, Dad named the things—in addition to the rods—that we needed in order to turn my kite into a reality:

brown paper bags (two or three large ones)
old pieces of bedsheet
pair of scissors
short piece of bailing wire
small bowl
string
water (a cup or so)
white corn flour (about two cups)

Before we began to build it, Dad explained that kites came in different shapes and sizes. "Yours," he said, "is going to be in the shape of a diamond." I didn't have the vaguest idea what shape that was, but I didn't dare ask. Many times I learned by asking questions; other times, I did so by intuition or observation. This time I would observe and learn in the process.

Mom kept a stack of large paper bags next to the wood bin. Sometimes we used them to start the morning fire in the woodstove. Dad picked the largest bag and began cutting it. He then spread the paper on the floor. He took two thin twigs (30 by 20 inches), arranged them in the form of a cross, and secured them at the cross-section with a short piece of bailing wire. Next he placed the cross on top of the paper to see if the paper was big enough, but he had to cut the second bag to have enough paper to fit the shape of my would-be kite.

As I observed my dad, he turned to me and said, "You pay close attention to how I do all this so that next time you can build your own kite, okay?"

"Okay," I responded.

"Now hand me the flour and the water. We're going to make some *poleadas*, paste, to glue these two paper sacks together."

I knew about poleadas because my paternal grandmother at the ranch used it to wallpaper her vigas, or beams, in her bedroom with sheets of paper from a Sears, Roebuck catalog. I had seen her mix the flour and water just as Dad was doing. Perhaps he learned how to make poleadas from her. I didn't ask, but the process was simple enough. The important thing was to get the paste's consistency just right. The paste could not be too thick or too runny.

Dad took out his pocketknife, dipped it into the bowl of paste, and spread the white substance along the edges where the pieces of paper came together. The paste didn't take long to begin to dry. Next he cut the paper to fit the shape of the kite frame, allowing an inch or so to fold over the twigs. I could see that Dad had built kites in the past. When he finished, here's what the kite looked like:

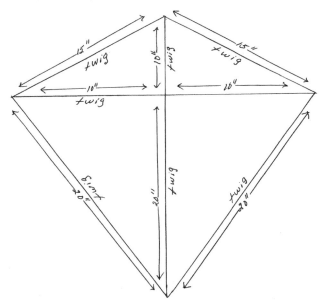

Drawing of a homemade kite.

He carefully picked up the kite with both hands and took it inside and put it under my bed to make sure the paste dried properly overnight. Before going to bed, he showed me how to cut short, thin strands of bed-sheet to make a tail for the kite. We knotted the pieces together. I did ask Dad why the kite needed a tail. His answer, as I recollect, was more tongue-in-cheek than serious.

"Look, horses have tails, right? Cows have tails, right?" he said as I nodded my head in agreement. "And your dog has a tail. They use their tails for balance. That's what the tail will do for the kite also."

I listened and scratched my head, because I thought horses and cows had tails to swat away the flies. As for my dog, I thought he wagged his tail to express happiness. Nevertheless, I took Dad at his word.

"There you are! The tail's complete. Tomorrow if there's enough wind we'll try out the kite. Now on to bed." And off I went.

I knelt next to my bed and said my prayers before Mom came in to bless me and to say goodnight. I had another restless night, but this time it was because of my wondering if the kite was going to fly or not.

The next day we had to wait until the evening breezes kicked up from the west. Dad had me fetch the kite from under my bed, while he got a ball of string that he was using to line up the adobes for the extra room he was building onto our little casita. With the point of his knife he cut a tiny hole through the paper where the vertical and horizontal twigs came together, and he tied the string to the twigs. Now the kite was ready for its first flight and my first excitement. He also attached the tail to the bottom of the kite. While Dad held onto the string, which was wrapped around one of Mom's old wooden rolling pins, about seven inches long, he asked me to hold the kite up above my head. I put my right hand behind the cross-section of the kite—not in front—where the vertical and horizontal rods met. He stood on top of a small hill next to the corral. I was farther down the hill with the kite still in my hand but with it attached to the string that Dad hung onto.

The evening winds were beginning to act up. We didn't have to wait long. Suddenly a gust of wind came and Dad shouted, "Turn loose!" He let the rolling pin drop to the ground, allowing the string to run through his cupped hands, the string gaining more and more slack. Like magic, the kite climbed higher and higher while Dad held on tight to the string wrapped around Mom's rolling pin.

Even Chopo, my dog, was excited. He wagged his tail and barked at the kite as it moved magically in the air. The gentle breeze coming off the nearby butte made the kite flutter ever so gently. "Come!" Dad shouted as he waved at me. "Come and fly your kite."

When he uttered the words "your kite," I knew the kite-building experiment was a success. I was proud of Dad. In my estimation, he was a master kite builder, indeed. I remember to this day those wonderful, exciting moments at the ranch. The following bilingual poem reflects my sentiments of flying a homemade kite.*

Mi papalote†   **My Kite**

Mi papalote   My kite
bandera en el aire   a banner in the sky
rascando las nubes   scratching the clouds
con buen donaire   with great elegance
para llegar al cielo.   reaching for the heavens.

Mi papalote   My kite
papel de parquete   made from paper sack
pegado con poleadas   glued with flour paste
cruzado con jaras   with slender twigs
del oriente   from east to west
al poniente.   in cross-like fashion.

Me jala y jala   It tugs and tugs at me
queriendo subir   wanting to ascend
mientras más escala.   the more it scales.
Le doy cordón   I give it
y más cordón.   more and more string.

Rasguña las nubes   It scratches the clouds
cuanto más sube   the higher it goes

con su sinuosa cola   with its wavy tail,
tejida en chongo   queue style from

....

*   From *Tiempos Lejanos: Poetic Images from the Past.*

†   "Comet"; a term of Nahuatl origin.

de pedazos de sábana	pieces of bedsheet
y baja y sube	waving up and down
como le da la gana.	as it darn well pleases.
¡Ay, qué alegría si yo	Oh, that I were also
tamién juera papalote	a kite so that I could fly
pa volar bien altote!	way up high into the sky!

I asked my father where he had learned to make a kite, and his answer was straightforward. "I learned on my own," he responded, showing utmost confidence. His next kite was a box kite, a much more complicated enterprise. He flew his box kite, and I flew the one he made for me. Flying homemade kites together was great fun.

At one point Mom joined us. In her right hand she had a piece of white paper with a hole cut out in the middle. "Here," she said and handed me the paper. "Send a message." She showed me how to put the spool of string gently through the hole in the paper. Slowly at first but quickly gaining speed, thanks to the wind, the paper climbed and climbed until it reached the flying kite. Mom also knew something about kites.

7

Spring House Cleaning

THE FRIGID AND BRUTAL months of winter—above all febrero loco, Crazy February, as people called it, coupled with the blowing dirt and windy days of March—were now history. No more frozen feet and chapped hands, at least for another year.

April was here. Spring was definitely in the air. Except for doing diapers here and there for my little brother Juanito, Mom decided to forgo washing and ironing, which as a rule she did on Mondays and Tuesdays. Of more importance was to jump-start her spring cleaning to ensure that she finished the bulk of work by Friday, when Dad came home from his government job in El Rito de Semilla.

I had gone to help Grandpa Lolo take his cows and horses as well as Bayito and Prieto, my mounts, down to the river to water them. On the way back up the hill, I saw that the kitchen and bedroom windows to our house were wide open. At that moment I knew that spring-cleaning was definitely upon us because I heard Mom singing one of her favorite Mexican songs. I paused and listened to her beautiful voice. Immediately, I recognized the words that by now I knew by heart and still do to this day.

Hace un año	A Year Ago
Hace un año que yo tuve un sentimiento.	A year ago I felt an emotion.
Hace un año que yo tuve una ilusión.	A year ago I had an illusion.

Hace un año que se cumple en este día.	It was a year ago to the day.
Tú recuerdas que en tus brazos me dormía,	You recall how I lulled myself in your arms,
y que inocente muy confiado te entregué mi corazón.	and how I innocently entrusted my heart to you.
Ese tiempo tan feliz no volverá.	Such happy times will not return.
Mi cariño lo pagaste con traiciones.	You rewarded my affection with deceit.
Me has dejado sólo crueles decepciones,	You left me with only cruel deceptions,
pero anda ingrata,	but come, now, you ungrateful thing,
como pagas otro así te las pagará.	as you've treated me, someone else will do the same to you.
Ay, ay ay ay,	Oh, oh oh oh,
corazón te lo pido . . .	oh, dear, I beg you . . .

As I stepped inside the bedroom, Mom heard me and right away turned around. "Where you've been, hijito? I need your help. It's a nice day, and we have to air out, *aigrar*, the house so we can start cleaning it inside and out before your father gets home in a few days."

"I went to help Grandpa Lolo water the animals," I responded.

"And look at all the mud on your shoes. Go scrape it off before it dries."

I grabbed a kitchen knife and went outside and returned a few minutes later.

"What can I do, Mom?" I asked, knowing full well that a litany of chores awaited us.

"The first thing you can do is take out the two *jergas*, rugs, in the bedroom, drape them over the clothesline—one at each end, so the clothesline doesn't buckle in the middle—and swat them good and hard with the broom." .

I loved to whack the rugs using the broom's wooden handle. Seeing the dust and dirt fly off gave me a sense of gratification. The sight must have been something to behold, because Chopo stood nearby and looked at me a bit astonished, if not bemused. The rugs would hang on the clothesline to air out until after supper.

I went back inside and found Mom in the bedroom. She had already removed the drapes; they were now on top of the bed. The *celosías*, window shades, were still up to give us privacy at night, although that was hardly a concern since the only Peeping Toms around were Grandpa's hobbled horses, which he turned loose at night.

"Come, hijito. Help me push the beds away from the walls to the middle of the room. We need to wash the walls."

The beds, which were not on wheels or coasters, were not easy to slide on the wooden floor without leaving scratches, but we managed to move them inch by inch.

"Now go get me a bucket of water from your grandparents' water tank. Oh, yes, and bring the sponges with you that are in the bucket."

As Mom stood on a kitchen chair and washed all three whitewashed adobe walls in the bedroom, including the wooden partition wall separating the bedroom and the kitchen, she continued her medley of Mexican songs. I listened while I washed the windows.

Thereafter, besides entertaining my two little brothers, Beltrán and Juanito, on the kitchen floors so they wouldn't get in her way, I helped wash the bottom parts of the walls using a small sponge. By that time Beltrán was whining that he was hungry. Juanito, who was younger—scarcely two years old—started crying. I was hungry, too. It was time to eat lunch.

After lunch all three of us took a short siesta under the two beds. My brothers slept under our bed, and I napped under Mom and Dad's. When I woke up, Mom had opened a box of *calsamán*, calcimine, that she had purchased on our last trip to the Bernalillo Mercantile in Bernalillo. I was surprised that for the first time ever Mom would use the light green powdery stuff to cover the walls instead of *jaspe*, gypsum, which residents in the Río Puerco Valley were accustomed to using.

People actually hauled huge chunks of gypsum on horse wagon over rough terrain in excess of twenty miles from a place called Las Lomitas Blancas, southwest of San Ysidro and west of Bernalillo, all the way to my valley. (Today the gypsum pits, a commercial enterprise, are called the White Mesa Gypsum Mine.) At home the husband or wife broke up the gypsum into small chunks with a sledgehammer and heated them in the stove oven. The gypsum was now soft and easy and ready to hammer into a powder; now and then it was ground in a *metate*, a grinding stone, before the white substance was mixed with water to whitewash the adobe walls.

But with calcimine—which also came in other colors—becoming increasingly fashionable, many women of the Río Puerco Valley not only resorted to the product but also liked it. Thus jaspe, the old-fashioned standard bearer since time immemorial, soon was history, like countless other products concocted or found on a ranch.

Mom welcomed the convenience as well and therefore forsook gypsum for calcimine. When I woke up from my nap, she had already mixed some of the calcimine in a bucket full of water. She was now ready to beautify the walls. Instead of using a paintbrush, she dipped a small piece of sheepskin or wool into the bucket and dabbed the clean walls with it. The process was laborious indeed, but Mom liked the texture of calcimine and thought it was somewhat easier to apply than gypsum.

By the end of the day, she had finished the west wall. The remaining two walls—north and south—would have to wait until tomorrow. Unfortunately, whitewashing walls is not a chore I was old enough to undertake or help Mom with. Besides, Mom, like most women I knew in my village or nearby, was a master at the task. The best help I could offer was to play with my little brothers.

By Thursday noon, I could tell from Mom's weary face that she was a bit exhausted from applying the calcimine, but she finally finished the bedroom, quite an undertaking for one person. The only white spot visible to the naked eye was the *nicho*, niche, on the north wall, where she kept her Holy Child of Atocha. She decided to retain the nicho's original white color. In that way, she explained, "Whenever I light a votive candle at night it can brighten up the Holy Child's face." The Holy Child was her most venerated santo, religious statue, in addition to the Virgen de Guadalupe, whom she kept on top of her dresser next to her bed. La Virgen was the patron saint of Ojo del Padre, our village.

After Mom finished sprucing up the bedroom, the next huge chore was to take apart the two mattresses and four pillows. This meant removing the wool from the mattresses and the pillows, washing, drying, and fluffing it, then stuffing the wool back in. Tearing a mattress apart and reassembling it was something I enjoyed. It was fun. In fact, even my little brothers joined the party, as it were.

Mom walked over to Grandpa Lolo's house to borrow a *lona*, tarpaulin. The canvas was the same one that he packed as part of his camping gear whenever we went on cattle roundups in the spring and fall. He'd spread the canvas on the ground at the campsite; it served as our eating table. Luckily, Grandpa was home and was able to help Mom carry the heavy canvas, so Mom didn't have to drag it across the dirt by herself. Once Grandpa Lolo and Mom got to our house, they rolled the tarp out on the ground in front, by the door to the kitchen.

Grandpa knew what Mom was going to do. Consequently, he offered to help carry the first mattress outside from the bedroom. That was Grandpa's nature, a veritable gentleman. He was always willing to help you. He was also known for his altruism in the community.

With the mattress on the ground, Mom fetched a single-edge razor blade that Dad no longer used for shaving. She kept several blades in a jar full of buttons, safely away from my little brothers, in case she needed one. She began by carefully cutting the seams at the foot of the mattress, although she could also have started at the opposite end. After cutting and removing the line of stitching, little by little she began to expose the wool inside. Mom showed her artistic talent by the delicate manner with which she controlled the razor.

Once she exposed the entire bottom portion of the mattress, you could see the sheep's wool. The intent now was to take out all the wool, leaving only the mattress cover, but first she had to remove the *motitas de lana*, little woolen balls, which were strategically spaced throughout on both sides—top and bottom—of the mattress and connected by a string that ran from one side of the mattress to the other. By cutting the string, we could then easily remove the wool from inside the mattress.

Crawling inside the mattress to pull out the wool was something I enjoyed doing. (My little brothers were to join me later, when they got older.) Mom obviously saw a glimmer in my eye. I had taken the wool out the previous year; hence, she thought I was an old pro at the job.

"Come, come. What are you waiting for, my *tejoncito*, little badger? Get a move on," she exclaimed. I began to pull the wool out with my small hands so that she could put it in a tin tub of warm water ready for the wash. Hot water was not conducive because the wool tended to shrink, which made fluffing it later more difficult.

Inch by inch, I made headway. Before I knew it, I was deep inside the mattress. The blue and white mattress cover wasn't quite as dark inside as the caves near El Aguaje, nor was it as spooky either. But a sense of claustrophobia came over me. I even wondered if people who died felt claustrophobic inside their wooden coffins. Before I knew it, I quickly had removed all the wool from inside the mattress.

As the process of tearing apart the mattress and putting it back together unfolded, Mom and I had two tin tubs full of wool ready to be washed. I learned why—and how—washing the wool was important. The wool itself was not necessarily soiled, unless one of us boys was a bed wetter, but over a year's time the wool turned flat, became lifeless, and lost its oomph, even if the mattress was turned over periodically to prevent a depression from forming in the middle.

Before Mom washed the wool, she washed the mattress cover, which I helped hang on the clothesline. Then she washed and spread the wool on Grandpa's canvas to dry. From time to time, Mom would move the wool with a wooden rake that was usually used for threshing pinto beans. On a hot and sunny day the wool didn't take more than two hours to dry. Then the fun began for me.

"Are you ready, hijito?" Mom asked with a lighthearted smile, as though she needed to coax me.

In the meantime, she had borrowed a couple of *varas*, round pliable staffs, from Grandma Lale. These wooden rods, about four to six feet long and less than an inch in diameter, were cut from a large bush tree that was commonly found in the Río Puerco riverbed. (The twigs for making my kite came from this same bush.)

Mom used the rods to *varear la lana*, whip the wool, giving it life by making it fluffy before putting the mattress back together again. The idea was to hold a vara firmly in each hand and to strike the wool, first with the right hand and then with the left (or vice versa), in rhythmic fashion.

Part of the joy for me was to see the wool jump up and down like hail striking the hard ground and bouncing into the air. The fluffier the wool, the higher it bounced. I did this over and over until Mom felt that the wool was fluffy enough. By the time I was done, instead of having two tin tubs of wool as before, there were at least twice as many.

By now the mattress cover that had been hanging on the clothesline was dry, thanks to the shimmering sun. Mom and I spread the cover on top of the tarpaulin. She then turned it inside out and rolled it back toward the head except for about two to three feet. This is the where she and I would began painstakingly restuffing the mattress by hand. Mom cautioned me not to force the wool in; otherwise, the fluffiness would disappear.

Starting at the head of the mattress, Mom used a steel needle about seven inches long. She ran the needle and string from one side of the mattress to the other—from top to bottom—at intervals of about twelve inches. The small woolen balls that had been removed earlier were then sewn back on, both for decoration and for covering the small indentations created after the needle was run through the mattress and the string was pulled tight. The indentations were also done with a practical purpose in mind—to render a therapeutic effect to one's back. The mattress had more shape and bounce than a flat surface would.

There was only one drawback to these interspersed notches in the mattress: whenever *chinches*, bedbugs, found their way from the chicken coop to our bedroom, those little grooves were a haven for the pesky critters. They would hide, not to be seen by the naked eye, and emerge at night to bite us mercilessly when we were asleep. I hated them because, as Mom said, "They love your *sangre livianita*, your sweet or thin blood."

Bit by bit, Mom made headway until she came to the foot of the mattress, where she sewed the seams shut. Now she and my father—as well as my baby sister, Julianita, who slept with them—would have a clean mattress until the following spring.

Doing to the pillows what Mom did to the mattress was easy in comparison. In fact, she and I washed the wool to all four pillows at the same time, but the mattress my little brothers and I slept on would have to wait until the following week, after Dad had gone back to work.

Having finished the pillows and Mom and Dad's mattress, washing the bedroom curtains and windows, plus painting their wooden frames inside, seemed relatively easy, though it was hard work just the same. Scrubbing the wooden floors in the bedroom was a bit more taxing, but Mom got down on her knees and tackled the chore with a bristle brush, soap, and warm water. Most of the older homes predating my parents' home—which was built in 1935, the year of their marriage—had dirt floors.

The kitchen also had wooden floors. It was separated from the bedroom, as mentioned earlier, by a wooden partition that Mom painted blue in the bedroom and white in the kitchen. Of the remaining three kitchen walls, Mom applied a light powdery calcimine similar to that in the bedroom, although the color was pale azure.

Cleaning the stove and cupboard were the last two things that Mom had to tackle before spring house cleaning was declared complete, except for redoing the mattress Beltrán, Juanito, and I slept on. The entire cleaning process usually took no more than a week or so, because in Dad's absence Mom and I also had to take the time to tend to ranch chores, such as feeding and watering the chickens, rabbits (my responsibility), and horses.

Mud plastering the house and painting the outside of the windows frames would now wait until my father was home for the summer months from his government job. At that time Mom would also lend a helping hand in mud plastering. After all, women were known for—and more adept at—mud plastering than most men. That was true of my Mom, Grandma Lale next door, and Aunt Taida, whose house was a short distance down the hill, close to the Río Puerco.

For now, our casita sparkled and Mom's eyes twinkled knowing that our dwelling was ready to welcome friends who usually came by on their way home from church or from a fiesta in the placita. Mom loved to entertain guests and to show off her spick-and-span home. Who could blame her?

8

Wash Day Meant Pinto Beans

BEFORE I REALIZED IT, Sunday evening was upon us once again. Mom and Dad's friends Fernando and Virginia had left our home after eating lunch and spending the afternoon with my parents. Now it was time for Mom to pack the galletas, biscuits, she had baked on Saturday, along with tortillas and some nonperishable foods for Dad to take with him for the work week. He continued the same type of work for the government, that is, constructing roads and so on, even though his CCC camp job had ended.

While Mom packed each baked good meticulously into a large tin can that lard came in—gold color coated inside—I watched in awe. Not one inch of space was wasted. Mom was so neat about everything.

"Come, hijito. While I get some other stuff ready for your dad, you can clean the beanos," she said kiddingly, as if to cheer me up.

She knew I didn't mind cleaning beans as much as I disliked Mondays. For me Monday was a double whammy: it was the day Dad left us alone for the next five days, and wash day was upon Mom and me—my little brothers were too small to help. To me Monday morning was the least joyful day of the week. A certain tedium and agitation always came over me.

Cleaning beans meant filling a pan from the gunnysack in the food cupboard and spreading them on the kitchen table. I then had to separate the light-colored beans (the good ones) from the dark red ones that were shriveled and not suitable for cooking. Plus I had to toss out those that had broken in half or lost the skin when the goats or horses had stomped unduly hard during threshing.

59

Furthermore, I had to pick out the *terroncitos*, small pieces of hardened mud balls, that mistakenly got mixed in with the pinto beans and dispose of them. My last hurdle, in a manner of speaking, was to slide the good beans into a pan that rested on my lap. They were now ready to be soaked overnight for faster and easier cooking come Monday morning. The bad beans were victims of the deselection and were tossed away. Those beans weren't even saved for planting.

Mondays were wash days not only in my home but also up and down the Río Puerco Valley, when most households were set aglow with the multicolored clothing strung on clotheslines, fences, or both. For me the bright colors were perhaps the only blissful aspect to wash day.

Besides having an aversion to Mondays, another reason for my unhappiness was because I had to watch over the pinto beans as they cooked. That was my one abiding responsibility for the day, plus making sure the *pato*, teakettle, had hot water at all times to add to the beans. One did not add cold water, or else the beans and bean juice turned dark and ugly. I also had to stir the beans from time to time to make sure they didn't stick to the bottom of the clay pot. Mom, as mentioned in chapter 2, had gotten the clay pot from a woman at Jémez Pueblo in exchange for some of Mom's homegrown vegetables.

Knowing that there was nothing worse than the smell of burned beans, I was very assiduous in watching over them. They could stink to high heaven if you burned them! My maternal grandmother's words invariably came to mind. "Hijito, if someday you wish to marry," she used to say to me in a kidding sort of way, "never mind whether the girl is pretty or not, as long as she doesn't burn the beans." Since I was just a little boy and matrimony was hardly in the cards yet, marriage and beans somehow did not mix and therefore offered little comfort to me. But I knew all too well that Grandma was only half-serious.

Feeding the stove wood was another added chore—or a nuisance—that cut into my marble-playing time on wash days. But eating *frijoles enteros*, whole beans and bean juice, in a coffee cup with a modest sprinkling of salt was something Mom and I enjoyed together. For me as a kid, it was a luncheon's delight. While frijoles enteros were fully cooked, they differed from those cooked for an extra hour. The longer-cooked beans turned soft and were not whole or puffy like frijoles enteros.

But cold tortillas from the day before were something that was not to my liking on Mondays. Except for wash days, Mom made fresh tortillas every day. She had me and the rest of the family spoiled. Once in a while I would warm a tortilla on top of the woodstove, but we children were warned that if you ate too many scorched tortillas, your teeth could fall out. Myth or not, I recanted from time to time. The mere thought of being toothless was not terribly appealing, which was ironic because dental hygiene, except for periodically rubbing baking soda on your teeth, was virtually nonexistent in most Río Puerco Valley households. Toothbrushes were rare, to be sure, but dentists were not in existence.

On Sunday, before dusk set upon us, there were several things I had to do to lessen the flurry of activity that occurred early Monday morning after we'd bid Dad goodbye. Perhaps the most important undertaking was to chop as much wood as possible to keep the fire alive under the *cajetes*, tin tubs, although chopping wood continued intermittently throughout the day. Having enough wood available for the stove and the beans was likewise a necessity.

I always tried to have ample chopped firewood on hand, especially during the hot summer months. Chopping and splitting wood in the heat of the day was not fun at all. In fact, the ax, while a good friend and companion, could make the chore downright trying if the blade was dull and in dire need of a good sharpening.

Either my father or my grandpa next door had to sharpen the ax on the family's *mollejón*, sharpening stone. The job was too much to handle for a young boy like me. As for Mom, she was adept at numerous designated-male chores, but using the sharpening stone was not one she dared to tackle.

More often than not I was glad when the last batch of clothing was bound for the tin tub with hot water. By then I was anxious to help Mom fish each heavy garment—pants and shirts to be exact—out of the hot water using a long wooden stick that Dad had crafted from a cottonwood tree. Sometimes we used an old broomstick handle. Even Chopo wagged his tail as if to rejoice that wash day was almost over for another week.

On Sunday evening, three large number 3 tin tubs (number 2 and number 1 were smaller in size) were lined up a foot or so apart next to our house, facing the Mesa Prieta to the east, like a set of cymbals ready for a symphonic concert. But the setup was hardly music to my ears, unless it came from the cracking of wood burning. The gurgling of boiling water, too, was soothing.

Two of the three tubs were placed on large stones, with ample room between stones for wood to be fed underneath and for whatever breezes came to fan the fire. In due course the bottoms and sides of the tubs had blackened from the fire and hot coals.

The three tin tubs were used for different purposes. The first tub contained boiling water for dark and heavy clothes like Levi's, lonas, and *pecheras*, bib overalls. The second one had warm water for more delicate garments, such as dresses and blouses. And the third tin tub was full of cold water for rinsing the clothes before they were strung on the clothesline.

To remove the grime from clothing, particularly Levi's and Dad's working shirts, Mom at one time soaked them in homemade soap called *jabón amarillo*, pine soap. Later on, circa 1941, she began to use large bars of P&G soap. She discovered this soap, wrapped in blue and white wax textured paper, on one of the family's trips to the Bernalillo Mercantile Company, where we did our shopping for *provisiones*, groceries.

For the longest time, because of my very limited knowledge of English, I thought the letters *P* and *G* stood for "Pretty Good," in praise of my mother's good choice of wash soap (she knew no English whatsoever). Much later, when I started school and progressed beyond the ABCs, I came to realize that P&G meant Proctor & Gamble, the manufacturer's name.

What's more, without fail Mom would pour Mrs. Stewart's bluing into the third tub. It made Levi's and bib overalls look more natural. Bluing was another washing product Mom had adopted thanks to the owner of the Bernalillo Mercantile Company. I can still picture the elderly lady on the blue bottle with a white collar and wire-rim glasses. She looked like a typical grandma, inviting you to use her product—which Mom did.

But the back-bending work for Mom was on the *lavador*, washboard.

Scrubbing heavy clothes, above all Dad's Levi's and work shirts, was hard and unforgiving work. I always felt sorry for her as perspiration dripped from her brow during the hot summer days.

Women like my Mom scrubbed pants and other dark or heavy pieces of clothing on the washboard, which was placed in a cajete with hot, soapy water, before rinsing them in cold water. The light-colored clothing like blouses, dresses, and women and girls' undergarments, the ostensible delicate items, were usually washed by hand in warm water to lessen the wear and tear.

The following poem portrays the washboard through the eyes of a child, yours truly, as I envisioned it on wash days in my village of Ojo del Padre.*

El lavador	The Washboard
La vislumbre	The glimmer
del lavador	of the washboard
salta de cajete†	bounces from tin tub
a cajete	to tin tub
por el Ojo del Padre.	throughout Ojo del Padre.
Día lunes de lavar	Monday is wash day.
todas las mujeres	All the women face
con sus quehaceres	their chores
se ponen a trabajar.	and get to work.
Agua hirviente,	Boiling water,
tibia	lukewarm
y fría.	and cold.
Cada cajete de agua	Each tin tub of water
con su	with its
jabón,	soap,
añil	bluing
y lejía.	and lye in each one.

....

*   From *Tiempos Lejanos: Poetic Images from the Past.*

†   *Cajete,* a tin tub common in the Río Puerco Valley; the word derives from Nahuatl.

| *Tres cajetes* | Three washtubs |
| *forman la sinfonía.* | make up the symphony. |

Ropa oscura,	Dark clothes,
blanca	white,
y delicada	and delicate
aguardan su lavada,	await their washing,
enjuagada	rinsing,
y secada	and hanging
antes de ser rociadas	before being sprinkled
y planchadas.	to be ironed.

| *¡Ay, lavador* | Oh, you poor, hard-working |
| *trabajador!* | washboard! |

¿Por qué dejas	Why do you stop
de entretenerme	entertaining me
con tu relumbre?	with your sparkle?

The washboard, along with P&G soap and Mrs. Stewart's bluing, were part of so-called progress among Río Puerco Valley women; each item helped ease the task of washing clothes and leaving them looking smart. Women no longer had to carry tin tubs of clothing down to the riverbed, where they had used stones or logs of wood to beat the dirt out of men's and boys' pants and shirts in *charcos*, pools of water. These puddles settled after the roaring waters of the Río Puerco had subsided following the perennial summer rains and thunderstorms.

Listening to Mom's beautiful voice as she scrubbed clothes and sang her favorite Mexican songs—her words floating and disappearing into the air—eased my day's gloom. And the faster the song's tempo, the more quickly her hands moved up and down the washboard. At times I think she chose fast songs in order to finish the scrubbing sooner. One of her favorite songs was the ballad of Adelita, which was popular during the Mexican Revolution. The song went something like this, words that I still remember.

Adelita	Adelita
Si Adelita se juera con otro,	If Adelita were to leave with another,
la seguiría por tierra y por mar.	I'd follow her by land or by sea.
Si por mar en un buque de guerra	If by sea it would be on a warship
y por tierra en un tren militar.	if by land, on a military train.
Si toca que yo muera en la guerra	If by chance I die in the war
y si mi cuerpo en la sierra	and if my body is left
va quedar,	in the mountains,
Adelita por Dios te lo ruego,	Adelita for God's sake I beg you,
que por mí no vayas a llorar.	please don't shed any tears for me.
Si Adelita quisiera ser mi esposa,	If Adelita wished to be my wife,
si Adelita ya juera mi mujer,	or if she was already my wife,
le compraría un vestido de seda	I'd buy her a dress made of silk
antes de llevarla al cuartel.	before taking her to my quarters.

At every washing stage, the clothes were put in a smaller tin tub (a number 2 or 3) or straw basket; the clothing was then hung on the *percha*, clothesline, with *granpitas*, wooden clothespins. Different-colored clothespins made of plastic came later, but my mom never used them. While colorful, she thought they were superficial and lacked vitality.

Beyond the clothesline to the north loomed the majestic Cabezón Peak. Surrounded by sandstone-colored mesas and hillsides peppered with juniper trees, Cabezón Peak (the Navajos call it Black Rock) provided a magnificent background for the assortment of clothing displayed on the clothesline. Except for Levi's, long john underwear, *calzoncillos*, and heavy-duty shirts that Dad wore during the winter, the clothes did not take long to dry. The winds from the west helped to dry out most garments quickly. But the natural dryers, as it were, consisted of the hot and cold gentle breezes that Mother Nature regaled us with throughout the four seasons.

Helping Mom hang the clothing was something I enjoyed doing. For one thing, I thought it was rather humorous to see pants and shirts strung upside down. Somehow it gave me a different perspective on clothes and the people who wore them. This was particularly true of the *pantaletas*, baggy bloomers, that women like Grandma Lale wore. Many women, including Mom and my grandma, were careful not to hang their undergarments on the clothesline (they dried them in the kitchen on top of chairs). They were reluctant to display their "underworld" in public because of passersby or *majaderos*, wisecracking old men, who happened by on wash day. As for us children, we, too, made jokes about the underwear, adding to the comedic ensemble.

Hanging clothes during warm weather was not a challenge at all, but during the frigid winters it was a horse of a different color. Your fingernails would turn blue and your hands ice-cold like water in an *artesa*, horse's trough. Carrying the clothes inside the house was not a breeze. At times it was even comical because the stiff-frozen shirts looked like dried cowhides, while the pants resembled the solid pieces of beef we strung from the rafters in Grandpa Lolo's nearby *dispensa*, shed (see chapter 24).

I tried—on purpose, of course—to get the shirts through the screen door in a flat, horizontal position instead of carrying them upright. As a result, I would get stuck, and Mom had to come and rescue me. "*Ay, hijto. ¡Siempre lo de siempre! Te volvites atorar.* Oh, my dear boy. The same thing all over again! There you are stuck again." She tried hard to contain her laughter. Many times, above all in the winter, wash days that started off less than cheerfully ended on a humorous note.

POSTSCRIPT

In 1943, two years before we left my paternal grandparents' ranch for Albuquerque, Dad bought Mom a gasoline-operated Maytag wringer washing machine. The washer was loud enough to scare the living daylights out of my Angora cat, but the rickety-rack sounds coming from the motor and from the long, twisting, coiled pipe that stretched from the kitchen to the outdoors were music to my ears. I was especially happy for

Mom, because now she only had to use the washboard sparingly. The days of holding Dad's shirts like a long morcilla, blood sausage, and wringing the water out of them by Mom and me twisting them in opposite directions were over, as now her Maytag wrung out the shirts. Unfortunately for me, I still had to chop wood to heat water for the washing machine and for cooking the beans.

9

A Fleet of Flatirons

AT AN EARLY AGE, I may not have known all my days of the week, but I knew that Tuesday followed Monday. Tuesday was the day Mom ironed clothes and linens. For me it meant another day of chopping wood to heat the flatirons on the woodstove, but it was nothing like the amount of wood I chopped and split on wash days. In that respect, Tuesdays were rather anticlimactic—and less hectic—and boring.

Off in the distance, in what seemed a place far, far away but was only a scant hundred feet or so, I could faintly hear Grandpa's rooster crowing in the chicken coop as the sun began to peek over the Mesa Prieta. Upon hearing the rooster, Chopo started barking. I was still half-asleep. But between the competing noises of the rooster and Chopo's barking, I knew it was time to get up and light a fire to get the coffeepot going for Mom.

I emptied the cold, gray ashes into a bucket and fetched a couple of slender juniper logs and a bunch of palitos, kindling, from the wood box to feed the woodstove. I put a few palitos under the logs and some wood chips on top to get the fire going. I lit the wood with a kitchen match, and almost without delay the crackling sound of the fire replaced the uncanny silence in our two-room house.

Starting a fire was even quicker if we had *ocote*, torch pine, which Dad and I didn't always find on our trips to the *monte*, wooded area, where we searched for deadwood to burn at home (see chapter 12). So saving the small, incendiary pieces of pine for starting a fire quickly in the dead of winter was crucial.

Mom had emptied the *cunques*, coffee grounds, and washed the coffeepot the night before when she did the dishes. The tin pot was now ready for me to use to make coffee. Once the coffee had perked, I took a cup to Mom. She was still in bed with my baby sister, Julianita, who slept with her. I enjoyed taking coffee to Mom.

This is something I particularly relished when Dad was home for the weekend. They both took pleasure in a hot cup of coffee in bed, along with a bizcochito or two. Today there would be no bizcochitos, only coffee. More often than not I could sense that Mom didn't really enjoy having coffee by herself, but she went along with me so as not to hurt my feelings. I had established my own daily routine of making coffee and serving Mom even in Dad's absence.

What she and I delighted in doing every day was to have breakfast together. It was a pleasant way to kick off the day. I was an early morning riser—and still am to this day—which was also true of Mom. Once we woke up, we could both hit the ground running, as you might say. Mornings were more productive for us than the rest of the day, above all during the hot summer months.

One of the first things Mom did on Tuesdays after getting up was to *rociar*, sprinkle, water on the first tub full of clothing that she had to iron. She used a small pan of water, dipped in her fingers, and sprinkled the clothes piece by piece before putting each garment in a special small tin tub, a number 3. The last thing she did was to cover the clothing with a damp towel to keep the items moist until she was ready to iron them.

"Besides your oatmeal, what else would you like for breakfast, hijito?" Mom asked, knowing that I loved her omelets and that *huevos estrellados*, sunny-side-up eggs, made me gag. I especially disliked the ones with the yolk running all over the plate.

Also, over-easy or sunny-side-up eggs, like what Dad ate, left the taste of wet dogs—repulsive—on the plate when you washed it, unless you scrubbed the plate thoroughly. Dad also liked *huevos pasados por agua*, soft-boiled eggs, in particular when he was suffering from *la cruda*, a hangover. Seeing him crack the tip end of the eggshell and then swallow the whole egg in one swoop was not to my liking any more than runny eggs were.

Before I could say boo, Mom already had cracked an egg into a small glass bowl and begun beating it with a fork. She knew I loved black pepper, hence she sprinkled in a little bit before dropping the egg into the *comal*, iron skillet, which had been heating up while I ate my oatmeal. There was no milk because Grandpa's milk cow, Ninfa, had died a few days earlier after accidentally falling off the river's embankment and landing at the river bottom some forty to fifty feet below. As a result, I ate my oatmeal with white Karo corn syrup, another one of those new products Mom had discovered during her shopping trips to the Bernalillo Mercantile Company.

"There you are! An egg that's round and yellow like the sun! And here's a little bit of red chile to add to your palate's delight," Mom said as she dished out a couple of tablespoons full of the spicy sauce. I learned to eat chile by the time I was five years old. I was now seven. A hot flour tortilla that Mom had just cooked complemented my omelet and chile.

I ate slowly until Mom was able to accompany me. Before I finished my breakfast, I wiped my plate whistle clean with two or three pieces of tortilla in a clockwise and counterclockwise motion. By then Mom was on her last bite of egg and swallow of coffee.

The top of the stove was now clear and ready for me to line up the four or five flatirons that Mom used for ironing. She had only two, but we borrowed the others from Aunt Taida and Grandma. As I kept an eye on the irons on the stove, they conjured up a fleet of ships coming at me. (I had seen a similar scene sporting real boats in a travel magazine in somebody's outhouse in our placita.)

Mom didn't have an ironing board. To my knowledge, they were unheard of in most households in our valley. What she did was to place a bedsheet or a blanket on top of the kitchen table. Sometimes if the kitchen became unbearably hot, she moved the table close to the window that faced to the north, with Cabezón Peak in full view in the background. Mom liked that; it was a nice distraction for her. Or else she ironed on top of one of the beds in the bedroom, where it was cooler, but the kitchen table was more convenient because the flatirons were only four or five feet away from the makeshift ironing board.

There was nothing helter-skelter about Mom's ironing routine, which she always followed to a tee. First, she ironed the heavy clothing, that is, pants and most of the shirts, except for Dad's white dress shirts, which she liked to starch and iron later. Next she ironed her dresses and blouses. She did not iron socks; *ropa de abajo*, underwear; or her own undergarments—what she called "delicate" clothes.

But my job was to fold neatly all underclothing and to roll everyone's socks into small balls pair by pair. Everything was destined for the drawers of the *cómoda*, the dresser that Dad had bought Mom soon after they were married.

Unlike scrubbing clothes on the washboard, done in a more rapid fashion, ironing was relaxed and slower paced—and so were Mom's songs. A tranquil and melancholy mood set in when she ironed Dad's shirts. The song I heard most often was "Mi chaparrita," whose tempo was suited to the occasion. Mom's words to the song, as she moved the iron smoothly back and forth, seemed to provide comfort of sorts in Dad's absence. Here are the lyrics as I remember them.

Mi chaparrita	My Sweetheart
Adiós mi chaparrita,	Good-bye my sweetheart,
no llores por tu Pancho ,	don't cry for your Pancho,
que si se va del rancho,	for if he leaves the ranch,
muy pronto volverá.	he'll return soon thereafter.
Verás que en las tiendas,	You'll see that in the stores,
te compro buenas prendas,	I'll buy you fine jewels,
y el beso que tú esperas,	and [as for] the kiss you await,
muy pronto lo sentirás.	you'll feel it very soon.
Adiós mi chaparrita,	Good-bye my sweetheart,
no llores por tu Pancho,	don't cry for your Pancho,
que si se va del rancho,	for if he leaves the ranch,
muy pronto volverá.	he'll return soon thereafter.

As Mom finished her song, she caught a glimpse of me sitting in a corner of the kitchen by the screen door, where a couple of minutes earlier I had dropped a few more pieces of wood in the wood bin. Her beautiful voice had almost lulled me to sleep.

"*¿Tienes sueño? Ve acuéstate un ratito.* Are you sleepy? Go lie down for a little while." I did just that soon after eating lunch. Two consecutive days of chopping and splitting wood were beginning to take their toll. After all, I was barely seven years old.

Before I took my nap, I headed for the escusao, outhouse. It was on a downward slope about two hundred feet from our casita. I told Mom I would return in a jiffy. More sincere words were never spoken. Boy, was I in for a surprise!

From the outside our outhouse looked like countless others, but inside it was special because it had three holes (a "three holer," as some writers would describe it). The larger ones were for Mom and Dad and the little one was for me. Their toilet seats were round and large enough to accommodate adults; they were built on an elevated platform about twenty inches from the wooden floor toward the back of the outhouse as you entered. Mine resembled a modern-day portable baby toilet; it was made of lumber with a cutout hole. The toilet, which sat nailed to the floor to the right of Mom's seat, was just the right size for a kid like me.

That day, for whatever reason, I decided to be adventurous. I took the liberty of acting like an adult and propped myself on top of Mom's toilet seat. The instant I sat down my body sank, with half of me disappearing below the toilet seat edge. My knees were suddenly up against my face while I held on for dear life, thinking I was going to fall all the way through the hole. I tried desperately to extricate myself from my unforeseen trap, but my efforts were to no avail. Little by little my body seemed to be sinking more and more. I began to feel an unpleasant numbness along with a tingling sensation in the lower part of my legs. I was losing circulation as well as strength—and I was petrified, to boot.

At that point, I started to scream, fearful that I was going to fall completely through the hole and land in the outhouse's unsavory pit. My screaming was in vain. Mom did not come immediately to my rescue. I wondered whether she could even hear me amid her singing and ironing, but I kept calling for her. "*¡Amá, amá! ¡Ven! ¡Ayúdame!* Mom, Mom! Come! Help me!"

Unexpectedly, the door to the outhouse swung open. Mom burst through with a startled look on her face. "Hijito, what in the world happened to you?"

"I'm stuck!" I exclaimed.

"Yes, I see."

Before I could explain, Mom grabbed my arms and slowly tried to pull me up, but without success. "*Estoy bien atorao, amá.* I'm really stuck, Mom," I said and started crying, terrified that for sure I would fall into the caca pit below.

Mom calmly told me to breathe in and to hold my breath while she pulled me up inch by inch. Once she dislodged me, I couldn't stand up. My legs were wobbly and numb. Mom rubbed them and rubbed them until the numbness disappeared. By that time we both breathed a sigh of relief. She put her arm around me.

"Next time you better use your *escusadito*, little toilet, until you grow up, *¿qué no?*" And she winked at me with a slight smile.

Mom, who was very patient with my siblings and me, knew I had learned my lesson, thus there was no need for a verbal scolding, a rarity coming from her. I was now ready for my siesta.

I got under the bed. This was the only place Mom allowed me to take a nap during the day. (She didn't believe in messing up a tidy bed until nighttime.) As I began to dose off I could hear Mom singing softly the words to another beautiful song, a Mexican corrido called "Zenaida." She loved to sing this ballad while she ironed. It truly was one of her favorite songs. Here's the opening stanza; that's all that I remember.

Zenaida	Zenaida
Cuatrocientos kilómetros tiene	It is four hundred kilometers
la suidá donde vive Zenaida.	to the city where Zenaida resides.
Voy a ver si yo puedo encontrarla,	I'm going to see if I can find her,
para ver si me da su palabra.	to see if she'll be by my side.

When I woke up I sauntered over to the kitchen. There was Mom resting on the wooden floor next to the window as the breeze brushed her hair and cooled the perspiration on her forehead. "Mom, are you tired?" I said to her.

"Yes, hijito, it's hot."

"Why don't you take a nap like me?"

"I still have to iron and starch your father's dress shirts, but first I have to iron the bedsheets and pillowcases"—something few women did. She believed that pressed bedsheets and pillowcases provided a softer and more comfortable feeling for a tired body. It was therapeutic. "Come, help me iron."

"But Mom, I've never ironed before."

"I know. There's no time for learning like now. If boys can sleep on bedsheets and rest their heads on pillowcases like girls, then boys can learn how to iron just like girls. Come. First, we'll start with the pillowcases. They're easier and more manageable. Just watch me."

Mom grabbed an iron from the stove, moistened her first two fingers in a bowl of water, and touched the hot iron to test it. If the wet fingers made a kind of a hissing sound, the iron was ready. She moved it effortlessly back and forth on the pillowcase; the movement of her wrist was smooth. She went over the center part of the pillowcase first and then followed the seams, turning the pillowcase over once she was done on one side. She repeated the same process. If the iron began to lose its glide, it was time for another hot one. Seeing Mom iron made the task look like nothing. She was an old pro at it.

"*Ora te toca a ti.* Now it's your turn," she said with a smile of encouragement and confidence. "Remember how I did it . . . and don't let the iron sit too long on any one spot, or else you'll leave a brown mark on the pillowcase. Worse yet, you could burn a hole in it. Okay?"

I grabbed one of the small irons—there were two of them—with a hot pad, and I started my indoctrination into ironing. Except for a few creases I left along the seams, Mom said I did just fine. She was very patient and a good teacher. Little by little, I graduated from pillowcases and bedsheets to pants and shirts, but she reserved the dresses, blouses, and Dad's dress shirts for herself.

She was accustomed to putting starch on the collar and cuffs of his white shirts. "A show of dignity and pride can be seen in a man's shirts, so your mother has to make sure your Dad looks elegant in public. That goes for you and your little brothers as well. You have to look real *pantera*, dapper. Do you understand?"

My little chest puffed up like a crowing rooster as she uttered the word *pantera*, a term I had heard my maternal grandmother employ, thus I had an unambiguous idea what it meant. I was so proud of my mother. She never failed to make Dad, my siblings, and me appear neat in public. And she looked equally debonair whenever we went to church or attended a social event in our placita.

Holidays in our village, whether religious or secular, were special occasions for my entire family to dress up. Mom always made sure we all looked like a million dollars.

10

Cleanliness

A Sense of Character

OH, HOW I LOVED Saturdays! It was a happy day, the day before Sunday, our resting day. It was also bath day and time to remove the dirt from head to toe, as well as to hear grumbles and admonishments. Because water was precious, we kids—Beltrán, Juanito, Julianita, and I—bathed only once a week, and all four of us in the same tub water.

Mom was in charge, and my two brothers and I toed the line, sort of, because we didn't always adhere to her wishes or orders. Kids must be kids. When it came to personal hygiene, Mom was exigent and expected us to come out of the tin tub as clean as our hands were at the dinner table. "To be spotless, especially out in public," she remarked on more than one occasion, "is a sign of character and pride. People will judge you by how neat you dress and look. Fancy clothes are not necessary." She never failed to remind us of the importance of cleanliness. "*En esta casa la limpieza es riqueza.* In this house, spotlessness is richness."

But on this particular Saturday, the routine would be a tad different. Mom told me at breakfast that she had a surprise for me. Today she would send me down the hill for my uncle to cut my hair, a rite of passage for little boys like me. Heretofore, she had been giving me my haircuts. Now she felt I was old enough to have someone else cut my hair. I had recently turned seven. My uncle was the self-styled family barber who cut my three other cousins' hair at our rancho. He even claimed to cut his own hair, although he didn't have much hair on his head to brag about.

At any rate, I was excited about my new adventure. My uncle already knew I was coming. I walked into the kitchen, and there he was, stone faced, rolling a cigarette from his can of Prince Albert tobacco. He was casual and matter-of-fact about my appearance as he lit his cigarette and took a few puffs. He blew smoke through his nostrils, which looked like twin stovepipes hard at work. He was a walking stovepipe, in fact, and the yellow nicotine on his right thumb and forefinger were ample proof of his smoking addiction. He and Prince Albert were inseparable. The worn-out right rear pocket of his Levi's, where he carried his can of tobacco, was further proof of their togetherness.

"Mom sent me to get a haircut," I said somewhat timidly, since this was my first experience at having someone besides Mom cut my hair. "*Sí, ya lo sé.* Yes, I know," he remarked with a sour sort of disposition.

My uncle, from what I'd heard and knew of him, didn't seem to have too many cheerful days. That was his nature.

He grabbed a kitchen chair and signaled me to follow him outside to the front of the house, what the family called the patio, although it wasn't a patio in the traditional sense of the word. This was March; therefore, it was still pretty cool and a bit windy to be sitting outside. My uncle went to the *cochera,* storage shed, adjacent to his house and fetched an empty ten-pound tin can and set it on top of the chair. He also brought back a piece of light canvas.

"There. Sit on top." I climbed up one side of the chair, but I struggled as the can wiggled back and forth. Somehow I managed to sit down without tumbling over, thank goodness.

He put the canvas around my neck and clipped it with a clothespin. "And don't you move" were the next words that spewed out of his mouth. Easier said than done, as it turned out!

My uncle had an old pair of clippers that he used in addition to his scissors. The comb, except for its large size and blend of reddish-brown and off-yellow colors, was nothing unusual. He began clipping, but hair got into my eyes. I brushed it aside, and he scolded me. "Didn't I tell you to stay still?" Little did I know that I was in for the experience of my childhood! Every time he clipped, instead of cutting my hair, he was pulling it by its roots! The clippers were so dull that they were in dire need of sharpening. The scissors weren't any better. He clipped again and, true to form, he pulled my hair, but this time he doubled his knuckles of his left hand and whacked me on the head. By now, I was shaking on top of the tin can like a wet dog emerging from the waters of the Río Puerco.

"Don't you dare move again! I can't cut your hair if you keep moving." I nodded my head in obedience and tried to stop trembling.

The relentless clipping and knuckling continued until he finished cutting my hair. "There you are! Pretty as a *guaje*, gourd," he remarked, trying to exhibit a little humor as he tapped me on my right shoulder.

I climbed down from the chair and said nothing. I left his patio and started walking home, thinking of my ordeal. The more I thought about it, the angrier I got. Soon I began to sob, and tears streamed down my cheeks. My head hurt from all the knuckling. I touched it and felt a number of huge *camachos*, bumps. I took off running up the hill till I got home. I dashed inside the kitchen. Mom right away noticed the tears and my sobbing.

"Hijito, what in the world is wrong? Why are you crying?"

"I'm never going back to get a haircut with my uncle. Look at what he did to me," I cried as I felt my head.

"Heavens! How did you get those bumps?" she asked after feeling my head.

"My uncle gave them to me when he was cutting my hair."

"But why? Did you misbehave or what?" she asked anxiously.

I explained what little there was to explain, and after listening attentively to me Mom vowed never to send me back to my uncle to get a haircut. She would rather cut my hair herself or else send me to don José Sánchez at our placita. The day had not gotten off to a good start, but at least I had my bath to look forward to.

After my siesta, it was time for our weekly bath in a large round tin tub, a number 1. I was responsible for chopping wood and heating up the water outside, just as Mom and I did on Mondays for wash day. The family had kept growing. By now there were three of us boys, plus my little sister. The order in which we bathed was simple: from the youngest to the oldest. My little sister, who was just a toddler, went first. I was the last one. Logical? Yes, based on Mom's way of thinking and the fact that the youngest child was apt to be less dirty than the oldest. Water was scarce, and so we had to economize.

One by one, we got into the tub. Mom bathed my sister, but my brothers and I were more or less on our own except for washing our hair. Mom made sure we didn't just wet our hair. By the time she scrubbed it good and hard, the water was dark, and the ring around the tin tub was rather pronounced. The ring was pure *roña*, one week's accumulation of grime from playing and performing ranch chores.

With washcloth and soap in hand, we did what we thought was plenty of scrubbing, but that did not appease my mom. After we had finished bathing, she would line up my brothers and me. It was inspection time. This prompted Beltrán to complain.

"Didn't you say once that you played no favorites among us? How come our sister doesn't have to stand inspection?"

"Because she's just a baby and she can't STAND UP," she responded, emphasizing these last two words. "Besides, as I said before and I'll repeat it again, you're all different, just like the fingers on your hands . . . and your sister's different." She left this last comment hanging in the air without further explanation. "But I also said that I loved all of you the same. I play no favorites. Now, stand here with your brothers and no more whining," she told Beltrán.

Mom could be assertive whenever necessary. The first one to undergo inspection was Juanito. He was the youngest of the three boys. Mom was wise enough to know that if our ears were dirty inside and out, we had been less than meticulous in washing. Juanito did fine. One down and two to go! Beltrán was next, but he failed inspection. Mom looked at the crevices of his outer ears first, then at his inner ear as if she were looking into a microscope.

"Is this part of you or not?" Mom asked as she probed and dug into his ears with the washcloth. "Or are you saving this for next week's bath?" She showed him the dirt she had just discovered.

The brown dirt on the white washcloth was Mom's evidence to impugn my brother's washing habits. She scrubbed and scrubbed both ears until they turned red. They looked like they were on fire. Beltrán knew he was at fault. He didn't protest. It wasn't the first time he'd gotten in trouble for not washing well. Despite his obdurate nature, eventually he learned to be more assiduous in his bathing habits, just as I had. I had suffered through my share of red ear episodes before learning to emerge from the tin tub clean as a whistle.

"There you are!" Mom said with a smile as she looked at my brother. "Water doesn't kill anybody unless you drown in the Río Puerco."

Beltrán got the point and didn't say a word. To make light of the situation, he looked at me and made a wisecrack.

"Amá, did my uncle use a pair of shears to cut Junie's hair? Look at the *tijeretazos*, snippings, he gave him," and he burst out laughing. Junie was my nickname, from Junior.

"Don't laugh. You might be next," Mom cautioned him with a stern look.

"Oh, no! Not me. I'd rather have Grandpa cut my hair with his shearing clippers."

For the longest time I had wondered why Grandpa Lolo had his own clippers and why he cut his own hair instead of having my uncle do it. Now I thought I had the answer. Pity my poor cousins!

"And look," Beltrán added, begging for trouble. "How come Junie's got a *cola de gallo*, a rooster's tail?" but Mom ignored his wisecrack.

I did have a rooster's tail, what we called a *remolino*, literally, a whirlwind. Even after wearing a hat for long periods of time, I would remove it, and pop goes the weasel! There was the rooster tail sticking up, making me self-conscious.

One day Mom told me she had the perfect solution to my predicament. She got an old nylon stocking she no longer wore and cut it a few inches from the top and tied a knot at both ends. The hose looked like a cap. Mom made me wear it at night when I went to bed. This went on for several months to a year. By that time my rooster tail was gone. I was a happy little boy when I was no longer subject to my brother's teasing.

After bath time was over and everyone had undergone inspection, Mom had to scrub the kitchen floor. She did this without fail every Saturday, even during the winter months, unless the weather was truly unbearable. Seeing my mother down on her knees scouring the wooden floor with soap, water, and rags, with perspiration dripping down her brow, is the one thing I did not enjoy about Saturdays. I did not relish the idea of seeing Mom work so hard. I often wished for mud floors. My sadness went beyond empathy. I felt so sorry for her, but by the time she finished, the floor sparkled. I was perceptibly proud of her. As a matter of fact, the entire kitchen was spotless, in case people came to visit us.

Tomorrow was Sunday, and the priest was coming to our village from Jémez Springs to celebrate Mass. My siblings and I were clean, and our Sunday clothes were ready for church. Mom made sure we didn't look scrubby. "And remember: *No pueden andar en público con la flor arriba y la jedentina abajo.* You can't go out in public looking pretty on the outside and smelling bad underneath." It was an expression she invoked from time to time.

11

Gold in Lead Barrels

"*ABRIL LLOVIOSO HACE A mayo hermoso.* April showers make May beautiful." May, the month of flowers, according to local folklore tradition, was upon us. Except for wildflowers that peppered the landscape, people didn't have many flowers around their homes. Mom was a rare exception. Without fail she grew geraniums year-round. Somehow she managed to keep them alive inside the house through the winter, but come May she'd set them outside the kitchen door, and there they stayed until late September or early October.

She also loved *varas de San José*, hollyhocks, above all pink ones, showing perhaps an influence from Grandma Cinda, my maternal grandmother in Bernalillo, who loved hollyhocks. The hollyhocks faithfully started sprouting in late May, sometimes earlier, next to the adobe wall that faced the eastern sunrise. Both the hollyhocks and the geraniums brightened up our casita.

"We should have named you José," Mom once said to me with a wry smile, because I was born in March and March 19 was Saint Joseph's day.

"I like my name," I countered. "I think José is ugly. Josefate is even worse, and that's what kids would call me."

One more month and Dad would be home from his Works Projects Administration (WPA) job to spend the summer with the family. He would leave again in September to resume his construction work with the government. Until then, his presence would add a cheerful note to our household, and Mom could then relinquish many of the outdoor responsibilities. For now, numerous ranch chores fell on her shoulders, as was true with other women, including my aunt Taida, even though their husbands were homeward bound.

My aunt, as mentioned in an earlier chapter, lived along the Río Puerco down the hill from us. A dear friend of my mother, Aunt Taida was married to Uncle Antonio, one of my father's brothers (not to be confused with my step-grandfather in Bernalillo, whom we grandchildren also called Uncle Antonio). We all lived within proximity of one another on my grandfather's ranch. Neither my father nor my uncle owned the property the families lived on. This patriarchal arrangement was not atypical among many Hispanic households in the Río Puerco Valley.

During its heyday, our placita is where villagers and inhabitants who lived nearby, like my family, went after water. Women were just as adept at hauling water as the men. My mom and Aunt Taida were prime examples. My cousin J. and I tagged along and helped them in whatever way we could muster.

My father had a couple of fifty-gallon lead (*plomo*) barrels that we used for hauling water from our village. I don't know—nor did I ever ask—where he got the lead barrels. To be sure, they were the only lead barrels I ever saw. All others were made of wood with metal rings around them. If the barrels went dry for a long time, the wood shrank and the rings fell to the bottom, causing the barrel leaves to collapse. They needed a certain amount of water to keep them intact. Dad's lead barrels had no such problem. Of course they were heavier than wooden barrels, even when they were empty, but they were indestructible. The *noria*, water well, in our placita is what Mom used as the source of water for cooking, drinking, bathing, washing clothes, and housecleaning.

Water was a precious commodity throughout the Río Puerco Valley. "Water," my Dad once told the family, "is like gold in lead barrels; don't be wasteful." And the placita was the only public place where people could go for the treasured liquid.

It was Sunday evening. I was helping Mom set up the tin tubs for her Monday ritual of washing clothes. Each water barrel had a small cap at the top that unscrewed. Once removed, you could peer into the barrel to check the water levels, which Mom did, thinking both barrels were full. Regrettably, they were practically empty, but it was too late for Dad to remedy the situation. He would be leaving early Monday morning—and Mom didn't dare to inform him, or he would be upset. "*En boca cerrada no entran moscas*. Flies don't enter a closed mouth" (in other words, "Silence is golden") are words I had heard often among old-timers in the community. Surely they must have crossed Mom's mind.

Before it got much later, Mom told me to run down the hill to ask Aunt Taida if she could go with us to the placita for water. I ran as fast as my short legs could carry me, with Chopo running right behind me. I knocked on the screen door and went in. My aunt was doing dishes, but I delivered the message. She said she could go and to tell Mom that she would come up sometime Monday morning. Uncle Antonio had a team of sorrel horses, so Aunt Taida was usually the one who drove whenever she and Mom went to the village after water. We had embarked numerous times on similar journeys in the past. I really liked going after water at the placita.

When Aunt Taida showed up the next morning, she had already hitched up the horses to the wagon. Dad had a special place for loading and unloading the heavy lead barrels. Sometime back he had carved out a kind of bowl-shaped niche on the side of a slope close to the house; it was just big enough to permit the horse wagon to be backed up against the edge of the dirt on a level even with the wagon bed. Heavy boards were sometimes placed flat on the ground so we could roll the empty barrels onto the wagon. The same routine was used to unload the barrels off the wagon when they were full. They rolled more easily on a smooth surface than on the dirt.

Once we loaded the empty barrels, we laid them on their sides with the barrel openings facing forward to prevent them from rolling back or moving sideways very much. The barrels were perfectly positioned for my cousin J. and me to sit on once my aunt cracked the *chicote*, whip, and the horses took off. Cousin J. climbed on one, and I mounted the other. We pretended they were horses. "Giddyap, giddyap," we hollered as we slapped the sides of the lead barrels. "That's a sure way to get bowlegged," Mom said jokingly. "You're going to look like don Pedro," added my aunt, referring to a man whose legs looked like moving arches when he walked. Don Pedro lived not too far from us, near El Rincón del Cochino.

As we proceeded along the sandy and twisting road headed for our village, we came to El Coruco, alluded to in chapter 5. It was renowned for wandering witches who came out at night as passersby went home from a dance at the placita or from visiting friends. "Uuuh, uh," sounded my cousin J. "*Cállate, majadero*. Shush, you clown. Witches don't come out during daylight," I said to him. I had also heard of rattling chains wreaking havoc with people in the dark. A creepy feeling ran up and down my spine. I wished for Aunt Taida to step up the pace of the horses.

Soon we came to the crossing of the Río Puerco. *La bajada*, the slope, was steep and boasted a short bend halfway to the bottom of the riverbed. Descending was easier with empty barrels than with full ones. Coming up with them full would also be easier. Just the same, Mom and Aunt Taida took extraordinary precautions. My aunt, who handled the team of horses with self-confidence, was also in tune with the horses' temperaments.

Before we started the descent she said to Mom, "*Tú apaláncate en la breca con las dos manos mientras yo detengo las riendas*. You push the brake forward with both hands while I pull back on the reins," and she twirled each rein several times around her wrists. The brake pad was a wooden block covered with leather. "And you," she added, referring to my cousin and me, "pour water on the leather attached to the wood block in case it starts smoking when I brake. We don't want the wagon to catch on fire."

Farmers always carried a small can or bucket of water in their wagons because the brake could smolder and even catch on fire if the leather rubbed too much against the cast-iron rim of the wagon wheel. Starting a fire was an unlikely possibility, but people didn't take chances.

Slowly we inched our way down the slope until we came to the riverbed. Now it was time to cross the river, a not-very-challenging task at this time of year since the water level was low. The April showers had come and gone without too much of a fanfare, whereas the heavy July and August rains were yet to come. Then the Río Puerco waters would come alive, swell, and roar like a raging bull. For now the gurgling water bounced up and down on the small rocks as I looked down from the wagon. The flow was more symptomatic of a gentle and forgiving river than one that could punish you with relentless fury.

We crossed the river with ease and reached the top of the embankment as I glanced toward the village. Suddenly, it came into full view as if spreading

Río Puerco near Ojo del Padre (Guadalupe) with Mesa Prieta in background, 2012.

its wings to welcome us, with the church, the most prominent edifice, looming proudly smack in the middle of the smiling adobe buildings.

We were only a few hundred feet from the water well. The horses either recognized the surroundings or they smelled the water and thus picked up the pace of their own volition. They headed for the water trough, located on the north wall of the little house where the water well was housed. My aunt didn't even have to point them in the right direction; the horses knew where to find the water.

The villagers at one time had built a small stone house to protect the water well from whence the water oozed for people to fill barrels and buckets for personal consumption. Even the trough next to the stone house was always full for riders to water their mounts.

The local residents had also hooked up a hose to the upsurging water; the pressure was strong enough to fill up barrels on a horse wagon. Filling up Dad's two lead barrels required little time, perhaps no more than half an hour.

Once that was accomplished, Aunt Taida tied the horses underneath some shady trees close to the church. From here we all walked over to the church. It was closed, but both Mom and my aunt knew the caretaker, who lived practically next door to the church. She came and opened the doors for them to pray. They both lit a couple of votive candles before we left.

Now it was time to tackle the descent west of the Río Puerco, a more challenging and precarious undertaking with two fifty-gallon barrels full of water on board. The routine going back of braking, pulling on the reins, and all that was pretty much identical as it had been crossing over, with one noticeable difference. The barrels were now full and standing upright against the driver and passenger's seat, where Aunt Taida and Mom were seated. Caution had to be exercised for the heavy barrels not to tip forward and hence crush the women. To prevent that from happening, they ran a rope around each barrel and fastened it to the tail end of the wagon. For added protection, my cousin J. and I were to pull back on the rope to keep the barrels from moving forward.

The opposite action was needed once we crossed the river. Going up the *subida*, the ascent, we had to make sure the barrels didn't slide backward and roll out of control. To avoid that kind of a disaster, a rope was looped around each barrel and secured to the driver's seat. If either my cousin or I sensed that the barrels were gaining momentum as we climbed the subida, we were to step aside or jump to the side of the wagon, lest we get hurt badly. It was better for the barrels to end up in the riverbed or in the river than for us to be flattened like tortillas.

While the foregoing safety measures may sound a trifle dramatic, it was better to be sure than sorry. *"Mira bien y no acates a quién.* Be sure you look before you leap" was a dicho that aptly applied in our situation.

On our way home we stopped by the Aranda General Store, on this side of the Río Puerco across from the village. Aunt Taida wanted to buy light Karo corn syrup to make white divinity candy, one of her latest delicious concoctions, which she had discovered from her relatives in Martíneztown in Albuquerque. We didn't dilly-dally, because we were all hungry. The sun above our heads told us it was close to noon and time to eat.

Except for one short hill after we left the Aranda store, the rest of the road home for the most part was flat. When we got home we had to unload the barrels. My aunt backed the horse wagon into the same niche-like place where we had loaded them before we left for the placita. The barrels had to be tipped on their sides and rolled off the wagon and placed on the west side of the house. The nearby butte shaded my casita from the western sun in the afternoon; it kept the barrels of water somewhat cool in the summer.

My mom grabbed one the boards that we had used before and stuck it under the first barrel. She cleverly raised the board, prying the tipped barrel and moving it forward little by little, as if pumping a car jack. The maneuver was simple, seemingly tedious, but easy. It worked to perfection.

Once both barrels were situated in their proper place, Mom invited Aunt Taida and my cousin J. for lunch, but warned them that all she had was leftovers. "When hunger is at stake, even a dried tortilla does wonders," my aunt said, and we all sat down to eat.

12

A Trip to the *Monte*

DAD WAS HOME FOR the summer, which meant that the ranchers and farmers who had government jobs building roads, fences, and other construction projects could tend to their crops, animals, and other farm chores. Boy, was I happy! Dad and I did lots of things together. We enjoyed each other's company. He was quiet, reserved, and formal—the antithesis of my mother's persona, even though both were Virgos. Her gregarious and happy-go-lucky personality was radiant. Just the same, Mom and Dad complemented each other very well.

The first order of business for Dad and me was to replenish the supply of firewood that had depleted to the last remaining logs. The frigid and merciless winter months usually took their toll on the large stack of wood. This past cold and snowy winter bore a resemblance to previous winters. It was now time for a trip to the monte, wooded area, to fetch firewood. This is something Dad and I did several times during the summer to stock up for the next nine months or so. Going to the monte remains one of the most memorable experiences of my childhood.

The night before, in anticipation of our journey, I was so excited I could scarcely sleep a wink. Even Mom heard me tossing and turning, whereupon she got up and stumbled in the dark to see what was wrong. "*Hijito, ¿qué tienes?* My dear son, what's wrong?"

"*Nada, amá, nada.* Nothing, Mom, nothing," I responded and tried to go back to sleep. Her concern for my well-being was always soothing and reassuring.

The next morning I was the first up. I put on my overalls, shirt, and the high-top shoes called *mata víboras*, snake killers, and headed for the kitchen to light a fire in the woodstove. The coffeepot was ready. Mom had prepared it before going to bed. I put the coffeepot on the back plate because the front one is where we fed the stove wood, though we also used it for cooking and warming up food. I accidentally dropped the handle on the floor that we used to lift the iron plates. "What are you doing?" asked Mom, who by now was awake. "Is the coffee ready?" Dad hollered from the bedroom. "*Ya merito*," I answered.

Today, unlike other days, Dad did not wait for me to take him coffee in bed. We had a busy day ahead and consequently had to shake a leg. "*No hay que dormir hasta que se te inche el cuajo.* One mustn't shilly-shally and get up late" was a saying Dad invoked quite often if you slept in.

By the time he got dressed, the coffee was ready and Mom had breakfast prepared for us. She fixed me an omelet first. Mom also liked omelets, or scrambled eggs, which I enjoyed also. She and I were on the same weather vane when it came to eating eggs. For Dad she fried a couple of eggs over easy.

A stack of fresh tortillas was already on the table. One by one we sat down to eat. I ate fast but without gobbling up my food, even though I was eager to get going. Mom always insisted that I take my time to eat at the table. Such etiquette, she averred, was a way of being respectful to the food and to your body.

Before I could say boo, my father was on his last sip of coffee. "*¡Ándale!* Shake a leg!" he said as he got up and pushed his chair under the table. Without waiting for an answer he dashed out, banging the screen door, something he frowned upon if we children did it. Fathers being fathers, I was to learn as I got older that they could take certain liberties that contradicted what they preached. My own father was no exception.

The sun was beginning to peek over the Mesa Prieta. Dad was on his way to the corral to put the harnesses on Camastrón and Magué, two huge, jet-black horses that belonged to Grandpa Lolo. They were beautiful and graceful looking. Dignity was written all over them. Dad liked to borrow them whenever we went after firewood because they were strong and sure-footed. In terms of farm work, they were reputed to be the best and most versatile team in the Río Puerco Valley. Dad hitched them to the horse wagon. We were almost ready for the daylong trip.

He had already put on the *barandales*, sideboards, the previous day, although they weren't critical for hauling wood. He had also loaded two pairs of towing chains for securing the firewood in front and back of the wagon. An ax, a rope, a shovel, and a remnant piece of canvas rounded out the gear that we needed for the trip. These were the bare necessities as we departed for the monte to look for firewood near Cabezón Peak.

Back at the house, I helped Mom pack our lunch. Lunch was simple, but for a young boy like me it was heaven because I got to eat out in the campo, in the open air amid juniper trees, sagebrush, and cacti. Neatly arrayed on the table were a half-dozen flour tortillas, a can of Derby's potted meat, a dry yellow onion, a can of oil-packed sardines, a few strips of *carne seca*, jerky, a pint of Mom's canned peaches in a mason jar, and a canteen full of water.

In addition, she included a Hills Bros. coffee can with ground coffee inside for Dad to brew at noon on top of a campfire. She packed a tin coffee cup for him as well. Except for the water and the coffee, Mom put everything neatly in a large tin can. She secured the water and coffee in a small flour sack and tied a knot at the top. Dad and I were ready for our day's journey.

As if on cue, he dashed into the kitchen. "*¿Ya está el lonche?* Is lunch ready?" he asked as he saw me standing, holding onto the tin can in one hand and the flour sack in the other. Without either Mom or me answering, Dad said, "*Güeno, ¡vámonos!* Okay, let's be on our way!"

"*Vente, hijito.* Come here, my son," said Mom, beckoning me so she could kiss me on the forehead. "*Y ten cuidado con las víboras. No te vayan a picar.* And be careful with the rattlesnakes. Don't let them bite you," she warned me.

"Don't worry, Mom. I've got on my mata víboras," and I proudly raised my right foot to show her my high-top shoes.

Dad and I hopped on the wagon, but he noticed that the cushions we used for padding were missing. "Bring me the *cojines*," he said to Mom. She gave me one, and Dad took the other. We both sat on the only seat to the wagon. "*Güeno. Hasta la tardecita.* Okay. See you later this afternoon," Dad said as he bade good-bye to Mom. Hugging or kissing is not something I or my siblings ever saw between my parents.

As we started off Chopo began growling. He had a forlorn look on his face, wondering perhaps why he was being left behind. His tail wasn't wagging, an indication that he was unhappy. "*¡Llévenselo!* Take him with you!" Mom shouted.

Right away I clapped my hands, a gesture Chopo understood well, and he ran and jumped through the back of the wagon, where Dad had removed the sideboard so that the firewood could extend beyond the wagon bed. Chopo wagged his tail uncontrollably. He was ecstatic. And I was, too, because he was good protection against rattlesnakes, in particular when we lay down for a nap under a juniper after lunch.

Though Mom didn't say anything, I'm sure she was happy that Chopo was accompanying us, because she was petrified of rattlers and worried that one might strike us. Besides, Chopo was a good traveling companion, someone I could talk to and play with. Dad was a man of few words. He did not believe in idle talk. When he spoke, he always seemed to measure carefully what he said.

The trip north to the monte near a place called El Bordo, east of Cabezón Peak, was probably about five miles of winding dirt road from our ranchito. It bore the name El Bordo because it was at the top of the wooded area where the water ran to both the east and the west following rainstorms. *Bordo*, or "border," also meant a small dam for holding up pools of water for livestock. El Bordo was kind of a mini–Continental Divide.

The drive on horse wagon was slow going, typical of travel on dirt roads in the countryside and characteristic of rural life in general. Camastrón and Magué traveled at a modest trot but with a thump that left noticeable imprints in the ground.

As we passed La Cañada del Camino, not far from our house, the prairie dogs stood on their hind legs wagging their tails as if greeting us. Chopo barked at them, but the prairie dogs were oblivious, perhaps because they knew that they were safe with him in the wagon. Normally, when I was on horseback and Chopo tagged along, he ran feverishly from one prairie dog mound to another, scaring the dickens out of the poor critters. Today was not his day. He had to settle for a bark or two.

We went by El Aguaje, so called because when it rained the water cascaded down huge rocks, took a few bounces, and created an *aguaje*, a watering place for livestock. The overflow of water emptied into the Esquipula Arroyo that ultimately ran downstream and provided water for our cornfields about a half mile away.

As we approached El Ojo de Esquipula (the Esquipula Spring), my father noticed that the natural springs bubbled down below in the arroyo, where livestock drank water. Grandpa Lolo had given Dad the property when my father was around nineteen or twenty years old.

When we reached the top of El Bordo, I could see the majestic Cabezón Peak to the west and the Jémez Mountains to the east. Dad pulled the horse wagon a short distance from the road in open terrain. Next, on foot, he reconnoitered the immediate area for dry deadwood. Most of it was *sabino*, juniper, the best wood to burn because of the heat that it radiated and the fact that it burned slower and longer than pine. Searching for wood was time-consuming, particularly if other wood gatherers had been in the area recently. Then finding wood was more difficult. Wagon tracks were always a good clue if someone had been there before us. If we saw some, then Dad would move the horse wagon deeper into the monte, where the findings were sure to be more plentiful.

One thing for sure: neither Dad nor the other ranchers who searched for wood ever chopped down live trees. That was a no-no and part of their efforts to preserve the wooded area, long before protecting the environment became fashionable.

While Dad was on his walking tour, I waited under the shade of a juniper until he returned. "There's not much wood here. Let's head closer to that hill down below." We climbed back on the wagon and worked our way in and out between trees, aiming for the hillside that, from a distance, appeared to be thick with trees. That generally meant that more deadwood could be found on the ground. And sure enough! As the wagon bounced and ran over *terremotes*, thick clumps of grass, we began to spot more and more deadwood.

Dad tossed it over the sideboards and into the bed of the wagon. If the pieces were long, then he loaded them in from the back. My job, with his help, of course, was to stack the wood piece by piece. This went on for at least a couple of hours. The higher the stack of wood, the more difficult it was to keep it from rolling off the sides of the wagon, because the sideboards only

went up about three feet. But by interlocking piece by piece, Dad was able
to secure the wood. At some point, I was not much help to him. He had to
finish loading the wood before he wrapped the chains around it, front and
back, but that would come later. By then the wagon was loaded to capacity,
and it was time for us to head home.

"*Güeno. Ya con esta leña basta.* Okay. I think we have enough wood,"
Dad said, and I breathed a sigh of relief.

Not only was it getting hot (the noon sun was beaming right over our
heads), but I was also getting hungry. As if guessing my discomfort, Dad
said with a wry grin, "*Ya se comen las grandes a las chiquitas, ¿eh?* The big
ones [i.e., intestines] are about to consume the little ones, right?," suggest-
ing that I was ravenous.

He unhitched Camastrón and Magué, took off their harnesses, draped
them over some tree branches, and hobbled the horses so they wouldn't
wander off too far.

"Bring the food," he said to me. I fetched the tin can with our lunch, Dad's
coffee, and my canteen of water from under the seat of the wagon, while he
spread the small piece of tarpaulin we had brought with us on the ground.

I pried open the tin can and took out the tortillas, which were wrapped
in a dishtowel. Next came out the cans of sardines and potted meat, the
jerky, the onion, and the jar of home-canned peaches. Dad took out his
pocketknife and opened the sardines and potted meat by carving the cans
around the edges. Using his knife, I spread the potted meat on a tortilla and
took huge bites like a hungry wolf. Chopo must have been starving as well
because he kept looking at me. I gave him half of a tortilla and two sardines.
He was happy.

Meanwhile, Dad was performing surgery on the sardines. He disliked
eating the tiny white bones (I did too). The sound of bones crunching in
your mouth was disgusting. I knew the feeling, since on more than one
occasion I had accidentally failed to remove some of the bones. Besides,
sardines also had a tiny black sliver that looked like an intestine, which
didn't appeal to me. I removed it as well. Otherwise, I loved sardines and
onions slapped between a tortilla out in the open range. Somehow they
tasted better than at home.

After we finished eating our peaches (the jerky would have to wait till we were on our way home), Dad gathered a few pieces of wood and built a fire to brew his coffee. I knew he needed some small rocks, so I took him a handful to place on the hot coals. Then he balanced the can of Hills Bros. coffee on top of the rocks and let the coffee perk. There was nothing like the aroma of country-brewed coffee.

After Dad drank his coffee, he said to me. "Let's rest. It's time for a little siesta." He grabbed the two cushions from the wagon and gave me one. He picked a shady tree, and I did the same thing, and we used the cushions for our pillows. But before lying down, I remembered Mom's forewarning regarding rattlesnakes.

I proceeded to draw a large circle around the area where I was to take my nap. Grandma Lale, my paternal grandmother, had told me once that this was the best protective measure against rattlesnakes when taking a siesta out in the open range. Fact or superstition, I wasn't about to doubt my sagacious grandmother. Besides, next to the circle was Chopo. Nothing could be more real than his presence, and I had confidence that if a snake moved stealthily my way, he would snap or bark at it. Hence I would wake up. Either way, whether protection came from the circle or from Chopo, I was in good hands for a restful nap—and I needed one. I was tired, and Dad was, too. The cicadas, with their own symphonic and shrilly sounds, helped to lull us to sleep.

Dad and I slept for a short spell, not as long as I was accustomed to at home, but the ground was not a very forgiving place. The floor under the bed where I took my afternoon naps at home was a tad more comfortable, plus it lacked the threat of rattlesnakes or bull snakes in search of rodents. I looked over at Dad, and he still had his *saguaripa*, straw hat, over his face. It wasn't long before he woke up.

"Bring me some water, hijito. I'm thirsty." I handed him the canteen of water. He took one big gulp. I took a swallow as well. There wasn't much left.

"Go get the horses while I tie the chains around the wood. Then we'll be ready to head home," Dad said to me.

But before he secured the chains, he got the shovel, dug a hole, smashed the sardine and potted meat cans, and buried them. The hole was quite deep. In that way the coyotes, whose knack for smelling food was incredible, would not dig up the cans and cut their tongues or paws.

By the time I returned with Camastrón and Magué, Dad had secured the

wood with the chains. The chances of the wood tumbling down onto the
road because of the movement of the wagon were now minimized. I loaded
all our belongings. We were now ready for our journey back home. With a
full load of wood, the trip would take longer than coming out to the monte
had, but Grandpa's team of horses instilled confidence in my father.

Dad hitched up the horses. We meandered our way through the junipers amid sagebrush and other vegetation until we reached the dirt road.
Going downhill from El Bordo with a load of wood required knowhow
and precaution, but Dad, like most ranchers, was good at the task. At times
like this, Camastrón and Magué were most reassuring since they were
huge, strong, and sure-footed. From time to time Dad had to apply the foot
brake while I pushed the hand brake with both hands. If not, the wagon
could gain speed and the wood could not only shift but, more importantly,
move forward, startle the horses, and possibly strike them. That is the
main reason why we didn't sit on the wagon seat going home. Instead, we
perched ourselves on top of the wood. I liked it up there. I thought I was on
top of the world. Chopo liked it as well.

We stopped briefly at El Ojo de Esquipula to water the horses and for us
to get a drink of water. Chopo jumped down from the wagon and followed
us. It was late afternoon—the warm part of the day—and no doubt the
horses were just as glad as we were to get some cool, fresh water.

After Dad unhitched the horses, we took them down to the bottom of
the arroyo, where the water oozed from the natural spring. Nearby, bub-
bling water from the ground formed little pools under the pink bushes
indigenous to the area. Dad took out his clean handkerchief, unfolded it,
and spread it on top of the water. He then got down on his stomach and
sipped water through the handkerchief. After watching how he drank, I
did the same thing, plus I filled my canteen to take home. The water was
really nice and cool. El Ojo de Esquipula was one of only two natural
springs in the area. The other one was in our placita, where the villagers
went for their water for domestic use (see chapter 11).

From El Ojo de Esquipula to our little casita was about a mile, but it
took at least a half an hour to get home because the road was winding and
hilly. We also had to cross the Esquipula Arroyo, followed by a hill.
Crossing the arroyo was tricky because it was fairly steep. This time Dad

had to simultaneously pull on the reins plus lean on the foot brake to prevent the wood from careening forward. I was scared to death as I looked downward at the bottomless arroyo. I held onto the front chain for dear life. Little by little, we descended the arroyo and then successfully went up the other side. Camastrón and Magué were exceedingly strong and masters at the job. Pulling the wagon up the slope was no challenge for them. They did it with ease. A short distance away we came to La Cañada del Camino, but this time the prairie dogs were nowhere in sight. Evidently they were taking their own siestas.

By the time we got home, Grandpa's horses had worked up a sweaty froth, thanks to the heat and the heavy load of wood. Dad pulled up to where we kept the woodpile and unhitched the horses. He took them to Grandpa's corral and removed the harnesses before feeding them. They would spend the night in the *caballeriza*, stable.

I immediately went to see Mom, who had her hands in a bowl full of dough. She had her rolling pin ready to roll out the tortillas on the kitchen table—she had no breadboard. "*¡Mira nomás que nariz! ¡Qué tomate ni que nada!* Look at your nose! What a nice-looking tomato!" she commented, looking at my sunburned face.

I went to the bedroom and saw myself in the chest of drawers mirror. I came back out to the kitchen. "No, Mom. It doesn't look like a tomato; it's more like a radish." She just smiled and kept rolling out her tortillas. Supper would be ready in no time.

My little brother Juanito was on the kitchen floor playing with his guaje, rattle, when Dad walked in. He sat down on the floor to play with him until Mom set the table. The sardines and potted meat back at the monte were history until our next trip. For now it was time for a nice hot meal with some nice warm tortillas, which Mom was superb at making.

13

Wedding Bells and the
Whole Shebang

IT WAS JUNE, AND my uncle Ramón would soon be getting married. His wedding is the only one I ever witnessed as a small boy in Ojo del Padre. And what a day of gaiety, food, music, dancing, and laughter that was! From morning before Mass until way into the night, the entire community became one huge family. After all, everyone was a primo, cousin, in a manner of speaking, and no one was excluded from the festivity. From the old folks to the young children, each one partook in the joyous event.

Uncle Ramón married a woman from the Gonzales clan, whose ranch was southwest of our placita. The day's events, in particular the most impressionable aspects, are still somewhat fresh in my memory after all these years. Courtship—if one can even dare to call it that—leading up to my uncle's matrimony is something I was not privy to except for what I gleaned from conversations overheard between Grandpa Lolo and Grandma Lale. I listened, assimilated whatever they shared with each other, and tried to make sense of their discussions regarding the impending wedding.

Here's what I do recall without equivocation. My uncle's first wife, Aunt C., died from an illness a few years after they were married. They had one son, who is still alive. I vividly remember going with my parents to her interment in Albuquerque at the Santa Barbara Cemetery in Martineztown, where my grandparents owned a home. I was about four years old. To this day I can walk through the front entrance to the historic cemetery and point to her unmarked grave, long ago abandoned and neglected by both sides of the family.

Later on Uncle Ramón met his second wife (he married two more times). Since my uncle was a widower, the more formal and traditional custom of asking for her hand in marriage, as nearly as I can ascertain, was preempted and therefore not followed to a tee. Such a procedure was not meant as disrespect to the bride and her parents, but came out of a clear understanding that there were mitigating circumstances for my uncle and consequently the rules were different from those for first-time marriages.

Most marriages among Hispanics in rural communities seventy or more years ago followed certain ironclad customs. First of all, the parents by and large arranged most marriages, without the prospective bride or sometimes even the son having a word in the matter. At times the boy informed his parents regarding his intentions to marry a local young lady or someone from a nearby village. They expressed either their out-and-out approval or their disapproval, depending on who the girl was and the reputation she and her parents enjoyed among the general public. Oftentimes the son's prospective wife was rejected by his parents or the bride's parents snubbed the potential son-in-law. Such refutation was the ultimate humiliation not only for the boy or the girl but for their parents as well. I once heard a wise old man say, "A stick to your butt at home is better than one in the face in public."

CARTA DE PEDIMENTO

If the soon-to-be bride lived in another community, as was the case with my uncle's wife-to-be, a family member or the local scribe prepared a *carta de pedimento* on behalf of the boy's parents asking for the girl's hand in marriage. The letter was hand delivered (rarely mailed) by a family member or a friend—not the boy or his parents—with an answer expected within a reasonably short period of time, possibly no longer than a week to ten days. If the girl's parents rejected the suitor's pedimento, or request, a rejection followed. If that occurred and people heard about it, the phrase "*le dieron calabazas*, he was given pumpkins" (meaning he was snubbed) reverberated throughout the community and its environs.

The reasons for the rebuff, however fickle, could run the gamut from the boy's father being an idler or a drinker to the mother having the reputation of being a gossipmonger or of cracking her chewing gum in public—excuses could sometimes be out-and-out silly. In the main, the poor daughter fell victim either to her parents' undesirable reputations or to the perceived quirks people attributed to them.

Other times there was no letter requesting the girl's hand in marriage. Quite simply, the corresponding parents, because they enjoyed a long-standing friendship, arranged the marriage between son and daughter, and that was that! End of discussion. Though this kind of an arrangement was more the exception than the rule, it was not unheard of. Partly embedded in tradition—some people claimed convenience—such a practice was intended by the parents to ensure marriage stability, if not perpetual contentment, between the newlyweds.

PRENDORIO

To my knowledge, given the fact that Uncle Ramón was a widower, there was neither a hand-in-marriage letter nor one of *prendorio*, engagement. Grandpa Lolo and Grandma Lale presumably paid a courtesy call to the Gonzales family, at which time they asked for the daughter's hand on behalf of my uncle. The families did not know each other well, but their encounter most likely was cordial and respectful, typical under the circumstances.

A discussion would have ensued, no doubt vis-à-vis wedding arrangements. These included the selecting of *padrinos*, matrimonial godparents (sponsors of the bride and groom), the nuptial ceremony, the reception, a sit-down wedding meal, and the evening dance at the local placita of Ojo del Padre. The overall costs to be incurred and who would pay for what generally was also part of the discussion between my grandfather and his soon-to-be compadre.

The wives did not participate in the monetary deliberations. The women, judging from my experience and what I observed and heard in my immediate and extended families, did put in more than their two cents' worth, but they did so later, at home with their husbands, not in someone else's private home.

THE WEDDING

The *casorio*, wedding, was celebrated in the summer. The year was around 1944, maybe even a year earlier. My uncle Ramón, whose first wife came from Albuquerque, now resided there. He worked for the Albuquerque Iron and Scrap Metal Company, located on North First Street along the railroad tracks. Yet wedding vows between him and his second wife were recited in Ojo del Padre at the Virgen de Guadalupe Church, where the bride's family were members as well.

The mayordomos, caretakers of the church, as a rule apprised the priest of the impending wedding plans, because he only traveled from Jémez Springs, northwest of Albuquerque, to our village once a month to celebrate Mass. Since weddings never took place on Sunday, a Saturday before the Sunday Mass was always selected for marriages.

And so it came to pass. All the families at our ranch attended the church wedding: Grandpa Lolo and Grandma Lale, of course; Aunt Taida and Uncle Antonio and their offspring; plus my little brothers and sister and I accompanying my parents. With the exception of my grandparents and Uncle Ramón, we all rode horse wagons to the placita for the big event.

Uncle Ramón, who had abandoned farm life years earlier, took my grandparents in his automobile. They rode in style, to be sure. My uncle had a fancy-looking car. It was a light green Dodge whose front doors one opened by pushing them out toward the front. He would step forward from the car—just the opposite of what we do today in late model cars—with pride and finesse. He had his swaggering ways.

I also recall that to open the car's hood you first propped up one side and then the other. From the front of the car, the two leaves of the hood conjured up an image of a bird with giant wings ready to take off in flight. Each side of the hood also had three or four vents. Not only was Uncle Ramón's car fancy, it was also the only car at his wedding.

Parking his Dodge in front of the Virgen de Guadalupe Church made its presence even more conspicuous; it quickly became the talk of the village. My father, who tended to be quite formal and a no-monkey-business person, even jokingly remarked on the way home to my mother that nuptial vows between his brother and his bride had taken a backseat to the car. My mother cracked a smile.

Nasario P. García and
Agapita López-García, the
author's parents, 1935.

When people arrived at church, they were dressed in their Sunday best, but the most glamorous without doubt were the bride and groom. She wore a long white dress that barely touched the ground. He sported a dark suit. The parents of both parties dressed equally elegantly. This was one of the few times I saw Grandpa Lolo dressed in a suit and tie. As for Grandma Lale, she wore a beautiful pink dress and a round white hat. The padrinos, sponsors of the bride and groom, were just as debonair.

Aside from the fact that a couple was being joined in holy matrimony, the Mass was fairly straightforward. People went to confession before Mass, which the priest delivered in Latin and Spanish, and took Holy Communion. Noticeably different were the murmuring and the festive mood inside the church before the Mass commenced. The atmosphere was unlike anything I had ever seen in my little village, but after all, I had never witnessed a wedding before either. This was truly a novel experience for me—and I was soaking it all up.

Between the Garcías and Gonzaleses' immediate and extended families, half of the small church filled up. The remaining parishioners were friends and invited guests. It goes without saying that the highlight of the Mass was the exchange of wedding vows. The murmuring reached an apogee of sorts, in particular among the women—young and old—who reveled in the whole affair. It was merriment at its best and truly a community celebration. Even kids like me whooped for joy, without being fully cognizant of the total impact of one of the most sacred sacraments of the Catholic Church.

Outside the church following Mass were the musicians, a violinist and a guitarist, waiting to kick off the day's festivities. As my uncle and his bride exited the church, the music began amid an avalanche of congratulations from all the grown-ups. Grandpa's intimate male friends patted him on the back while at the same time congratulating Uncle Ramón, wishing both of them, especially the groom, good luck and happiness. The women, much more formal, expressed similar good wishes with a hug and a peck on the cheek. The young girls of marriage age grinned from cheek to cheek, steeped in envy. They no doubt wondered when their fateful day of matrimony would come to pass.

BLESSINGS, RECEPTION, AND LUNCH

As people dispersed and went home, the bride and groom hopped into Uncle Ramón's green Dodge and took off in a cloud of dust for my grandparents' home, the hub of the day's festivities. Grandpa Lolo and Grandma Lale rode back home with us in Dad's horse wagon.

Before we descended to the bottom of the Río Puerco to cross, I looked across the river and saw a trail of dust from Uncle Ramón's car. To me it looked as though he was flying. To be sure, he must have been on cloud nine. It was a great day for him, his bride, and everyone connected with the wedding.

By the time we reached home, my uncle and his bride were already at my grandparents' ranch house. Aunt Taida, Uncle Antonio, their children, and the rest of the invited guests did not take long in arriving. My grandparents' home was a modest dwelling—a large bedroom and a huge kitchen-dining area, with a portal that stretched across both rooms and faced the Mesa Prieta to the east.

Once the bride's parents arrived, they along with the bride and groom were seated in my grandparents' bedroom, which had been converted into a living room. Here a popular ritual took place. Both the bride and groom knelt in front of their parents for a formal blessing for good fortune in their holy matrimony; the blessing was uttered by the individual mothers as they made the sign of the cross on the couple's foreheads.

As soon as the blessing was given, the musicians erupted into a repertoire of joyous melodies. "¡A bailar, a bailar! Let's dance! Let's dance!" These words rang out from the back of the room from an unrecognizable voice. As was customary at wedding receptions, the padrino and the bride took to the dance floor first; the *madrina* followed suit with the groom. The parents of the wedding couple then cut in and danced with the new son-in-law and new daughter-in-law. Other people, both relatives and friends, joined in, kicking up their heels (*a tirar chancla*) soon thereafter.

While the dancing was going on, a flurry of activity was heard in the kitchen-dining area, where a long table was set up for the reception. The snacks consisted of drinks (coffee, mint tea, and lemonade), bizcochitos, *pastelitos* (small fruit pies), and molletes, sweet rolls, which Grandma and her two granddaughters, Catalina and Eremita, had baked two days before the wedding. Since most grown-ups and some children had fasted to receive Holy Communion, the reception was a good remedy to ease everyone's hunger pangs until the big meal was served after twelve noon.

Except for a few whiny kids who clamored for lunch but were appeased with an extra bizcochito, traditionally the first ones to eat were of course the bride and groom, their parents, and the padrinos. In essence, they were the stars for the day, with the spotlight on the new husband and wife. Lunchtime was also when the musicians took a break and sipped on something (a glass of wine or whiskey, which Grandpa had tucked away for special occasions) until they came to the table, joined by other family members, close family friends, and other guests.

Food for the occasion consisted of a combination of everyday cooking with a complement of special dishes usually prepared for specific seasons during the year, among them Lent and Christmas. Overall, everything was scrumptious, thanks to women like my grandma, my aunt, and my mother, all of whom were excellent cooks and bakers. Here is a list of foods and drinks that decked the luncheon table during Uncle Ramón's wedding:

cabrito asado (oven-roasted baby goat)

calabacitas (zucchini) fried with corn

carne adovada (marinated beef in red chile *caribe*)

caldito (broth with shredded jerky and potatoes)

costillas asadas de res (oven-roasted beef ribs)

chicharrones (pigskin cracklings)

chiles rellenos (made with green chile and raisins)

café solo (black coffee)

empanaditas (fruit and mincemeat turnovers)

flour tortillas (stacks of them)

galletas (biscuits)

home-canned peaches

lemonade

mint tea

natillas (custard pudding)

oven-baked chicken

papas fritas (fried potatoes)

pasteles (pies)

peas

pinto beans

quelites (wild spinach)

red chile sauce

red wine

rice pudding with raisins

torrejas (egg fritters dipped in caramel)

torta de huevo (egg fritters dipped in red chile)

water

A small, homemade wedding cake was placed auspiciously in the middle of the dining table, for everyone to admire when they sat down to eat.

LA ENTRIEGA DE NOVIOS

Following lunch, the grown-ups mingled outside and sat on the porch to chitchat, while kids ran around on full stomachs as though they were not apt to get sick. All the while, Uncle Ramón and his bride sat in the living room, but they never tried to steal a kiss, let alone hold hands. Outward manifestation of affection of any kind was deemed inappropriate. Such social behavior was not a matter of being prudish, but rather a reflection of their parents and grandparents' respectful comportment in public.

By midafternoon, right about the time people began feeling a bit heavy eyed, the musicians popped in to liven things up with a *ranchera* and other Mexican songs. The more energetic couples quickly took to the floor; others followed and even danced under the portal's shade. The dancing went on for a few minutes when out of the blue the padrino, wedding godfather, hollered in a boisterous voice, "*La entriega, La entriega.*" This signaled the "delivery" of the bride and groom to those present, an important cultural episode in the lives of the newlyweds.

The madrina, wedding godmother, then stepped forward, and with the help of the mothers of the bride and groom, they spread a bedsheet on the floor. Once the musicians started playing "La entriega de los novios" (The Wedding Song), relatives, friends, and guests began tossing money on the bedsheet as part of the celebration. The more money, the better; it was to help the wedding couple start their new lives.

Recounted below in regional dialect are the beautiful lyrics to an entriega from a booklet that Grandma Cinda, my maternal grandmother, bequeathed to me before she died. (To this day I still recall many of the words as well as the *tonada*, tune.). The symbolism throughout the wedding song is striking, but it is worth noting that the entriega likewise had its moral underpinnings to help the bride and groom lead a productive and respectable married life in their community.

La entriega de novios

1
"Ave María," dijo la ave
para empesar a bolar.
Y "Ave María," digo yo
para comensar a cantar.

2
Atención pido a toditos
en este público honrado
para festejar el acto
de los recién esposados.

3
Para empesar a cantar
a Dios le pido memoria.
Que me conseda en su fe
como San Pedro en la gloria.

4
De la iglesia van saliendo
de mañana cuatro rosas,
el padrino y la madrina,
el esposado y la esposa.

5
Ya salieron de la iglesia
con muchísima alegría.
Ya salieron esposados
como San José y María.

6
Hiso Dios con su poder
Adán con su sabiduría.
Hiso que Adán se durmiera
y le saco una costilla.

The Wedding Song

1
"Holy Mary," said the bird
before starting to fly.
And "Holy Mary," say I
before I start to sing.

2
I ask everyone's attention
in this honored audience
to celebrate the act
of the newlyweds.

3
To begin to sing
I ask God to help me recall.
May He have faith in me
like Saint Peter in heaven.

4
Leaving the church in early
morning are four roses,
the godfather and godmother
and the groom and bride.

5
They have left the church
each with exceeding joy.
They have left as newlyweds
like Saint Joseph and Mary.

6
What God did with His power
Adam did with his wisdom.
He made Adam fall asleep
and extracted one of his ribs.

7

Hiso que Adán se durmiera
en un hermoso bergel.
Y le dio una compañera
para que se estubiera con él.

7

He made Adam fall asleep
in his beautiful garden.
And He gave him a companion
so she'd be with him.

8

Ya vuelve Adán de su ser
con una voz admirable.
"Te resibo por esposo
por obedeser al padre."

8

Adam has now returned
with an impressive voice.
"I greet you as my husband
prepared to obey the priest."

9

¿Qué sinifican las belas
cuando se van a ensender?
Sinifican el mesmo cuerpo
que allí va a permaneser.

9

What do the candles signify
when they're about to be lit?
They signify the body itself
that's to remain one whole.

10

¿Qué sinifican las belas
cuando las van a apagar?
Sinifican el matrimonio
y el anillo pastoral.

10

What do the candles signify
when they're to be extinguished?
They signify matrimony
and the pastoral ring.

11

Ese manto, esa corona
que a esta novia le pusieron,
fue el honor de sus padres
y buen cuidado que le
tubieron.

11

That shawl and that crown
the bride has received,
they symbolize her parents' honor
and the good care she received.

12

La corona sinifica
una rosa de Castilla.
Y ese manto sinifica
la pureza de María.

12

The crown signifies
a rose from Castilla.
And the shawl signifies
the Virgin Mary's purity.

13

Oiga, el recién esposado,
que le quiero hacer saber.
Ya no hay padre,
ya no hay madre.
Ahora lo que hay es mujer.

13

Listen, recently wed husband,
for I want you to know.
A father is no more,
nor is there a mother.
What you have now is a wife.

14

Oiga, recién esposada,
escuche lo que le digo.
Ya no hay padre,
ya no hay madre.
Ahora lo que hay es marido.

14

Pay attention, dear newlywed wife,
listen to what I say.
A father is no more,
nor is there a mother.
What you have now is a husband.

15

El sacramento divino
tan blanco como una rosa.
Viva [el nombre del novio]
manifestando a su esposa.

15

The divine sacrament
as pure as a rose.
Long live [the groom's name]
showing off his wife.

16

No crea usted [esposo] que
    por mandar
en este punto veloz.
La criansa la dan los padres
y el natural sólo Dios.

16

Don't think of yourself [husband]
    as boss
even for one fleeting moment.
Parents are the ones who raise kids,
but only God can give us children.

17

En la puerta de la iglesia
el sacerdote les desella.
Tienen que ser esposados
como San José y María.

17

At the threshold to the church
the priest extends his wishes.
You must be husband and wife
like Saint Joseph and Mary.

18

Si dejas tu cruz por otra
has de pegar un suspiro.
Usted ha de ser responsable
en el tribunal divino.

18

If you should forsake your cross
you must let out a sigh.
You must be held responsible
before the divine tribunal.

19
El estado no es por un rato
ni por un día ni dos.
Es para una eternidad
mientras estén vivos los dos.

19
Marriage is not just for a while
nor for a day or two.
It's for an eternity
while the two of you are alive.

20
El estado no es muy duro;
es como un vaso de cristal.
Comoquiera que se quiebre
ya no se vuelve a juntar.

20
Marriage is not very hard;
it's rather like a crystal glass.
However it may break
you cannot put it back together.

21
"¿Ya van a tomarse el dicho?"
el padre les preguntó.
"¿Qué si con voluntad
se presentaban los dos?"

21
"Are you ready to take the vows?"
the priest asked each of them.
"Is it of your own volition
that you come before me?"

22
Entre suegros y consuegros

no deben de haber enojos,
porque se han consagrado
los dos niños de sus ojos.

22
Between in-laws and co-inlaws of
     the couple
there must be no discord,
because the two children of their eyes
have been blessed.

23
Óigame usted, el esposado,
le hablo con delicadesa.
Usted se parese al rey
y su esposa a la princesa.

23
Listen to me, dear husband,
I speak to you delicately.
You resemble the king
and your wife is the princess.

24
Nuestro Dios los ha juntado
con su santo matrimonio.
No le den cabida al diablo
ni le den gusto al demonio.

24
Our Beloved God has united you
with his holy matrimony.
Don't give the devil wings
or for that matter pleasure.

25

Entre suegros y consuegros
manifesten la verdad.
En este dichoso día
cambellen de voluntad.

25

Among in-laws and co-in-laws
show nothing but the truth.
On this fortuitous day
begin to show goodwill.

26

Vajo este suelo divino
corre el agua cristalina
donde se laban las manos
el padrino y la madrina.

26

Underneath this divine surface
runs crystal-clear water
where the godfather and
godmother wash their hands.

27

Los testigos de estos novios
manifestan la verdad.
Se presentan en la iglesia
con toda su voluntad.

27

The witnesses to the newlyweds
represent the truth.
They come to the church
of their own free will.

28

Padres de los esposados
escuchen, les voy a hablar.
La bendición a sus hijos
ya se la debe de echar.

28

Now listen, parents
of the newlyweds.
The blessing of both of them
you must now grant.

29

El padrino y la madrina
ya saben su obligación
de entregar a sus hijados
y echarles la bendición.

29

Godfather and godmother,
you already know your obligation:
to deliver your godchildren
and give them your blessing.

30

Aquí acabo cantando;
ya con esta me despido.
A todos les doy las gracias,
despensen lo mal serbido.

30

Here's where I finish singing
and I now bid you farewell.
I thank each and every one,
forgive me if I failed in my role.

Of the two musicians, only the guitarist sang the entriega. Moreover, if the *cantador*, singer (I never heard a female singer, *cantadora*) was about to run out of verses—which he knew by heart—and the atmosphere was lively, the people prompted him to continue. And true to form, he was able to invent new verses on the spot. Improvising verses before concluding the entriega was a gift most *entregadores* (deliverers) were blessed with. That's why they were oftentimes called *puetas*, poets.

All the while the guests, including kids, kept tossing more coins (no paper bills) on the bedsheet. The more spirited the action, the longer the musicians delighted in prolonging the entriega, so that the pile of money grew bigger and bigger. This money probably wasn't much by today's standards, at best ten to fifteen dollars, but it did provide the bride and groom with a nice chunk of cash with which to begin a new life of challenges.

EL ROBO DE LA NOVIA

Amid all the excitement and hubbub surrounding the entriega, the bride disappeared.* "Someone stole the bride! Someone stole the bride!" These words reverberated throughout the house. The propitious moment for such an act to take place was during the bride's visit to the outhouse, even though the godmother was supposed to safeguard her at all times so as to avoid the so-called kidnapping.

Stealing the bride was usually concocted and carried out by friends of the groom and the padrino in collusion with the godmother. But the persons responsible for paying the ransom to rescue the bride were none other than the padrino or his own buddies (*cuates*), something that had been agreed upon before the abduction. The ransom probably didn't amount to more than a few dollars.

And who stole the bride, how, and what was involved besides money? Everybody was keen on the idea that at some point the bride would disappear surreptitiously. That was a given. On the one hand, the padrinos—

---

* See "They Stole the Bride!" in *Grandma's Santo on Its Head: Stories of Days Gone By in Hispanic Villages of New Mexico / El santo patas arriba de mi abuelita: Cuentos de días gloriosos en pueblitos hispanos de Nuevo México.*

above all the godmother—and parents of the bride and groom supposedly kept an eagle eye on the bride. But at the same time, whenever it was convenient, they also tended to look askance.

The idea of abducting the bride was typical in my village and others along the Río Puerco Valley. The prank, because that's what it was, was done in jest, a game grown-ups played, yet it also served as one more way of raising money for the newlyweds on their wedding day. The groom was also aware of the ploy and was therefore a good sport in the total scheme of things. His married friends would lure him into having a beer or a shot of whiskey on the pretext that they, old hands at married life, were prepared to offer a few pointers. At that point his bride disappeared from the scene.

A principal in the kidnapping invariably was a close friend of the groom, who whisked the bride away on horseback. That happened at my uncle Ramón's wedding. His bride disappeared, whereupon a search party dispersed in different directions to rescue her. The searchers combed the area—from the family dispensary (shed) near the corral and the corral itself to the horse stables and my parents' house nearby.

The one place they failed to search was my father's garage, where he kept his old jalopy. Half of the garage, which had been carved out from a small hill next to his corral, was always dark and gloomy inside; it kept cool in the summer. That's where a member of the rescue party had the presence of mind to look, but the suspicion that someone, perhaps the godmother, had tipped off the searcher was undeniable. The bride, looking forlorn tucked away in the dark, was also a good sport throughout the entire episode.

Once the padrino paid the ransom, the bride was returned to the groom, accompanied by shouting and hand clapping. The musicians also broke into a fast-paced song. People danced to celebrate the moment and sang along with the musicians before guests started saying their farewells to head back home and get ready for the wedding dance at my village. The dance, the last big event of day, was scarcely a few hours away.

EL GRAN BAILE EN LA PLACITA

My mother, Aunt Taida, and my cousins Eremita and Catalina helped Grandma Lale clean up the kitchen; then they rested prior to getting ready for the *Gran baile*, the Big Dance, which started at dusk. But people began arriving at the Romero Dance Hall in the placita before sundown to get their choice seats. These consisted of *tarimas*, wooden benches, lined up against the walls on either side of the hall. Underneath the benches was where babies and small children slept in makeshift beds when they got tired.

The musicians always occupied the back wall, with a couple of chairs to sit on between dances in case they needed to pause and rest momentarily. Some musicians were up in years and consequently needed to take a break as the night progressed.

When my family and I arrived at the village, there were already a number of horse wagons in front of the church, adjacent to the dance hall. The horses were unhitched but tethered to the wagon wheels. Most owners, including my father, carried a bale of alfalfa for the horses to eat throughout the evening until we returned home.

In the meantime, the dance hall was full of relatives, friends, and other guests. The same violinist and guitarist who had played during the day at my grandparents' home arrived slightly ahead of Uncle Ramón and his bride, their respective parents, and the padrinos.

Once everyone was situated inside the hall, the padrino signaled the musicians, and the dance began with the traditional *marcha*, wedding march. The padrinos took the lead, followed by the bride and groom and their parents. After that everyone—from the old folks on down to the small children—participated in the intricacy of the march-dance.

Most padrinos were adept at leading the march, but in rare cases a couple well known in the community for their swirls and twirls was invited to take the lead. The wedding march involved a series of simple moves at first, followed by intricate formations in which dancing couples were separated into two lines—men in one and women in another—then breaking up into groups of four or six, reuniting with their original partners, and so forth. Many of the moves were similar to square dancing.

Once the marcha was over, tradition took another step forward. My uncle Ramón and his bride took to the floor before anyone else. This was a courtesy accorded the newlyweds. The musicians then played a slow waltz for the bride and groom to dance to. Once they had danced from one end of the floor to the other, accompanied by people clapping and shouting, dancers of every age joined in.

At that point other couples cut into the newlyweds' dance, and the males danced with the bride, and the women with the groom, but not before the women had pinned a dollar on the groom's lapel and the men had done the same on the bride's dress. Dancing with the newly married bride or groom was an honor, but you had to pay for the privilege. This was another way of raising money for the newlyweds.

The Big Dance continued for several hours. Unlike other dances in my village, which sometimes lasted until the wee hours of the morning, wedding dances rarely went beyond midnight—they took place at the end of a long day of activities. People didn't wear watches, but one of the musicians usually had a pocket watch and therefore was keenly aware of the time. Most musicians played without charging money, so they were not duty bound to play any later than necessary. Once they struck an old-fashioned waltz, the tarimas emptied onto the dance floor, people congratulated the newlyweds and bid adieu to their friends, and the dance ended.

Uncle Ramón and his bride hopped in his Dodge, left the village, crossed the Río Puerco, and headed for Albuquerque, where they would start a new life. As I saw the headlights moving north alongside the hillsides toward the Cerros Cuates, Twin Peaks (Santa Clara and Guadalupe), they reminded me of moving sky lights, which people purported were flying witches. But in this case there was one noticeable difference—my uncle and his bride were not supernatural creatures of the night, but rather newlyweds headed into the twilight of happiness!

14

May I Sharpen My Pencil?

LIFE ON THE RANCH for Mom and me changed bit by bit. By now, at the tender age of twenty-four, she had borne four children, three besides me: my little brothers, Beltrán and Juanito, and my baby sister, Julianita. Babies appeared to come from nowhere. Having more kids increased Mom's pressures; she was responsible for running a household and tending to our animals in Dad's weekly absences.

But even at her young age she had a superb knack for adapting to most family situations. Mom was always upbeat; at least that was my own perception and assessment. Moreover, she engaged us kids at a very early age in even the most minute of chores. We were always busy as we got older, but still with ample time to play. We were hardly ever bored to death. Mom wouldn't allow it.

One thing for sure, Mom's expression of love for her children did not vary one iota as the family grew. Her affection remained as constant as her composed nature. I recall vividly as if it were yesterday a complaint from my brother Beltrán. As Mom got my clothes ready for my first day of school, somehow he felt that her overt attention toward me in anticipation of my "big event" was excessive. "You like Junie more than you like me," he muttered, pouting a bit.

Pout or no pout, Mom would hear none of that nonsense. Her response was swift and to the point. "Look here, hijito," she said to him, eyeball to eyeball, even though he was only four years old. "Children are like the fingers on my hand. They're all different, but I treat them all the same."

The analogy left him scratching his head and gave me something to ponder as well. After all, we were too young to comprehend such adult-type stuff, but somehow episodes like this stuck to you like pine tar on your fingers. You didn't forget them overnight.

Realizing that neither he nor I quite grasped what she meant, she proceeded to illustrate a young mother's innate wisdom. Her playful nature came through from time to time. She grabbed my little brother's hand in hers, with the palm right-side up, and said to him,

"Here you have five little fingers. One, two, three, four, five." He listened and I watched, because Mom had played this game with me in the past. She then started with the index finger and followed through one by one. "This fat little finger [the thumb] found an egg. This one boiled it in hot water. This one peeled it. This one put salt and pepper on it. And this itty-bitty one [the pinkie] ate it all!"

My brother looking a bit bemused but, seemingly satisfied, said to her, "And why did the little finger eat all the egg?"

"Because he was real *cuzco*, greedy. That's why! And that's the whole point of the story, hijito. One day you'll understand."

"And when do I learn to count, amá?" he asked, changing subjects.

"When you start school like your brother."

Dad came home that Friday, as he did routinely. But besides hard candy, which by now was giving me multiple cavities and toothaches (dentists were unheard of in my valley), he also brought me a Big Chief tablet, a pencil, and a box of crayons consisting of eight different colors. He knew school would be starting on Monday because Mom made sure he remembered, although he hardly needed a reminder. Dad had a phenomenal memory; he almost never forgot anything. One thing my siblings and I learned very young was to be truthful for fear that he'd catch us fabricating a story to cover our wrongdoing.

Weekends at home were pretty busy for the entire family, sometimes even more so for Mom, but Dad thrived on ranch chores. These were quite different from his backbreaking pick-and-shovel job of building roads and fences. He made sure Mom had enough hay handy to feed the horses and the milk cow during the entire week. He didn't like for her to haul any hay from the haystack. In watering the livestock, something Mom and I did at least once a day, we'd go down to the riverbed, where pools of water could still be found from the summer rains. Dad and I took up those chores on Saturdays and Sundays.

I helped my parents in whatever ways I could, but one of my primary jobs throughout the week was to feed and water the chickens and my rabbits. Grandpa Lolo and Grandma Lale collected rainwater from their flat roof in a huge tin tank they had bought eons ago. (Until recently the lonely tank was still there after all these years!) That's where I fetched the water for our chickens and rabbits. In return for the water, I helped Grandma with her chickens, while Beltrán got in the way and caused mischief. Even at age four, he was a character.

He did help, in a manner of speaking, by collecting the eggs from the chicken coop in a dish towel, a makeshift basket, unless he decided to crack one or two to make sure they weren't *vanos*, that is, hollow. You could generally tell if an egg was no good because its *cáscara*, shell, was *güera*, blond color. In that case, the egg never reached the breakfast table.

But nothing was ever lost at the ranch because Chopo, who usually tagged along on my trips to the chicken coop, lapped up the broken eggs. He was my accomplice, so to speak, in hiding from Mom the so-called evidence in case we accidentally broke an egg or two and she questioned why so few eggs had made it home in the dish towel.

Following Dad here and there as he performed his ranch chores was a joy, but at the same time it was tiring, because of the energy he possessed. Moreover, he was well organized and methodical in everything he did; he capitalized on every minute of the day. As a consequence, he got more work done in half a day than most people accomplish in a whole day. His self-discipline caused him to exude self-confidence, something he tried to instill in all of his children. One of his favorite sayings was "*Haz las cosas al revés y las haces otra vez*," the equivalent of "Haste makes waste."

A respite for Mom from the animals and chopping wood did not lessen her household work over the weekend. She still had to cook our meals; bake biscuits, bizcochitos (anise and cinnamon cookies), and a pie or two; plus prepare a variety of foods for Dad to take with him come early Monday morning. She also had to wash and iron his clothes, but she tried to do this on Saturday.

Sundays were basically a day of rest or a time for family and friends to get together. Few ranch people worked on Sundays unless it was to perform small chores or to rescue crops from threatening rainstorms or frost that oftentimes struck from nowhere in late summer or early fall. Attending Mass during the priest's monthly visit to the village from Jémez Springs or Cuba was of course obligatory.

On Sunday evening, the day before I started school, Mom, Dad, and I sat around the kitchen table. On top of the table were my Big Chief tablet, pencil, and crayons. Next to my school supplies was an empty La Paloma flour sack. That was to be my knapsack for carrying my prized possessions to school.

Mom also brought out my brand-new pecheras, bib overalls; a white long-sleeve shirt; a pair of brown high-top shoes; and my socks. Beltrán was already tucked in bed, so he couldn't aver favoritism. After all, it was all part of a rite of passage that he, too, would enjoy three years hence.

While we sat at the table chitchatting about my first school day, Dad took out his pocketknife and asked me if I wanted my pencil sharpened.

"No, apá," I said. "Cousin J. has told me that they have this little machine at school that the escueleros, school kids, use to sharpen their pencils. I want to do the same thing. It's called a sacapuntas, pencil sharpener."

Aside from the pencil sharpener and the fact that eight or ten students went to school in Uncle Antonio's school bus, I was pretty much in the dark as to what to expect. I was on the brink of discovering a brand new world, to be sure. To say that I was very excited with the adventure I was about to embark upon was an understatement, but no one was happier than Mom. In fact, she was ecstatic, whereas Dad was much more reserved. That was his nature. Both of them, however, stressed the importance of school. I sensed that Mom in particular was overjoyed at seeing her first offspring attend school, since she never had that opportunity. Dad had fared a bit better, despite having to quit in the fifth grade to help his parents with their farming and ranching responsibilities.

By the time I got up Monday morning, Dad was gone. He rose earlier than usual so that he could milk the cow, thereby sparing Mom and me that chore on my first day of school. Before getting dressed, I ate my breakfast—a bowl of oatmeal, a tortilla warmed over the woodstove, and a cup of fresh milk.

Uncle Antonio's school bus, which the author rode to school, c. 1943–1945.
First row, Cousin J. is on the far left. Second row, Cousin G. is hiding his face.

Once I had eaten, I put on my new clothes. Mom made sure my face, hands, and ears were clean. The last thing she did was to comb my hair. She tried to mat down my unruly cola de gallo, rooster tail, but with little success. "There you are!" she said. "You're as handsome as a prince." I didn't know what this last word was, but I figured that it was something I would learn in school. One thing for sure, her gesture of love and affection was something that Mom tended to show regardless of the circumstances.

"Let's go. It's time for the school bus. It will be here any minute. But first, come here," and she made me kneel down so she could bless me.

By now Mom knew what time it was because she had the new Westclox clock I had bought her after my Angora cat broke the previous one when he knocked it off the chest of drawers. The bus usually stopped at the top of the hill around eight o'clock. We walked to the dirt road, about one hundred feet from our little house. Mom handed me a brown paper bag. I knew it wasn't candy! "Here's your lunch and something to drink. Don't open it till lunchtime." I put it in my La Paloma flour sack along with my school supplies.

Up the hill came Uncle Antonio's yellow bus. He had gone north to Santa Clara to pick up the Jaramillo kids along with the Gonzaleses, all of whom lived across from the placita this side of the Río Puerco. He stopped, opening the doors to the back of the bus for me to hop in. Mom's parting gaze as I looked out the rear window was accompanied by a happy smile on her beautiful and loving face.

Except for Dad's old car, I had never ridden in a vehicle. The school bus was a new adventure for me. From my house to La Mesa School in Rincón del Cochino was about three to four miles on a dirt road. My uncle zipped down the bumpy and winding road, leaving a cloud of dust behind us. We bounced and jostled each other along the way; seat belts were unheard of. The safety of schoolchildren did not seem uppermost in my uncle's mind.

The only kids familiar to me on the bus were my cousins (Uncle Antonio's children) and the Gonzales kids. At least I didn't feel like a total stranger. On the way to school, we stopped to pick up one of the Montaño children, Loyola, whom I knew because his parents and Mom and Dad were good friends.

Once we got to school and off the bus, the scenario changed dramatically. In addition to the García, Gonzales, Jaramillo, and Montaño schoolkids, there were those from the Valencia and Armijo families. I had seen those kids at church, but didn't really know them. Everybody scattered throughout the playgrounds to greet their old schoolmates, except Cousin J., who was now in the second grade. He took me by the hand to show me inside the school. As we walked in, there was Miss Montoya, the schoolteacher. "This is my cousin," he said to her in Spanish. "*Bienvenido*," she responded.

Cousin J. also showed me what was to be my home away from home. The one-room schoolhouse was a rectangular adobe structure with a main entrance in front and two windows on either side. Inside the schoolroom, the blackboard was located on the back wall. I noticed that all the walls were whitewashed. A potbelly stove for the winter months stood almost in the middle of the room. The small wooden barrel with drinking water and a communal jumate, dipper, sat on top of a chair next to the teacher's desk at the front of the classroom. A dish towel hung on the chair for students to wipe the dipper every time we drank water.

There were approximately twenty-four desks. Each wooden desk had decorative black wrought-iron legs, and it could seat two pupils if necessary, an especially useful feature when the older students helped the younger ones with their classroom assignments. The desktop had an inkwell holder on the upper right-hand corner for a bottle of Sheaffer's Skrip ink, plus an elongated groove long enough to place a pencil and a fountain pen or two pencils.

Suddenly I heard Miss Montoya ringing a hand bell. She asked everybody to form two lines in front of the schoolhouse, in no particular order, but this would change after the teacher assigned desks to everyone. Once inside Miss Montoya called out our names and pointed to the desk where each student was to sit. A piece of white paper bore each student's name. She spoke in Spanish for the benefit of the first graders, like me, who knew no English. Next were the names of the second graders, followed by the third graders, and so on until she got to those in the eighth grade. This last grade was the highest level of education you could achieve at a one-room schoolhouse like La Mesa School—or anywhere else in the Río Puerco valley.

As Miss Montoya assigned desks, she switched between English and Spanish. I understood what she said in Spanish, of course, but I didn't have the foggiest notion what she was saying in English. She must have said something about pencils, because everybody held a pencil high in the air. Sensing that we were going to use our pencils, I raised my right hand. A multitude of eyes beamed upon me as Miss Montoya came over. Without hesitating, I said to her, "*¿Puedo hacerle punta a mi lápiz?* May I sharpen my pencil?"

"Look, hijito," she said in Spanish, "from this day forward we're going to learn English."

Needless to say, her use of Spanish at that very moment made me feel more comfortable than the actual challenge or ordeal that was to follow in subsequent days, weeks, and months of trying to read, speak, and write in English. Miss Montoya insisted on the use of English inside and outside the classroom without scolding, embarrassing, or punishing us if we resorted to Spanish. All the students were in the same boat, struggling to cope with English. This included the older students, who forgot over the summer whatever English they had learned during the previous academic year.

Of the three skills—speaking, writing, and reading—the latter was the most enjoyable, albeit problematic for most of my classmates and me. The first book that I read in school and one I was able to take home to practice on was *Run, Spot, Run*. When I read this book the first few times, what came out of my mouth was, "Rrun, Espot, rrun." The pronunciation was hardly smooth; it sounded like my father's car when it missed, but the other kids also had the same problem as I did. Nobody laughed, though. No one could avoid trilling the *r*'s or adding an *e* to *Spot* or to words like *school*, which sounded more like "eschool." These were but two isolated cases of troublesome pronunciation, but the *v*'s also became *b*'s ("very" versus "bery") and the *ch*'s sounded like *sh*'s ("church" versus "shursh"). It was also not unusual to hear sentences like "Tank yu bery mush."

As time went on, it was difficult to tell whose challenge was more daunting—teaching for Miss Montoya or reading for us students. Either way, everyone, including her, seemed to be running in place from one school year to the next. Trying to learn a foreign language (and English was a foreign language!) was tantamount to trying to fit a square peg into a round hole. Even the pronunciation of bad words in English from Cousin J.'s cousins from Martíneztown, who visited the ranch on occasion and who presumably spoke better English, wasn't any better. "Chicken shit" (*miedoso*) came out sounding like "shiken chit." Somehow we thought, however unconsciously, that reversing the pronunciation of the *ch*'s and the *sh*'s would make words sound better and more correct, when in fact it made matters worse.

The clock went off on Miss Montoya's desk. It was 10:30 and time for recess. We were allowed fifteen minutes to play games or to use the outhouse. Baseball was popular among the older boys and girls. The younger boys shot marbles, and the little girls played hopscotch or jacks. Fifteen minutes were gone in no time at all.

Miss Montoya spent the rest of the morning assigning books and explaining what a typical school day would consist of, based on her lesson plans. Having to teach multiple grades meant she had to set aside blocks of time for each grade level, but the older students were encouraged to help the lower grades whenever we younger kids needed assistance. We all learned together and from one another. The camaraderie system, if one could call it that, was an extension of the so-called primo phenomenon in the community, whereby you treated and helped your fellow man as if he were your own blood cousin. And the scheme worked.

For lunch we were allowed one hour—from twelve to one o'clock—and encouraged to eat our homemade lunches (there was no such thing as a cafeteria) on the school grounds, provided the weather was bearable. I grabbed my lunch from a nook underneath my desktop and headed outside with the rest of the kids my age. Cousin J. joined me. There were no tables or benches; therefore, we found a shady spot northeast of the schoolhouse, facing the Rincón del Cochino Canyon. (A man at one time reputedly raised a bunch of hogs in the canyon for family consumption—hence the name.)

I opened my brown paper sack to see what Mom had packed me for lunch. The first thing I saw as I peeked was a *mantelito*, a cloth napkin that she had crocheted. She knew I really liked scrambled eggs and fried potatoes; that's what I found neatly wrapped in a flour tortilla, the old-fashioned version of today's burrito or wrap. To hold the tortilla together she had stuck a *popote*, or broom straw, through it (our version of a modern-day toothpick). A pint-size mason jar of water was my drink. For dessert Mom had packed two bizcochitos.

Before I started eating, I made the sign of the cross and said grace, something Mom had taught me and that she insisted upon ever since I was able to speak. Her words, "*Gracias a Dios, que nos da el pan de cada día. Amén,*" were simple and to the point. They were the same words we recited as a family at the dinner table. I thought of her as I ate my lunch and thanked her as well. When I finished I folded my napkin, put it back in the paper sack, and folded the paper sack as well to use again.

Miss Montoya also packed a lunch, even though her living quarters were just a short distance away, at the Valencia home. She ate at her desk by herself, unless some student didn't feel well and stayed inside. About five minutes before one o'clock, she emerged from the schoolhouse, ringing her little bell. The time had come to line up in two columns, except that this time she put the young kids in front and the older students toward the back, according to grades. As we walked in we did not have to scramble for our desks; everything was done in an orderly fashion. My desk was next to the window, facing the Mesa Prieta to the east.

We spent the rest of the afternoon listening to Miss Montoya outline a series of don'ts in class. Some of them, which I can still recite from memory, were as follow:

1. You will not talk unless you're asked to by the teacher.
2. You will not chew and crack gum.
3. You will not bother your classmate in front or behind you.
4. You will not build or fly paper airplanes.
5. You will not shoot spit wads at your classmates.

The foregoing don'ts were not all clear to me, but I got the gist of what was intended. Shooting spit wads is one that threw me for a loop. I didn't have the faintest idea what she meant. Much later, I learned that some mean-spirited boys used *tetones*, green pods from the cottonwood tree, with rubber bands as shooters to strike the girls on their butts.

The list of don'ts was the teacher's way of setting the parameters for discipline and classroom behavior. The boys who broke these rules (girls were hardly a problem unless provoked) spent time in a corner either standing or kneeling, sometimes with their pants rolled up above their knees, depending on the severity of the infraction or the number of times he had misbehaved and been disciplined. Discipline was rarely a problem for the teacher, who commanded the utmost respect in the classroom as well as in the community. She was, after all, the maestra, master of her craft and a paragon of knowledge.

No sooner had Miss Montoya finished with the don'ts list when one of the students, obviously trying to be funny, raised his hand.

"Yes, Alberto, what is it?"

"If we can't throw espit wats, can we throw *pedos*, farts?"

Everybody burst out laughing, breaking the silence for the first time that day. But all Miss Montoya could do was to stare daggers at Alberto, who, as it turned out, was not only a cutup but also very intelligent.

"Okay," said Miss Montoya, "it's time for the afternoon recess. You have fifteen minutes."

Once we were back inside she asked everyone to put their heads down

on the desks and to rest for three to five minutes. After we rested, Miss
Montoya had one last etiquette reminder. To drive her point home, especially
for the newcomers, she held up a book and recited in Spanish this clever and
delightful short ditty, whose words I still recall. It went something like this:

Si yo este libro me perdiera,	If I should lose this book,
como puede suceder,	as it is bound to happen,
le pido al que lo hallara	I ask the person who finds it
que me lo sepa devolver.	to have the decency to return it.
Y si fuera de uñas largas	And should he have sticky fingers
y con poco entendimiento,	and be a bit unprincipled,
le pido que se acuerde	I ask him to remember
del séptimo mandamiento.	the seventh commandment.*

Miss Montoya had barely finished when Alberto stood up and asked permission to speak.

"Yes, Alberto. What is it this time?"

"Miss Montoya. Last year you also taught us another poem. Can I recite it?"

"Yes, Alberto. Go ahead."

Alberto cleared his throat, put his hands in his front pockets as if to assert
his posture and self-confidence, and began his recitation.

Si una cosa yo me encontrara,	If I should find something,
cuatro veces lo diré.	I shall repeat it four times.
Si su dueño no se plantara,	If the owner should fail to come forward,
con ella yo me quedaré.	I shall keep it for my own.

In other words, "Finders, keepers; losers, weepers." Again the class got a
chuckle out of Alberto, but this time more in recognition of his ability to remember something that most of the class probably had forgotten.

By the end of the day, I had a good feel for what school was going to be like.
I enjoyed my first day but was anxious to get home to share my experience
with Mom. From my desk, I looked out the window and saw Uncle Antonio's

* Thou shalt not steal.

school bus. He was already waiting for us with the back doors popped open. Miss Montoya dismissed school promptly at three o'clock, when her alarm clock went off.

The ride home seemed less bumpy and winding but longer, perhaps because I was eager to see Mom, in spite of all the school excitement. I particularly missed playing gin rummy with her at noon, something we had been doing almost on a daily basis ever since she had taught me the game two years earlier.

When I got off the bus, I didn't even say good-bye to my cousins or my other schoolmates. I dashed home and flew inside the kitchen, where Mom was playing on the floor with Julianita. I squatted and hugged Mom.

"¡Ay, hijito! How was school? Tell me all about it. But first go put on your playing clothes. You have to wear your school clothes again tomorrow."

After I changed clothing, I grabbed a piece of tortilla, slapped a light layer of lard on it, and sprinkled it with a little salt. This was my version of the modern-day peanut butter and jelly sandwich. Many kids in my valley enjoyed the same concoction once they got home from school. In between bites, I recounted almost verbatim what had transpired at school. By the time I finished, I was exhausted. The day had been long but eventful and exciting. School brought a new dawn for Mom and me, mainly for her, since she had never attended one day of school in her life.

15

La Matanza

A Festive Occasion

AT SCHOOL, WHENEVER I heard the word *matanza*, hog butchering, my face warmed up with joy and my heart beat a happy sound. It was a heavenly time for me. Images of sizzling chicharrones, crisp, meaty cracklings, and fresh oven-baked morcillas, blood sausages, made my mouth water. These were two of the delicacies and by-products that came from the venerable animal ungraciously called the pig. *Marrano, cochino,* or *puerco* in Spanish were no more flattering. (*Cerdo,* a more contemporary term in Spain, was alien to Río Puerco Valley residents).

Every year in late October or early November, when temperatures began to dip and winter peeked around the corner, a matanza was celebrated among the three families at my grandparents' ranch, with an occasional guest or two joining us. My immediate family, Grandpa Lolo and Grandma Lale (*mi papá grande y mi mamá grande*), and Aunt Taida, Uncle Antonio, and their offspring formed the nucleus for the festive occasion. Counting my siblings and me, who at one time numbered five (three more were born later, after we moved to Albuquerque); my five to seven cousins, depending on when one counted; plus the respective parents and Grandpa Lolo and Grandma Lale, our so-called community at any given time hovered between sixteen and eighteen people.

From the eldest down to the youngest, each one of us fulfilled a role on the day of the matanza. Whatever the contribution, major or minor, it did not matter. You were still a key player in the overall scenario. A matanza traditionally meant the butchering of a hog. It did not preclude a cow, a young steer, or a heifer, but these animals did not conjure up the excitement of a hog. Slaughtering a hog was a big event at our ranch; it was a genuine happening, a festive occasion indeed.

Grandma Lale took charge of raising the hogs, but we all helped her fatten them. This included Grandpa Lolo, my family, Aunt Taida, and Uncle Antonio, as well as their children. No scorecards or timetables were kept among the caretakers as to who fed, watered, or locked up the hogs. We all pitched in to help Grandma.

According to my father, Grandma Lale at one time boasted around eighty pigs, more than anyone in our valley. During my childhood, though, she never had more than eight to ten hogs at any given time. These included piglets born in the spring. Come fall, after harvest season, in September she would turn loose her herd of pigs in the cornfields so they could feed on the *rastrojos*, corn stubble. But as winter struck in earnest she did something special for her hogs—she fed them warm boiled corn or *salvao*, wheat bran, at least two or three times a week to keep them fat and healthy throughout the cold months. She loved her hogs. They were like pets to her.

In the spring and summer, her hogs roamed and mingled with the goats, cattle, and horses in the open terrain along the Río Puerco, where fodder was plentiful. In the evening the grandchildren made sure the hogs were back safely in their pens, away from the cornfields, to protect them from the coyotes. Caring for the hogs was indeed a family affair. In that way, when matanza time arrived, everybody felt a sense of kinship toward the swine that was to provide us with enough meat to supplement other meats during the winter.

Preparations for the matanza were hardly helter-skelter; they were methodical and carried out with utmost precision. The event was spearheaded by none other than Grandpa Lolo, with assistance from my father and Uncle Antonio.

Grandpa was a master at seeing that all the preliminary groundwork was in place the day before the matanza. He also took charge and oversaw the actual matanza from beginning to end. Without fail the butchering took place at Aunt Taida and Uncle Antonio's place, because they had a huge cottonwood tree close to their house that was used for hoisting the pig with a set of Grandpa's winches. Sometimes the tree hadn't quite lost all of its fall leaves, and it provided patches of shades if the day was warm.

The women, too, had their fair share of responsibilities. First and foremost, they made sure ample pots and pans were on hand to ensure that the butchering process did not skip a beat. They also never failed to have enough fresh coffee for the men to drink and warm tortillas to munch on throughout the day. Hot coffee, especially on cold days, was essential, and men delighted above all in the aroma outside coming from a Hills Bros. tin can sitting in a fire pit instead of a coffeepot on the woodstove inside the house.

The women's role, as we shall learn more in this chapter, was fluid and therefore changed during the day. They also performed some of the least glamorous work, while the daughters usually lent a helping hand, a learning experience that would put them on a path toward assuming a similar role later in life as wives and mothers.

Grandpa Lolo always assigned my father and my uncle certain chores as part of the overall preparations. One of the main items—and my grandfather usually possessed all of them—was to set up a makeshift table to put the hog on after it was slaughtered. This entailed fetching five or six long boards from underneath the *entarime*, wood floor, in my grandparents' kitchen or from under the portal in front of their house. The sturdy boards, about eight to ten inches wide and one and a half inches thick, were washed with hot, soapy water, rinsed, and placed across two or three so-called burros (a kind of scaffolding). They were interspersed according to the weight of the hog. While seemingly crude, the setup was practical and reliable. Boys like me, depending on age and ability, helped our fathers in whatever ways possible.

Near the table my cousins and I chopped wood to keep the fire going from dawn until the last batch of chicharrones was cooked and the matanza came to an end later in the afternoon.

Aside from the large copper vat or cauldron, which sat on top of hot rocks above the fire pit and was used for frying the chicharrones, a large cajete, tin tub, containing very hot lime mixed in water also sat on top of stones. The concoction was poured on the *guangoches*, gunnysacks, or old pieces of *carpa*, canvas, that covered the hog to soften the bristle for easier removal.

But given the entire assortment of items needed for a matanza, none was more important than knives, which Grandpa Lolo owned and was very proud of. You could bet that the evening before the matanza, as if to carry out a yearly ritual, right after eating supper he could be found pedaling a mollejón, a round sharpening stone. The stone, measuring about twelve to fourteen inches in diameter, was like the front wheel on a bike. A small tin can full of water dangled in front of his contraption. He ran both sides of a knife against the stone and sparks flew; the water dripped from time to time as he tipped the can by hand to make sure the stone remained damp. With his right thumb he tempered the blade gingerly, until each knife was sharpened to his liking and ready for the poor pig.

Grandpa Lolo had three or four large knives that were more like kitchen knives; they were used around the house for cubing or cutting up meat. They were also utilized to scrape the hog's bristle or to cut long strips of *lonja*, layers of fat from the hog's back that were turned into lard and used for cooking.

In his collection of knives, Grandpa had one that was special. It was long, sharp, and pointed like a *lezna*, awl, and he used it to reach the hog's heart soon after it was knocked senseless by being struck in the forehead with a *marro*, sledgehammer, the more humane way of killing a hog, according to him. Shooting the hog between the eyes with a .22 caliber rifle, as some ranchers preferred, many times was totally ineffective. What this did was to anger the hapless animal, causing it to shake loose and go berserk, while the older kids attempted to tackle the poor thing. This prompted more than a few chuckles. But the sight was hardly a laughing matter, especially for someone like Grandpa Lolo, an easygoing person for whom the matanza was no monkey business.

The night preceding the big event, I tossed, tumbled, and wrestled with my pillow all night long, restless from the anticipation and excitement of the festive occasion to come. Before the sun began to peer over the Mesa Prieta, I momentarily fell asleep and awoke as if from a trance.

I heard Grandpa Lolo's voice outside our kitchen door. "*¿Ya estamos?* Are we ready?" he asked through the screen door. "*Ya voy.* I'm coming," my father answered. He and Mom were already up and dunking small pieces of tortilla in their coffee. A hearty breakfast on this special day was

La matanza, Nasario P. García family, c. 1922–1924.
The author's father is second from left. Grandma Lale is fourth from left,
and Grandpa Lolo is holding the rope attached to the hog.

out of the question. Snacking on chicharrones or what have you later on constituted part of the breakfast, however late.

As one and all congregated around Aunt Taida and Uncle Antonio's house, there stood my grandfather with a short rope in his right hand, giving instructions to my dad and my uncle and making certain that all arrangements were in place. The fire had begun to crackle and pop in the open fire pit.

The rest of us, above all my cousins and me, blew on our hands to keep them warm, while Mom, Aunt Taida, and Grandma Lale stuck their hands in their apron pockets. The morning was brisk, ideal for a matanza.

My father and uncle and all the boys paraded behind Grandpa Lolo to the pigpen, where Grandma's hog had been kept in solitary confinement without food—only water—for the past twenty-four hours. This was done to keep the digestive tract as clear as possible, since some of the intestines would be used for blood sausages.

When we got to the pigsty, the star—or, rather, potential victim—seemed a trifle forlorn, as if the hog sensed his impending demise. As Grandpa Lolo glanced at my cousins J. and G. and me perched on top of the fence looking down at the pen, my grandfather looped the rope and put it around the hog's neck. The pig oinked and oinked. At that moment I thought to myself, "Poor pig. If he could talk, he no doubt would ask, 'What are you going to do with me?'"

For some unexplained reason, I felt sorry for the poor animal. A contradiction suddenly flashed across my mind. One way or another there was something wrong with the whole scenario, an incongruity of sorts. For over a year or so we treated the hog almost as if he were human, feeding him boiled corn and warm wheat bran in the winter, but now we were about to cajole him into getting whacked with a sledgehammer. Words that Mom had once said to me sprung forward in my mind: "*Pa vivir hay que morir.* To survive you have to die." A paradox or not, I accepted it, nonetheless, because hot chicharrones wrapped in a warm flour tortilla were much more enticing than any philosophical viewpoint of mine at my age.

I'm sure the squealing pig could be heard back at Aunt Taida's house where she and Mom stoked the fire nearby to make sure that the lime water in the tin tub would be ready to facilitate removal of the pig's bristle. It was only a matter of minutes before one of the boys took off running to tell the ladies that the pig had been hoisted on the winches up the cottonwood tree. Soon thereafter my grandfather grabbed his long, sharp knife and pierced the pig's heart. Right away my father placed a *bandeja*, pan, beneath to catch the blood that was to be used for morcillas. Grandpa Lolo was an expert at bleeding a hog. He was also known for having *sangre liviana*, thin blood, which meant that the meat would be tender (someone with *sangre gruesa*, thick blood, was thought to be prone to butchering tough meat). There was something ineffable but favorable regarding the chemistry between the pig and a butcher like my grandfather.

Beyond the proper bleeding, he routinely removed all the pig's entrails. Everything was salvaged except for the stomach and *bofes*, lungs, which were considered nonedible even for the dogs (we boys had to bury them deep enough so the dogs couldn't find them). Once Grandpa cut open the hog in front, he, Uncle Antonio, and Dad placed it facedown on the makeshift table, with all four of its legs spread out, and Grandpa split its back down the middle.

After this happened, everybody got into the act. This was when the real fun started. Kitchen knives could be heard clanging among the grown-ups as they prepared to do battle removing the bristle, while children stood by with sharp-edged tin can lids, ready to do the same. By now the hog was covered from head to toe with gunnysacks soaked in lime water to soften the tough bristle. Little by little everyone went to work. The grown-ups applied their knives as though they were drawknives for more effective scraping, holding the knife with both hands from tip to handle (the same technique that was used in removing the bark off vigas). This enabled the *pelador*, scraper, to put equal weight on the entire knife edge.

We children sort of held up the rear in the scraping process until the pigskin was visible. My favorite part for removal of bristle was the feet, because you could concentrate on a small yet difficult part of the pig.

Next Grandpa Lolo used his sharp knives to cut the long strips of lonja, the fatty hog's back. Dad and Uncle Antonio then dumped the strips into a tin tub; sometimes they strung them on the clothesline, provided they were not too heavy. The cool temperature hardened the strips, which made it easier to remove the *cuero*, pigskin, from the lonja. The *cueritos*, strips of pigskin, were hung from the beams in the dispensa, shed, to dry; later they were cut into small pieces and cooked in pinto beans to add flavor.

The lonja, or layers of fat, were diced into small pieces—with meat on them, of course—the day of the matanza to make chicharrones, the meaty part of the fat that was deep fried to crispness in Grandpa's copper cauldron. Whatever fat or lard was left in the cauldron was what Mom, Grandma, and Aunt Taida saved in lard cans and used for cooking.

We watched Grandpa Lolo slowly turning the wooden paddle clockwise and counterclockwise to make certain the chicharrones cooked evenly. The paddle was also what he used to scoop up the chicharrones and dump them in a *cernidor*, sieve, to drain, whereupon he spread them on a dish towel on top of a small table until they cooled enough to be eaten.

For me this was the highlight of the matanza; my cousins and I were the first to put our hands on the meaty delicacies. There was nothing more delicious than a few chicharrones wrapped in a flour tortilla, similar to today's burritos. They were also mouthwatering warmed over with refried beans for breakfast or lunch.

Chicharrones, the staff of life on the day of the matanza, was something we kids could eat faster than uttering the word. A large hog like Grandma Lale's could yield enough chicharrones for each family to take home in a five- to seven-pound can lined with a wax base to prevent them from turning rancid. A large hog could sometimes produce enough lard for a single family's cooking and baking needs for at least one year, that is, from one matanza to the next.

While Uncle Antonio and Dad took turns helping Grandpa Lolo tend to the chicharrones, Mom, Grandma Lale, and Aunt Taida were busy scrubbing and washing the pig's intestines in hot water to make blood sausage. Cleaning the intestines was a messy job, perhaps the least attractive aspect of the matanza. Most women had strong stomachs, however, and were up to the challenge.

The ingredients for making morcillas were simple and unobtrusive. And measuring the exact amounts was not fashionable or typical among rural women; good cooks like my mother, aunt, and Grandma sensed and knew how much of each ingredient to put in. Here's a rough rendition of my mother's list of ingredients for blood sausage as I remember it.

pig's intestines
pig's blood
chopped white onions
red chile seeds
chopped garlic
oregano
salt
fat (tiny pieces)

The intestines were tied with a piece of string at one end. Then, little by little, Grandma, Mom, and Aunt Taida filled them by hand with the pig's blood, chopped onions, red chile seeds, and the other spices. When the morcillas were ready, strings were tied at the other ends and they were boiled in hot water. (Some women preferred to mix the blood and other ingredients in a bowl and then stuff the intestines.) Extra caution had to be taken or else the morcillas, which looked like balloons, might overcook in the stove oven, in which case they could rupture or perhaps even explode if they got too hot, although that rarely happened. Mom, Grandma, and Aunt Taida were old hands at making morcillas; they even knew intuitively how long to cook them. Back then there were no cooking thermometers or temperature gauges on the old-fashioned stoves.

Getting a taste of the hot morcillas did not take long—about forty-five minutes to an hour. By then we were all ready to graduate from chicharrones to blood sausage, the small boys in particular—we liked cutting up and showing off our blackened teeth, which looked like they were filled with dark cavities because of the cooked blood that got stuck between them. This was just part of the fun throughout the day. The grown-ups took our mischief in stride. After all, a matanza was a joyous affair, and we kids provided the lighthearted moments whenever the opportunity arose.

While the morcillas cooked, the men cut long strips of pork rinds (cueritos) to be used during the winter in menudo, tripe stew. Here's a simple but true-to-form list of ingredients for menudo.

> dried pork rinds (cueritos), 3 inches long and 2 inches wide
> lime-treated hominy
> pig's feet (optional)
> red chile pods (optional)
> water
> salt
> chopped clove (*diente*) of garlic (optional)

Pigs' feet were customarily added to the menudo, for the most part, when it was made for Christmas vespers, Nochebuena, but since there were only four pig's feet, my parents and my uncle's family got two apiece—a front and hind foot for each household. Grandpa, who was in charge of supervising the matanza, also divided the hog among the three families, but the prized trophy from the event was the pig's head. And that without question went to Grandma Lale, because she was the expert in making tamales.* She roasted

---

* See *Grandma Lale's Tamales: A Christmas Story / Los tamales de Abuelita Lale: Un cuento navideño.*

the head in the oven and used the meat for her tamales, one of her culinary specialties (more on this in chapter 17) and a tradition at Christmastime.

The pig's head, like the rest of the hog once quartered, was destined for my grandparents' dispensa. Made of adobe bricks, measuring no more than eight by ten feet and boasting an eight-foot ceiling, the pantry was situated between my grandparents' house and ours. It served in lieu of a refrigerator because there was no such thing as refrigeration in the Río Puerco Valley. In the summer the pantry was ideally suited for perishables, like meat and home-canned fruits and vegetables. Inside were wooden shelves plus *ganchos*, hooks, on the beams so we could hang flour sacks full of jerky, dried fruit, different cuts of beef and pork (e.g., front and hind shanks), long strips of pork rinds, and my grandmother's pig head.

The pantry was community property; it belonged to my grandparents, my parents, and my aunt and uncle. Except for a wooden peg on a string attached to the door, the pantry was rarely locked, much to the delight of us urchins (the boys), who sneaked in once in a while and helped ourselves to jerky or dried fruit, even if Grandma's pig head dared to stare at us straight in the eye. In the semidarkness it could be a spooky and intimidating scene, to say the least, but during daylight hours the pig's head was part of the matanza and something children like me became accustomed to in ranch life.

By the end of the day, the fire was dying down and the coals were turning to white ash. The makeshift table was dismantled, the winches were brought down from the tree, the tin tub, cauldron, and knives washed and put back in their proper places. By then, everyone was ready to call it a day.

As my parents, my three siblings, and I accompanied my grandparents up the hill to our homes, not far from my aunt and uncle's place near the river, each one of us carried our share of chicharrones in tin cans and the morcillas in bandejas, large pans. When we reached the top of the hill Grandma Lale, who was a very religious person, rejoiced. She made the sign of the cross and gave thanks to God for another successful matanza, even though she had blessed the pig when it was placed on the makeshift table.

After Dad and I helped Mom put away the blood sausage and chicharrones, I went outside our casita, sat down on the ground, and leaned against the adobe wall. I stared at the Mesa Prieta, whose stark and mystical beauty engulfed me as I reflected on the day's festive activities. The hustle and bustle, laughter, eating, and chatting now formed part of my bank of wonderful childhood memories.

"*¿Qué pasa, hijito? ¿Estás cansao?* What's wrong, my dear son? Are you tired?" Mom asked as she looked out the screen door.

"*Sí, amá.* I'm tired," I answered with a wistful smile.

"*Pero contento, ¿eh?*" she countered.

Mom had a magical gift for tuning into my thinking frequency whenever I was in a pensive mood. She was so intuitive and understanding regarding my emotional feelings. She probably even sensed that I yearned for another celebratory event like the matanza.

With Christmas just around the corner, how could she be wrong? The Yuletide season was one of my favorite times of the year, and nobody knew that better than Mom.

16

A Diaper, Sliced Potatoes, and Vinegar

FAR OFF IN THE distance—or so it seemed—on this brisk November morning, I could hear faint noises in the kitchen. The clattering sounds coming from the iron stove lids as Mom fed the stove kindling and wood made my head throb as though it were going to burst. Something was definitely wrong. My condition made me hug the sheets when suddenly I heard Mom's voice, a rueful reminder that the time to get up was upon me. No more than a few seconds elapsed before I heard her again.

"Come, hijito," she said, pulling at the blankets that weighed heavily on my sore body and weighty head. "The school bus will be here soon, and you still have to get dressed and eat breakfast."

Perhaps noticing that there was no movement coming from underneath the blankets, except for my little brothers tossing and turning, she came and uncovered my head.

"Good heavens! What monster do I have here?" she asked. "Look at your unruly hair. What a *tapeiste*, haystack! And your rooster tail is sticking up in the air. It looks like you got caught in a dust devil. Is something wrong?"

"Yes, amá," I answered. "My head feels like the size of a pumpkin, and it's not from a headache."

"Okay. Let's see what's wrong," She felt my forehead. "There's an old saying, 'When there's no cure for an illness, the best remedy is death,'" she uttered with a playful smirk as she pinched my left cheek.

"Does that mean I'm going to die if I don't get well?" I countered quizzically.

"We're all going to die, hijito, but not today. I'll make sure of that, okay?"

"If you say so," I responded.

She determined that I had a fever and it was best for me to stay home. "Listen. Your uncle's school bus will be here any minute. Keep your ears perked in case he honks. I can then go tell him that you're not feeling well and for him to inform the teacher. In the meantime, I'll think of something to get you well."

I listened for Uncle Antonio, and sure enough it wasn't long before he honked. He did this whenever I wasn't on the side of the road at the top of the hill waiting for him. If I wasn't there, he usually surmised that something was wrong, but he always sounded the horn to make sure. If Mom went out, my uncle had his answer. This time, unlike previous times, he didn't just honk two or three times; he must have been in a bad mood, because he "sat" on the horn. The piercing sound made my head feel ten times worse.

After Mom talked to Uncle Antonio, she came into the bedroom and once again felt my forehead. "*Ojalá que no sea calentura de pollo por comer gallinas.* I hope you're not faking it," she commented with a wry smile. "But don't worry. I'll take care of you in no time."

I heard her in the kitchen, but not for long. Shortly thereafter she came into the bedroom holding a small aluminum bowl with slices of potatoes floating in vinegar diluted with water. Draped over her left forearm was a diaper. She set the bowl on top of a chair next to the bed.

"Okay, hijito. This is your Grandma Cinda's remedy that will take care of your fever"—words that were music to my ears since I was feeling so lousy.

Mom never once mentioned flu. Such an illness by name was unheard of in the Río Puerco Valley. If it was the flu, mothers, including folk healers like Grandma Cinda, simply treated the illness as if it were a *romadizo*, head cold. My mother was no different.

She propped up a couple of pillows behind my back and had me sit up straight. Then she folded the diaper two or three times lengthwise. By now the potatoes had been soaking in water and vinegar for several minutes;

they had begun to turn slightly brown around the edges. One by one Mom placed enough slices of potato on the diaper to cover my forehead. Once she did that, she carefully secured the diaper and potatoes across my forehead and tied it in a knot behind my head.

"Mom, I thought potatoes were only to eat. What good will they do me on my head instead of in my stomach?" I asked with a touch of sarcasm.

"Ah, with a question like that, I now know either you're not very sick or you're already getting better! Now, sit upright and rest. The potatoes and vinegar will bring down the fever. They will draw out the fever, just like pine sap drawing a splinter from your thumb. That's the magic of potatoes, vinegar, and water; they work together like mutual friends."

"Okay," I said, somewhat dejected, since I didn't like being sick and having to miss school. On the other hand, Mom was doing what she knew best, which was to apply one of Grandma Cinda's remedies, one that her patients raved about.

The potatoes, vinegar, and water felt soothing enough to put me to sleep, but the hot chamomile tea Mom gave me no doubt helped as well. I guess I slept for quite a spell, particularly since I hadn't slept very well the night before. Sometime later Mom came into the bedroom again; I had just woken up. I guess I looked improved, because Mom cracked a smile.

"Well, well. Who wounded you? You look like you've been to war, with that diaper around your head," she observed kiddingly.

The next day, after a restful twenty-four hours, I was well enough to return to school. Mom's treatment had done the trick. I was feeling much better. This time Uncle Antonio didn't have to honk. I was at my bus stop, anxious to hop on the school bus, as soon as Mom had hugged me and sent me away with her blessings.

The day at school started off pleasantly enough, nothing out of the ordinary, but during recess an incident occurred that changed my life for the next several months. One of the so-called games—although it was more of a prank among the older boys—was to "depant" the younger boys in front of the girls. The bullies thought it was hilarious, but the rest of the schoolmates, especially the girls, didn't look upon their urchin behavior as funny or entertaining. The teacher didn't relish the idea either, and the onus was on her to discourage the older boys from such unsavory antics, but controlling certain activities on the playground during recess was not always easy. The older boys were cunning.

Morning recess came around ten o'clock or so. The November sun had long since peered over the Black Mesa. Up to now, because of the cold weather, we had enjoyed only one or two recent recesses. But today was sunny and relatively warm. The tepid air that came out of the nearby Rincón del Cochino made the day even more pleasant and tolerable. There were no particular games or activities on this day. The teacher felt that we should just enjoy the outing, until my cousin G. hollered at one of the Jaramillo boys from Santa Clara. That's when my nightmare started.

"Hey, Casimiro. It's a perfect day for depanting. What do you say?"

"You're right. Who's it going to be?" Casimiro asked. His real name was Conrado, but he had earned the nickname of Casimiro because of his poor vision (*casi miro*, I can hardly see).

"Junie," responded Cousin G. "That's what he gets for not coming to school yesterday. Besides, we've never taken his pants off, right?"

I had seen this prankish act once before, so when they came after me, I took off running. I headed for a corral that the Valencia family had not far from the playground. I approached the main gate and quickly climbed to the top, just before Cousin G. could grab my feet to pull me down. From there I jumped down on the other side. Unfortunately, as I landed my right elbow struck a large rock, hitting my crazy bone (*el huesito sabroso*).

At first I screamed in agony. I then started crying as I held my arm, but I couldn't get up. My cousin G. and Casimiro were on the opposite side of the corral gate. My cousin jumped over to see what was wrong. I was on the ground crying and holding my arm in obvious and excruciating pain.

"Are you all right?" he asked. His question, needless to say, was rather hurtful—and stupid.

Casimiro joined him. They opened the gate and picked me up as I held my right arm with my left hand. By that time the teacher had started looking for us. She ran quickly to see what was wrong with me. She had a frightened look on her face. As we walked into the schoolhouse, the rest of the students looked at me. I continued to hold my arm. They could tell that I was in pain.

"If it's broken, my father can help him," said one of the Valencia boys. Right away the teacher sent him to get his father.

Mr. Valencia came and looked at my arm, felt with his hand around the elbow area, and somehow determined that it wasn't broken. But that was hardly comforting to me, given that I was in such agonizing pain. He thought the elbow was probably *desconcertao*, dislocated. Since it was still a few hours before my uncle would come to pick us up after school, Mr. Valencia suggested that my arm be kept warm by wrapping a diaper or some other material around the elbow area. Warmth was to soothe and alleviate the pain. The teacher had a scarf, and she warmed it up periodically on top of the potbelly stove and wrapped it around my elbow.

The rest of the day seemed endless, not only for me but also for my cousin G., thanks to his bright idea. The teacher had already had a word or two with him and the Jaramillo boy about their senseless horseplay.

Going home that afternoon was no picnic. The bouncing up and down on the dirt road didn't help the pain, which by now had traveled to my shoulder. The entire right arm felt like it was going to fall off. Uncle Antonio seemed rather oblivious to my situation. Once he stopped for me to get off, Cousin G. helped me home. He was feeling somewhat guilty.

"Good heavens, hijito! What's wrong? What happened to your arm?" asked my startled mother.

"He had an accident," my cousin interjected before I could say anything.

My version of the purported accident came later. Mom was angry at my cousin. Moreover, I told her what Mr. Valencia had said about alleviating the pain. Mom thought that was an excellent suggestion, but the pain lingered. I spent two restless nights and missed school, to boot. Then Dad came home Friday evening.

By Saturday morning, we had packed a few family belongings and headed for Grandma Cinda's house in Bernalillo. My step-grandfather—the other Uncle Antonio—was a *sobador*, a chiropractor and bonesetter. Without much examination he determined that I had a dislocated elbow. He had the reputation of being gentle with his hands, but all that was relative. As he tried to put my elbow back in place, I screamed and screamed in agony.

"Stop, stop!" shouted Grandma Cinda, who was in the same room with my parents. "That's enough! You're hurting my hijito."

The worst part was yet to come. The frigidity of the days and nights of winter felt like stabs of cold steel penetrating my elbow. When spring came and went, so did the pain. The summer was even more helpful. Little by little the hurt subsided, and eventually it went away. My mother was sure my elbow had fallen back into place without my knowing it.

One thing for sure, the depanting game was history; it was never to be practiced again at school. The teacher had taken decisive action to end the silly game. I was the last victim, and Cousin G. and Casimiro, the perpetrators, had learned their lesson. The older boys would no longer antagonize and humiliate first-grade boys like me. There would also be no more blushing faces among the girls.

Any illness or injury at the ranch was no joyful experience. There were no doctors or dentists around. Traveling to Albuquerque for medical treatment was only for those families with money. And the only folk practitioner in our midst lived in the placita, a couple of miles away from our home. Therefore, Mom became our primary health care provider, treating us with the appropriate home and herbal remedies that she learned from Grandma Cinda prior to the advent of commercial products.

Here is a list of the most common sicknesses and injuries that I can recall, followed by the manner in which they were treated in my household.

Common Illnesses and Injuries and Their Folk-Medicine Treatments

SPANISH NAME	ENGLISH NAME	FOLK-MEDICINE TREATMENT
almorranas	hemorrhoids; piles	treated with suppositories (*calillas*) made from ground *yerba del manso*, a plant of the lizard's tail family.
basura en un ojo	foreign matter in the eye	a small, smooth pinto bean was inserted in the eye; it would roll around the eyeball to pick up the matter before the bean was popped out

blandura	loose bowels; diarrhea	*atole*, blue corn gruel, always came to the rescue for any stomach problems
catarro	runny or stuffy nose	tea made with leaves of *poleo*, pennyroyal, was snuffed up the nose to ease congestion
chilito de perro	sty	a hot pad was applied before bedtime (I often heard that a sty came from seeing a dog pee or because you wished for something you couldn't have, like a BB gun)
cólico	colic	chamomile tea made from *manzanilla* leaves was popular for babies or children
cortaduras	minor cuts	the blade of a cold knife or compressed cobwebs helped stop the bleeding
dolor de cabeza	headache	stamps from sacks of Golden Grain tobacco were applied to the temples (on each side of the head)
dolor de cintura	backache	hot towels were applied to sore areas; men with backaches from horseback riding, like my father, wore a special wide leather belt (like a corset)
dolor de estómago	stomachache	popular remedy was *atole*; tea of *yerba buena*, mint, was also good (most grandmothers had small patches of mint growing in their home gardens)
dolor de garganta	sore throat	ground *rosa de Castilla*, rose petals, mixed with water and sugar was drunk; drinking *yerba del manso*, the dry ground root mixed in water, was also good
dolor de muela	toothache	ashes of cottonwood tree bark were applied to the aching tooth

dolor de sentido (*oído*)	earache or ear infection	lamb's wool, oil, and snuff were applied in the ear or tobacco smoke was blown into the ear
empacho	constipation (in babies)	the skin of the baby's back was pulled to snap back
estreñimiento	constipation	castor oil was given to kids as a remedy
garrapatas	ticks	small drops of kerosene oil or sweet oil in the ear forced the ticks out
grano enterrado	pus-filled boil	a paste made from saffron, water, and flour was applied to the boil to open up the infected area for drainage
liendres	nits	the head was shaved and the scalp rubbed with kerosene oil to keep nits away
lumbrices	tapeworms	drinking sweet pickle juice eliminated the worms
piojos	lice	the head was shaved; at times kerosene oil was applied to the bare scalp
postemilla	tooth abscess	a paste made from flour mixed in water and applied to the cheek reduced the swelling
resfrío	simple cold	hot chamomile tea was drunk at bedtime
romadizo	head cold	hot chamomile tea reduced head pressure; sliced potatoes dipped in water and vinegar could be beneficial in treating flulike symptoms
torceduras	sprains (e.g., ankles)	volcanic oil was applied on sore areas or sprains

Commercial or Patent Medicines

Baking soda—Arm & Hammer baking soda was used in lieu of
   toothpaste. It was applied to the teeth with a forefinger and rubbed;
   toothbrushes were unheard of.

Castor oil—Given to kids for constipation.

Citrate of magnesia—A laxative used in moderation for constipation;
   mostly for grown-ups (it was Dad's favorite).

Iodine—Antiseptic for cuts; moderately helpful.

Mentholatum—Applied to the chest area to relieve chest congestion,
   stuffy noses, and coughing due to colds.

Mercurochrome—Used on cuts as an antiseptic but not very effective.

Merthiolate (thimerosal)—Rubbed on cuts as an antiseptic; it burned like
   the dickens but was effective.

Rosebud salve—A lip balm, sometimes used on body sores.

Rubbing alcohol—Had multiple uses ranging from an antiseptic for
   blisters and skin infections to a rubbing compound for aching muscles
   or joints.

Vicks VapoRub—Applied to chest and throat to relieve coughing and aid
   breathing; helped relieve aches and pains of muscles and joints.

Volcanic oil—A liniment applied to aching joints or sore muscles.

Illnesses, as can be seen from the list above, included a wide variety of
ailments, but no one sickness sticks out in my mind more than tapeworms,
something I was plagued with between the ages of five and six. Following
a bowel movement, I would notice these short yellow things that looked
like flat spaghetti. Upon informing my mother, she and Dad determined
that I had *lumbrices*, tapeworms, and thus the reason for my not gaining
weight was discovered.

In a matter-of-fact sort of way, my father said I needed to drink sweet
pickle juice. By then, sour pickles in a jar, along with other commercial
foods, had entered our diet, but not sweet pickles. My father had learned
that sweet pickle juice was the perfect remedy for curing tapeworms. Thus,
for the next year or so, my parents bought jars of sweet pickles, and I drank
and drank the juice—and checked and checked for tapeworms—until I
found the juice repulsive. Ultimately, I got rid of the pesky tapeworms and
began to gain weight. I was a happy little boy, and Mom was overjoyed, too.

In looking back at the years that my family resided at the ranch (1935–1945), I recollect that my mother had a remedy for every common illness or injury. After all was said and done, the cure at times seemed secondary to Mom's love and affection. These two human qualities are what tipped the scales when she was curing her children. A state of mind in getting well was crucial, whether we realized it or not. Mom's words and actions spoke volumes. Her prayers more than anything else were never absent whenever an illness befell one of us.

It's Posole Time!

WITH THE FADING OF the fall season, the cold westward winds in predictable fashion had begun to blow on and off all day long. By the time the customary darkness of the evening struck, we were forewarned that frigid nights were imminent. Once the cold penetrated your bones down to the marrow, it seemed to hang on forever like a relentless leech. The bitter winter was not my favorite time of the year. Even the foothills, buttes, and peaks seemed to freeze in time, but somehow the Christmas season and the New Year made the months of December and January more bearable. Though inclement weather depressed me, the arrival of febrero loco, crazy February, and marzo aigriento, windy March, eased the discomfort somewhat.

LA VIRGEN DE GUADALUPE

La Virgen de Guadalupe, our patron saint, was honored on December 12; it was one of the most significant religious holidays of the year. On the evening of La Virgen de Guadalupe's feast day, a pilgrimage led by the mayordomos and the *rezador/a*, the prayer leader, took place around the church and the village; this signaled the advent of the Yuletide season, and old-fashioned *luminarios*, small bonfires (not to be mistaken for *luminarias*), were lit.

A bonfire was lit each night between December 12 and Nochebuena, Christmas Eve. With more and more luminarios burning each night, the village looked brighter and brighter as the flames from the bonfires aimed for the nightly skies. On Christmas Eve villagers attended the Misa del Gallo (literally, Mass of the Rooster), Midnight Mass. On this special night Guadalupe, our placita, was aglow, and pride dangled in the cold air. Tonight the thirteen luminarios were lit about half an hour before Midnight Mass began. This brought not only warmth to all Guadalupanos but also joy as they celebrated the birth of the baby Jesus.

Each evening the sacristan was responsible for lighting the luminarios. They were stacks of juniper or *piñón* wood arranged upright, like a teepee. A large piece of ocote, torch pine, was placed in the center and served as a fast starter in the winter. One or two families in the village usually provided the wood—oftentimes because they had made a personal religious vow—but finding pitch was not always easy. People kept a keen eye out for this special wood so that the sacristan would have enough to light all the luminarios on Nochebuena.

Every evening without fail my father hitched up the horse wagon and we headed for our placita. There we joined the prayer leader and other villagers in reciting the rosary as we paraded in procession-like fashion around the church, pausing momentarily at each luminario before returning inside the church. This ritual went on nightly until *las vísperas*, Christmas vespers, were upon us, which put people into a state of anticipation for the celebration of the Misa del Gallo.

MISA DEL GALLO

The Nochebuena was pretty cold. Mom got my little brothers, my sister, and me all bundled up with extra blankets before we took off for the village. She prepared a makeshift bed in the wagon for Beltrán, Juanito, and me in case we got sleepy. Julianita was still a toddler. Mom held her in her arms until we got to the church.

Filled with the eagerness of attending the Misa del Gallo, coupled with the excitement of eating posole, hominy (see ingredients on page 153), and opening our Christmas gifts when we got back home, I knew going to sleep was a doubtful proposition. What is more, the bitter cold was not conducive to sleeping.

As we rounded the bend to El Coruco, renowned for its stories regarding witches and rattling chains (see chapter 5), I covered my head with one of the blankets. The spookiness that overcame me did not disappear until we finally reached the Río Puerco about a quarter of a mile away. We started to descend to the river bottom, and I stood up as soon as I heard the wagon wheels groan when Dad applied the hand and foot brakes. There was enough water running in the river for the moon to create an icy reflection right before we crossed. By then my teeth had begun to chatter from the frigid night.

"Are you sleepy? Are you cold?" Mom asked us as we moved along the sandy road after crossing the Río Puerco. All I could hear were the horses' hooves and the soft sound of the sand hitting the wheels. A short distance away was the Virgen de Guadalupe Church.

Perhaps Mom heard my teeth chatter, prompting her to ask if I was cold. When we arrived at the church, Mom immediately took us inside. She huddled us around the potbelly stove before Midnight Mass started.

The fire was crackling, and the heat felt nice on my red palms. While I rubbed my hands together to warm them up, I looked around. The perspective from the back of the church was quite different from what I was accustomed to—Mom and the rest of us always sat up front. Besides the tall, white, skinny candles flickering at the altar, the colored prints of the stations of the cross hanging on the wall were lit up but with small, fat, yellow votive candles. The entire church seemed brighter than usual on the special night of Nochebuena.

The other thing that struck me as I cast a glance about was the fact that, unlike the typical practice during regular monthly church services, men were not standing at the entrance. They were sitting down with their families. Women jokingly claimed that men usually leaned against the back wall, not because they were being gentlemen by relinquishing their seats, but because they wanted to watch the young girls come in.

Except for a few men, most grown-ups went to confession before Midnight Mass started, including my mother, who was very religious. Fasting for her and other parishioners on this festive occasion was not necessary, although some people declined to eat anything after dusk. At the time of receiving Communion, you could tell who had fasted and who hadn't just by the way they chewed on the host. After I made my First Holy

Communion, I wondered silently if some overzealous parishioner kept track of such things.

Following Communion, and before the Midnight Mass ended, Grandma Lale, who long ago had started a choir in the community, led the singing of the traditional Christmas song "Vamos todos a Belén." It was beautiful! I still remember the rhythm as well as some of the lyrics.

Vamos todos a Belén	Let Us Go to Bethlehem
Vamos todos a Belén	Let us go to Bethlehem
con amor y gozo.	with love and joy.
Adoremos al Señor,	Let us pray to our Lord,
nuestro Redentor.	Jesus Christ, our Redeemer.
Relumbra una estrella,	A star shines brightly
divino dulzor.	on our sweet divine one.
Que bonita y bella,	A pretty star shines
nuestro Salvador.	brightly on our Savior.

Another popular song at Midnight Mass was "Noche de paz," known in English as "Silent Night." The night indeed seemed more peaceful as the Mass ended for another year, with people filing out and heading home to indulge in their traditional Christmas foods and modest gifts.

NATIVITY FOODS AND CHRISTMAS GIFTS

Once we left the church and climbed on the horse wagon, I could tell Dad wasn't in any mood for idle talk. He cracked the whip one or two times, and the horses picked up their gait. Upon crossing the river, the moon still shone on the water. Far off in the distance, I could hear the coyotes howling. I was used to their harmless noise, which kept me awake going home. Mom didn't utter a word either. Either she was tired, or she yielded to Dad's mood. My little brothers and sister were dead to the world, despite the occasional bouncing of the horse wagon.

By the time we got home, it was way past our bedtime, but Christmas Eve was one occasion when children were allowed to stay up the whole night, if we could last that long. Dad rode the wagon practically to the kitchen door and climbed down, and Mom handed him Julianita and got off. Beltrán and Juanito, who were now only half-asleep, didn't require any help. Neither did I. All three of us hopped off—or slid off—the back of the wagon.

Meanwhile, Dad went to lock the horses in the corral. While Mom put my little sister and Juanito to bed, Beltrán and I waited at the table to eat our traditional posole. This was a requisite before we could open our Christmas gifts, but the wait didn't matter much because I was starved—as Dad would say, using his favorite expression when he was famished, "*Ya se comen las grandes a las chiquitas*. The big [intestines] are about to consume the little ones." I loved not only posole but menudo as well. Both were on the menu. Here are Mom's ingredients.

Posole	Menudo
Garlic clove (optional)	Garlic clove (optional)
Hominy	Hominy
Pig's feet (optional)	Pig's feet (2 to 4)
Pork (cubed)	Pork
Red chile sauce	Red chile (optional)
Water	Rinds (cueritos) and/or tripe
Salt	Water
	Salt

Mom's posole and menudo had cooked for more than three hours before we left for Midnight Mass. By now they were practically ready to eat, although still simmering, being that she had fed the stove two or three good-size pieces of wood prior to departing for Midnight Mass. All she had to do was to bring the posole and menudo to a low boil. She had two medium-size pots of posole, one with red chile and the second one without for Beltrán and me, even though at my age (seven years old) I already ate red chile, provided it wasn't too spicy. A third pot containing menudo was ready as well. Mom sometimes added pig's feet for good measure, which Dad really enjoyed (later in life he ate Hormel's pickled pig's feet, which came in a jar).

Mom came back from the bedroom after putting my little sister and Juanito to bed. "It's posole time!" she said as she walked into the kitchen, where Beltrán and I were munching on tortillas from a stack that was in the middle of the table, within easy reach of everyone. Mom dished out posole for him and me. As for Dad, he ate a good size bowl of menudo, followed by posole with chile, although Mom oftentimes fixed menudo with red chile. I didn't take long to eat my posole, because I was hungry and also anxious to open my Christmas gifts.

Christmastime was one of the happiest and most joyous episodes of my life. Sadness, albeit fleeting, seemed to strike me when I dreamed of receiving several gifts but usually got only one—and invariably it was a pair of socks or a piece of clothing. My parents believed in being practical, not in flamboyantly going in debt just to shower us kids with an array of gifts that they could ill afford on their meager budget.

In my household, as was true in other valley homes that I was familiar with, there was no Christmas tree to bedeck the living room (there was no living room in our home!) or bedroom. In fact, Christmas trees were unheard of until we saw them at friends' or relatives' homes in Bernalillo or Albuquerque.

Apropos Santo Clos (Santa Claus) or even the Three Wise Men, they were esoteric, at best. As a rule Mom put everyone's Christmas gifts out in the open on top of her cómoda, dresser. By doing so she tended to lessen the temptation for us to tear a hole in one corner of the package—which could get bigger and bigger—just to peek inside.

This particular Christmas, I yearned for a BB gun. I had dropped enough hints on my mother's lap, as well as showing her pictures of BB guns in the Sears catalog. After Mom cleared the kitchen table, she brought out everyone's gifts one by one. She handed me a softly wrapped package, but this time it was not a pair of socks. Instead, inside I found a leather cap with straps to secure it under my chin; it was insulated with sheep's wool to keep my ears warm. I had seen these caps in the Sears catalog. They looked like those worn by airplane pilots. I liked it because it was different, but I was disappointed, since I had not received a BB gun.

"And what did you want a BB gun for?" Dad asked after he heard me muttering under my breath.

"So I could shoot birds," I responded without hesitation.

"And why the poor birds? They have a right to live, just like you and me.

Why not the hawk that comes around from time to time to pluck the chicks? Besides, you have your slingshot," he added, knowing full well that even if you were a sharp shooter with a sling, it was not an easy enterprise to bring down a target compared to using a BB gun.

Suddenly Mom reappeared in the kitchen with a big box in her arms and exclaimed, "Look what I have for you and Beltrán!" She sported a huge smile.

My eyes almost popped out of their sockets. They must have looked like saucers to her. I was surprised, if not shocked. I didn't know what to make of the enormous box.

Little by little my brother and I dug into the package, which was bigger than both of us, or so it seemed. I glanced at Dad. He had a curious look on his face. After several minutes of struggling with the box, which seemed like an eternity, we finally unraveled the mystery package. It was a tricycle! It was made entirely of metal except for the rubber around the wheels and the tips of the handlebars. I was excited. The idea of a BB gun quickly faded from my mind. Dad, too, had a happy look on his face. I now had a new toy that I could enjoy with my brother.

(I should add parenthetically that until about 2007, the forlorn tricycle hung from my grandparents' portal, sixty-plus years after my family and I left our valley in 1945 for Albuquerque. I never had the presence of mind to rescue it from oblivion. I can only hope that it has found its way into a museum.)

I was suddenly ready for another bowl of posole before going to bed; I had to get up early the next morning to wish Grandpa Lolo and Grandma Lale and Uncle Antonio and Aunt Taida a merry Christmas. It was now about three o'clock. I must have been quite tired, because once my head hit the pillow I fell asleep. Unlike other mornings, when Grandpa's rooster customarily woke me up, it was Mom who had to shake me out of bed.

"Come, hijito! The sheets are going to stick to you like pitch on a pine tree. Up, up. Here's your flour sack."

"Okay, amá."

I quickly ate a couple of bizcochitos, grabbed the small, empty sack, tossed it over my right shoulder, and rushed out the kitchen door.

I had a pretty good idea what Grandma Lale was going to put in my sack.

Two days earlier I had been over to her house and saw her baking molletes. These were small, sweet loaves of bread with anise seeds in them; she baked them every Christmas and sometimes for Lent. Now and then she used the horno, the outdoor adobe oven, but this year she baked them in her wood-burning stove. Grandma had two sets of tin pans that held eight soft, yellow molletes each. These tiny loaves, a tradition in Grandma's culinary special-ties, were absolutely out of this world.

One minute at most is what it took me to walk over to my grandpar-ents' kitchen door. I knocked.

"Who is it, who is it?" came a voice from inside that sounded like Grandpa Lolo's.

"*¡Felices Pascuas! ¡Felices Pascuas!* Merry Christmas! Merry Christmas!" I hollered, invoking the traditional holiday greeting.

"*¡Felices Pascuas, hijito!*" Grandma Lale echoed as she came to the door.

After she and Grandpa exchanged a few Christmas pleasantries with me, she grabbed (sure enough!) two golden molletes from the top of her kitchen table and cautioned me not to put them in the bottom of the sack. Better said than done! These were the first tidbits I received for my morn-ing Yuletide jaunt. Grandma Lale also gave me a few bizcochitos. Baked goods were the traditional gifts in my extended family. Once in a while hard Christmas candy was thrown into the mix.

I thanked Grandpa Lolo and Grandma Lale, but before I took off she asked me to come back in a little while to watch her make her tamales. I had done this the previous year on Christmas vespers. That was exciting. I therefore promised to be back after visiting Aunt Taida and Uncle Antonio down the hill.

When I got to their house with my flour sack slung over my right shoul-der, I shouted at the front door without knocking.

"*¡Mis Crismes, mis Crismes! Si no me dan algo, habrá munchos chismes.* Merry Christmas, merry Christmas! If you don't give me something, gos-sip will run rampant," I said jokingly. I was using my own little rhyme that I had invented instead of reciting the traditional rhyme children used when they went knocking at doors expecting Christmas treats, such as baked goods and other tidbits: "*Oremos, oremos. Angelitos semos. Si no nos dan regalitos, ventanas quebraremos.* Let us pray, let us pray. We are little angels. If you don't give us treats, we'll break your windows." It was all said in jest, of course.

"*¿Y los de nosotros?* And where are ours?" Aunt Taida and Uncle Antonio responded in unison as I walked into the kitchen, where my uncle was eating a bowl of posole for breakfast.

Aunt Taida saw that I had my little sack, and she promptly reached for some white divinity candy with walnuts from the top of the kitchen table. Divinity candy was a specialty of hers. She also gave me two bizcochitos and some pastelitos, small pumpkin pies that she baked in a flat tin pan. Unlike regular pies, they were square and thin.

About that time my cousins emerged from the bedroom, where they obviously had been enjoying their own Christmas gifts. Cousin J. showed me a small bag of marbles; in it he had some beautiful shooters, including an agate, the pride and joy of any marble player. He was anxious to try it out.

"How do you like it? With this agate I'll be able to win every game," he said proudly while sporting a smug look.

"*Ya veremos.* We'll see," was my brusque response before I bid him good-bye, as I had promised Grandma Lale I'd watch her make tamales. I thanked my aunt and uncle for the candy, bizcochitos, and pies and went back up the hill to my house.

"Well, how many goodies did you get?" Mom asked. I emptied my sack's contents on top of the table.

"Now I won't have to do any baking for a while," she added with a smile.

"Mom, where's Dad?"

"He went over to your grandma's."

"Good. That's where I'm going. She asked me to come over so I could watch her make tamales."

"And when are you going to ride your tricycle?"

"I'll do that after I come back from Grandma's," and I took off.

When I walked in the kitchen, one large room used as kitchen and dining room, Dad was talking to Grandpa Lolo. Both were drinking coffee and dunking their bizcochitos. No sooner had I sat down than Grandma said to me, "Are you ready, hijito? The pig's head is almost cooked."

I had completely forgotten about the pig's head that she had stored away in the shed right after the matanza (see chapter 15) a few weeks earlier. She opened the oven door, and there was the pig's head, big ears and all. I wasn't scared. After all, the pig was dead, but its bulging eyes were not shut. Its eyeteeth were visible; they looked like those of an angry javelina. The pig had a menacing look.

Grandma Lale put on a pair of Grandpa's gloves to use as hot pads and took out the pig's head and set it on the kitchen table. "Are you ready, hijito?" she asked as she took off her gloves. "We're going to pluck the meat from the head for the tamales," and she handed me Grandpa's sharp awl, which he used in repairing his shoes. The awl, Grandma assured me, would make my job of pulling every piece of meat off much easier than it would be if I used a kitchen knife or a pocketknife. This was a new experience for me.

Making tamales with meat from the pig's head was a Christmas tradition as well as a delicacy. Grandma Lale never used any other kind of meat. It had to be the pig's head or nothing at all. I removed the strings of meat and sneaked one or two pieces before we finished. Then Grandma asked me to fetch the corn husks from the flour bin.

These were the husks the grandchildren had carefully selected and set aside whenever we husked corn. Grandma Lale steamed them in an Indian clay pot full of hot water until she was ready with the *masa*, cornmeal dough. Once she had spread the dough on two overlapping corn husks, she spread the meat and pure red chile sauce on top. Then she rolled up the corn husks and tied each end with short pieces of husk. She repeated the process until she had at least a dozen tamales. That's about all the scarce meat the pig's head would yield, but each mouthwatering tamal was a delicacy.

Once Grandma and I were done, she gave me three tamales to take home, one each for Mom and Dad and the third one for me.

Before I left I asked Grandma Lale if I could see her Nativity scene, because we didn't have one at home. She kept hers in the bedroom, and it was very popular with her grandkids. The animal figures were all made of dark wood, with the cow and the donkey occupying center stage to show that they were the ones that kept the newborn baby Jesus warm with their breath. The cradle was made of a lighter wood, but the baby Jesus was made of rosy-pink-colored plaster. He looked like a little doll.

When I got home, I saw that Mom was going to make her traditional chiles rellenos and empanaditas, turnovers, something I wouldn't miss for the world. I quickly went outside and tried out the tricycle. Not once did I tumble over. I was very proud of myself. But it was, after all, a tricycle; the three wheels provided the necessary balance. As for my little brother, I had to push him on the tricycle until he grew big enough to reach the pedals and ride by himself.

Mom asked if I wanted a bowl of *sopa* that she had made Christmas Eve. Of course I couldn't refuse her scrumptious bread pudding made with raisins, caramel, and the homemade cheese called *requesón*. In addition to her chiles rellenos and empanaditas, the sopa (some New Mexicans call it *capirotada*) was another one of Mom's Nativity foods, although she did make it on other occasions throughout the year, above all during Lent.

I sat at the table to eat my sopa. Cooking in a pot of boiling water was a cow's tongue from a cow that Dad, Grandpa Lolo, and Uncle Antonio had slaughtered sometime in late November, in addition to the hog. It was a rarity to have slaughtered both, since they usually alternated one or the other from year to year. The cow's tongue, like the hog's head, had been kept in the dispensa until now, when it was Mom's turn to make her delicious empanaditas. Otherwise, Grandma Lale had the honors.

Once the tongue was cooked, Mom placed it on the cutting board. While it was still hot, she cut fine incisions into it with a very sharp knife and then peeled off a thin veil of skin. She cut the tongue into small pieces. Afterward, she set up the hand-grinding machine for me on the kitchen table. It made the turning of the handle of the meat grinder easier. I ground the whole tongue, and now it was ready for the turnovers.

Mom gathered the ingredients, which consisted of raisins, cinnamon, sugar, and shelled piñón nuts. She mixed all of them with the tongue meat. Next she rolled out a small round flour tortilla and put a spoonful of the ingredients on top. Then she folded the dough over into the shape of a half moon and sealed it by pinching together the two sides using her thumb and forefinger all around the edges.

The next step was to drop each empanadita into a pan of hot lard to fry until they were golden brown. She repeated the whole procedure time and again, until all the ingredients were gone. Mincemeat empanaditas, so

called, were another one of Mom's Christmas delicacies. By the time she
finished, she had between twelve to fifteen empanaditas to complement
other Nativity foods.

Although she sometimes also made pumpkin or fruit turnovers with
boiled peaches or sun-dried apricots that she and Dad got from the
Indians in Jémez Pueblo, at Christmastime she preferred to only make the
cow's tongue version.

Her fruit pies were not made in regular round pie pans. She made them
in a rectangular pan with a thin layer of dough lining the bottom. A layer
of cooked fruit about a quarter-inch thick was spread on top. She topped
the fruit with another layer of dough and then sealed all around the edges
using a fork. Fruit pies could be eaten at breakfast, for lunch, or as snacks
in the evening. In that respect, fruit pies were very versatile. I liked them.
I thought Mom and Aunt Taida made the best fruit pies in the world.
Some of the fruit came from their canning (see chapter 25).

But the most unique dish in Mom's repertoire of Nativity culinary
delicacies was her chiles rellenos. They were made with chopped roasted
green chile, stuffed with mincemeat, raisins, and sugar, enveloped in
flour dough so that they looked like small, elongated dumplings, and
deep fried in fat. If the chile was too hot or spicy, only grown-ups ate
them. The sweet raisins and sugar made the rellenos more bearable on
the tongue.

By noon on Christmas Day, an abundance of delectable Nativity foods
that Mom had prepared dressed the kitchen table; at the end of the day she
would put the leftovers in large tin cans to keep them fresh. All total, the
foods and pastries included the following:

Empanaditas	Pastelitos
Baking powder	Baking powder
Cinnamon	Cinnamon
Flour dough	Flour dough
Ground cow's tongue	Fruit preserves or pumpkin
Lard	Lard
Piñón nuts	Salt
Raisins	

Sopa	Chiles Rellenos
Cinnamon	Chopped roasted green chile
Homemade cheese (cow's milk)	Flour dough
Raisins	Mincemeat
Sugar	Piñon nuts (optional)
Toasted homemade bread	Raisins
Water	Sugar

The memories of the foregoing potpourri of mouthwatering Christmas delicacies remain embedded in my psyche to this day.

Christmas day, being one of the most religious days of the year, was when families and friends commingled and ate to their stomachs' and hearts' content. The old adage of *"Panza llena, corazón contento.* A full stomach yields a happy heart" was true.

On Christmas day Mom did not have a formal sit-down luncheon. Everyone ate whenever we felt the slightest hunger pangs. Posole and menudo simmered on top of the stove all day long. It was my duty to keep adding water to them lest they burn or stick to the bottoms of the pans.

By the end of the day, I was stuffed to the gills. Christmas day, with my new cap and tricycle, had been a memorable one indeed. Now I looked forward to Dad ringing in the New Year with his .45 caliber pistol, the traditional way to symbolically kill the old year and ring in the new one.

El año viejo	The Old Year [*]
Esta noche	Tonight
a las doce	at twelve o'clock
saca papá	Dad takes out
su .45.	his Colt .45.
Le pone	He loads it
dos cartuchos,	with two bullets,
uno pa matar	one to ring out
el año viejo,	the old year,

....

[*]   See *Tiempos Lejanos: Poetic Images from the Past.*

otro pa saludar	another to ring in
el año nuevo.	the New Year.
Por todo	Throughout all the
el Río Puerco	Río Puerco Valley
zumban	shots
y retumban	zoom
tiros	and firearms
y balazos.	echo.
¡Bum! ¡Bum!	Boom! Boom!
Mi apá dispara.	My father fires.
El estruendo	The racket
lo estremece	shakes him
de los pies	from head
a la cara	to toe
como un trueno.	like a thunderclap.
Hasta los animales	Even the animals
se despiertan—	wake up—
las gallinas	the chickens cluck,
caracaquean,	cluck,
las bestias relinchan,	the horses whinny,
mientras que	while
los perros	the dogs
y los coyotes	and the coyotes
compiten por	compete for
su lugar en	their own place
la confusión	in the medley
de voces.	of voices.
Desde San Luis	From San Luis
a Salazar	to Salazar
y de Guadalupe	and Guadalupe
al Cabezón,	to Cabezón,

con pistolas y rifles	with loaded
de munición,	pistols and rifles,
matar el año nuevo	ringing out the old year
era costumbre	was a custom
y tradición.	and a tradition.

The New Year was a joyful time for resolutions that most of us were quick to make but just as quick to forget. It was a time of *esperanza*, hope—hope for rain, hope for better crops, and hope for an easier way of life for all the humble, proud, and hardworking people of my valley.

18

From Cleaning Ditches to
Planting Crops

EARLY, WINDY MARCH WAS a preamble to spring and a stark reminder that the planting season was just around the corner. The rastrojos, stubble, that the horses, hogs, and goats had chewed practically down to the ground, were the only visible signs of crops left from the previous sowing season. The fields, dormant throughout the fall and winter months, now beckoned us to wake them up from their prolonged nap.

The time was upon us once again to bring the soil back to life, a process that commenced around mid-March. Now and then the routine was begun a bit later, depending on weather conditions, and it continued until sometime in April, when we planted our crops. The variance in time and when to get started hinged on my Grandpa Lolo's analysis of the weather, gleaned from his readings in his loyal companion, *The Old Farmer's Almanac*, in Spanish (he had taught himself to read). He banked on the information, and the rest of the family followed suit. His good judgment on planting matters was hardly ever off target or even doubted, for that matter.

The parcels of land where the three García families planted their crops were clearly understood according to how my grandfather, the landowner, parceled out the farmland. Only two sons, my father and my uncle Antonio, both married with children, lived at the ranch. The traditional pecking order was invoked.

Since my father was the younger of these two sons, as well as the youngest of three brothers and three sisters overall, he was allocated the less fertile land. The soil on Uncle Antonio's land, on the other hand, was just as rich as that on Grandpa Lolo's tract. This was evident in the volume of crops their fields produced. The farmland, as noted above, all belonged to my grandfather. Hence, whatever land my father and uncle cultivated for raising crops was on loan, as it were.

Despite the seemingly arbitrary, though traditional, manner of distributing land, a cooperative effort prevailed among the three families, from the tilling of the soil in early spring to the harvesting of the crops in late summer and early fall. The women and children's helping hands were vital as well.

The land that the families shared at Grandpa's modest ranch was situated about three to four miles directly south of Cabezón Peak, a historic sight in the region and visible for miles around. To the southeast of Cabezón Peak is another peak called Cerro Chivato. The Esquipula Arroyo, whose headwaters are at El Bordo—a few miles east of Cabezón Peak, where Dad and I went after firewood—runs between both peaks; it carried large volumes of water during the monsoon season in July and August.

From El Bordo, the Esquipula Arroyo meandered southwest for several miles, flanked on either side by hills, junipers, buttes, and smaller arroyos that served as its tributaries until it emptied into a ditch well within my grandfather's property. The ditch had been carved out on his land, perhaps by him, long before I was born. It was not part of the acequia system that was connected to the dam several miles north of our village. The man-made dam gave way to a torrential downpour in the late 1930s and was never rebuilt, principally because of lack of support from the federal government.

At one time not only was my grandfather very active in the Río Puerco Valley acequia system, but he also had been the mayordomo back in 1921. His responsibility, like that of other mayordomos, was to oversee everything from ditch cleaning in the spring to the allocation of water for summer crops. By the time I was old enough to work in the cornfields, the acequia network that once upon a time had provided much-needed water to farmers and ranchers up and down the valley was no longer part of the irrigation system. The dam, as mentioned above, had ruptured and was never rebuilt.

The farmers now relied exclusively on dry farming (*de temporal*) with runoffs channeled into the preexisting ditch system farmers had built on their land or, as in our case, water from arroyos that fed into our cornfields.

Whenever it rained, the waters from these arroyos were the main source of irrigation for our crops. Helpful, too, during the rainy season was water that surged down La Cañada del Camino, north of my grandfather's property. This ravine ran parallel to the Esquipula Arroyo and consequently helped flood our fields. A large hill bordering my grandfather's cornfields to the south served to dam up the water that in many cases backed up and soaked all three families' cornfields for two to three weeks.

Though my grandfather and uncle had the prime land, if the rains didn't come, good land was of little consolation. Only the weeds, rattlesnakes, and prairie dogs thrived during dry, hot summers.

Come March, the first order of business was to clean my grandfather's acequia, which cut across both sides of his farmland. He usually took charge of doing so, because my father continued manual labor for the government, while my uncle drove the school bus and tended to other farm chores.

"Ah, hijito, you're home from school," exclaimed my mother. "I didn't see your Uncle Antonio's school bus coming today. I guess he didn't raise a lot of dust—ha!" she remarked as she gave me her usual big hug to welcome me home. "Change your school clothes quickly and go see your papá grande, who's waiting for you."

"Do you know what he wants, amá? Perhaps he wants me to go fetch the eggs from the chicken coop," I said, attempting to answer my own question. Grandma Lale, who usually gathered the eggs, was still in Albuquerque, where she spent part of the winter. Soon she would join Grandpa Lolo and the rest of us for the planting season.

After putting on my work clothes, I moseyed over to his house, a stone's throw from ours. I did not find him in his rocker, from where he usually liked to look out to the fields facing the Mesa Prieta. Rather, he was on the edge of the porch, dangling his feet, almost touching the ground. He was a tall man. I could tell he had just gotten up from his siesta, a custom we all adhered to except us children when school was in session.

"Hello, Grandpa. Mom said you wanted to see me" were the first words out of my mouth. I was really curious to know what he wanted.

"Yes, go get your cousin J. so you two can help me clear out the ditch. But don't take too long."

I was curious no more and wound up like my mother's Westclox alarm clock, since Cousin J. and I usually provided the muscle for clearing the ditch of all debris. I took off down the hill like a bolt of lightning with Ligero, Grandpa's dog, right behind me. Cousin J. was changing clothes when I dashed through the door to his bedroom.

"Grandpa Lolo wants us to go help him clean the ditch."

My cousin got all excited and quickly put on his socks and work shoes before running to the kitchen. He stepped on a chair and handed me a tin can where Aunt Taida kept her leftover tortillas.

"Did you get a bite to eat when you got home? Here," he said, before I could answer his question.

He gave me a tortilla and then slapped on a thin layer of lard and sprinkled a dash of salt on his. I did the same thing. Since I hadn't had a chance to snack on anything after I got home from school, the tortilla was a blessing.

We walked out the kitchen door eating our tortillas and hurried back up the hill to join Grandpa Lolo. Because it was a bit brisk, I first had to get my *cachucha*, cap with side flaps, and tell my mother that Cousin J. and I were going to help Grandpa clean the ditch.

We were overjoyed. For one thing, Grandpa Lolo was a patient and fun person. If we caused mischief, which we did from time to time, he didn't scold us. He hardly ever got mad or got keyed up about anything. (Little wonder he lived to be one hundred years old!) Moreover, clearing the ditch was more of a pastime than a job to be reckoned with. Cousin J. and I were raring to go.

The first thing we had to do was to tackle the *cizañas*, tumbleweeds, that had blown into the ditch and accumulated on account of the winter winds. Getting rid of the prickly bundles was the fun part of the cleaning process. My cousin and I would each light a match simultaneously underneath the inflammable tumbleweeds, taking care to pay attention to the direction of the March winds. We never failed to get a kick out of watching the crackling flames first shoot high into the air and then travel the contour of the ditch, zigzagging really fast, like a jackrabbit desperately trying to escape its prey. The only precaution Grandpa Lolo gave us was to make sure the fire didn't burn out of control, setting the nearby trees on fire, and didn't go beyond our fence and into the Montaño property down range.

Once the tumbleweeds had burned to the ground and the ashes quit smoldering—an hour or so later—Grandpa Lolo hitched up Uncle Antonio's sorrel horse to the *escrepa*, scraper. He used it for clearing the ditch residue called *ensolve* (*azolve*), which consisted of different kinds of debris left after the gushing waters of a deluge had washed through. My uncle's horse was quite savvy and knew exactly what to do. The beauty of an escrepa was that one could scrape the ditch bottom for a good stretch, then the debris was pushed up the side of the embankment and dumped on the banks. Eventually the entire stretch of the ditch, about a quarter of a mile within Grandpa Lolo's property, was clean as a whistle and ready for the next flow of water to run its course devoid of any obstruction in its path.

The scraper was a handy piece of farm equipment, but it was not for kids like me. Its use called for strength in the forearms and coordination between the horse and the person behind the scraper, usually a man, although some women were quite adept at—and not at all reticent about—tackling the job. Beast and human had to work in unison. Grandpa Lolo and Uncle Antonio's horse were perfect for the undertaking. Watching them work together was a joy; it was practically musical. I could tell Grandpa was an old hand at using the scraper. I wondered how many years he had been doing this type of work?

A *fresno*, although larger in size than the escrepa, comes from a classical word that means ash tree or wood from this tree. Both the fresno and escrepa were made of heavy metal, sort of oval shaped, with two wooden handles at the back for the farmer to hold onto. Two chains on either side were linked together in the form of an inverted *V* and connected to the horse's harness. The fresno, however, was wider and deeper and could carry more dirt than an escrepa. Both were used to clear out debris in ditches, to shore up bordos (the rims around man-made lagoons), and to dam running water to redirect its flow when it rained.

Once the ditch was cleared, and before planting took place, the soil had to be turned over, as you might say, to let it air out and rest for a few days.

We called this *barbechar la tierra*, to cultivate the land, as opposed to *arar*, to furrow, which is what we did when the actual planting took place (more on this later). Regardless of which of the two tasks one undertook, once again, like utilizing the scraper, it was a team effort between the farmer and the horse.

Grandpa Lolo, Uncle Antonio, and Dad owned horses suited for furrowing. My father helped on weekends when he came home, whereas my grandfather and uncle plowed in the mornings, when Cousin J. and I were in school and before the heat of day descended on them.

Even though it was still early spring, the March desert breezes were already upon us. The blowing dirt and perspiration on the tiller's brow were not a pleasant sight. Hard work was at hand.

After cultivating the land, the next step was utilizing the *jaira*, harrow. Jaira (pronounced HIGH-rah) is an Anglicism. The use of the harrow, which raised even more dust than plowing did, was hardly a welcome relief, but it came after cultivation and was used for leveling the soil. The appearance of the jaira meant that we were one step closer to the actual planting of crops.

For me, as may be the case with other people familiar with farm life in rural New Mexico, the term *harrow* conjured up two words in Spanish: *jaira* and *rastra*. In my family the two terms in essence signified three different pieces of equipment. There were two iron harrows, the spike and disk harrows, and they performed the same task albeit in slightly different ways. The rastra, or drag harrow, on the other hand, was made from wood. They were vastly dissimilar in appearance, size, and shape. A team of well-trained horses pulled all three types of harrows.

The spike harrow, as the name indicates, sported sharp iron spikes for uprooting weeds, breaking up chunks of soil, and softening the dirt; it had a square-shaped (or sometimes rectangular) iron frame. In contrast, the disk harrow, also made of iron, was elongated, about ten feet in length, with one continuous row of disks that could cut and slice through the soil with relative ease. The drag harrow was a crude piece of timber (more later). It was used to level or flatten the plowed ground, above all *terrones*, big chunks of earth.

Of the three farm implements in question, the jairas, spike and disk,

Old-fashioned iron spike harrow belonging to the García family. Drawn by one horse.

were the more modern type, made in a factory and able to be drawn by one horse or two, depending on the size of the implement. A one-piece spike harrow was pulled by one horse or, if two small spike harrows were banded together, by two horses. Grandpa Lolo's spike harrow, which was large, needed two horses. He also owned a disk harrow as well as a homemade wood drag harrow.

To drive the spike-tooth harrow drawn by one horse, my father or Uncle Antonio would stand in the middle for added ballast, pull back on the reins for leverage, and egg the horse on. In the case of the larger harrow, like what Grandpa Lolo owned, my grandfather would position four large rocks—one on each corner of the iron frame—for weight distribution instead of standing on it himself, although at times he did stand in the middle. As expected, the rocks were more effective than the standing farmer; also, by using the rocks, the farmer was less susceptible to falling and injuring himself.

Unlike the perilous spike harrow, the farmer using the horse-drawn sharp-edged disk harrow simply walked behind the contraption or to one side without much fanfare or danger to himself.

And what can be said about the rastra? It is a classical word that takes us back to Spain in time and history. The rastra could be cut from a cottonwood tree and turned into a rather crude piece of lumber resembling a railroad tie; it measured six to eight feet in length and about twelve inches in height and in depth. Embedded a foot to fifteen inches from each end of the rastra were two *argollas*, iron rings, or ganchos, hooks, with heavy-duty chains connected to the crosspiece of a wagon leading to the horse's harness.

The rastra was a one-man operation, but a two-horse rastra was not unusual. If confident enough and adept at the challenge, a *rastrero* like my grandfather, already an elderly man—so I thought at the time—of seventy-plus years of age could balance himself on the rastra with little difficulty as the horse pressed ahead.

If Grandpa Lolo could do it, why couldn't grandchildren like Cousin J. or me duplicate the feat? The answer came out of the blue one day when Grandpa went home for a pair of barbed wire pliers to mend a fence and left us alone under the shade of a tree next to the ditch. The ditch was adjacent to a flat sandstone mesa that looked down on us as we rested. Cousin J., who was about ten years old, a trifle older than me, and feeling a bit of bravado, said to me, "Listen, Junie, now that Grandpa Lolo's gone, I'm going to see what it's like to get on that rastra. I've been watching how Grandpa rides on it. I don't think it's all that difficult. If I can ride a horse, I can ride that crude piece of lumber," he added with assurance and an air of cockiness.

"You're crazy! What if something happens?"

"Nothing's going to happen. You just watch me," and he went after the horse that was enjoying the shade of a tree nearby.

He hitched the horse to the rastra, but the horse must have sensed that the weight was lighter than usual, because when Cousin J. climbed on, the horse took off at a pretty good clip.

"Look, look, I told you I could do it," hollered Cousin J. while I watched somewhat anxiously.

He waved his right arm in the air as he held onto the reins in his left hand, balancing himself rather gingerly on the rastra as it bounced on the ground. The uneven soil was coarse in some places and sandy in others.

No sooner had Cousin J. shouted at me than the horse got startled and took off running, causing my cousin to lose his balance, whereupon he tumbled forward and landed on his back in front of the rastra. In a split second the rastra ran over him. Scared to death that something horrible had happened, I ran to him as the horse scampered across the fields; the rastra bounced up and down until the horse came to a stop. By now Cousin J. was getting up from the ground and dusting himself off, pale as yogurt.

"*¡Híjole! ¡Qué rebato llevé!* Boy! That scared the shit out of me! That terrón was big, wasn't it?"—as if to blame a clump of earth for causing him to lose his balance.

"*¡Mira! Te repelates toa la nariz. ¿Qué va dijir El Lolo?* Look at you! You scraped your nose all up. What's Grandpa Lolo going to say?"

Oddly enough, when Grandpa returned, he must have had other things on his mind, like mending the fence that the cows had knocked down by the Esquipula Arroyo. He didn't even notice Cousin J.'s swollen nose and the missing skin, whereas my Aunt Taida right away saw his bruised nose when we got home. He had a bit of an explaining to do. My aunt put some Rosebud salve on his wounds to keep them from getting infected. She added nary a word of sympathy, because she was upset about the mishap and Cousin J.'s stupid stunt.

"Don't go eat pinto beans," she advised him, presumably because beans could cause infection, a feeling among many folks.

His scars lasted for a year or two, a rueful reminder that being daring and macho had less than redeemable rewards. The brush with the rastra earned him the nickname El Repelao, the Scraped One, at school. The sobriquet was hardly complimentary.

It should be noted that in my village and throughout the Río Puerco Valley, whenever somebody was good at performing a special feat, people would say, "*¡A ése sí que le arrastra!* Boy, he's really good!" Perhaps there is some relationship between *arrastrar* (to be good at something) and the ability to balance oneself on the rastra.

Grandpa Lolo and Uncle Antonio finished using the jaira and rastra; it was now time for the *rastrillo*, the last step before planting began in earnest. Rastrillo comes from *rastro*, rake, or *rastrillar*, to rake. Drawn usually by two horses, the rastrillo was made of iron and had two large wheels on either end of an axle; attached to a wooden bar between the wheels were sharp half-circle rings that touched the ground. The farmer sat on an elevated metal seat in the middle of the rastrillo. He raked, piled up, and burned everything from stubble and cornstalks to tumbleweeds.

The fields were now ready to be planted with crops; these included above all else corn and pinto beans, two staples for most families. In addition to the popular yellow-corn seed, my grandfather also planted a variety of special corns. Among them was *maíz azul*, blue corn, for *nixtamal*, a blue dough from whence came blue corn tortillas; *maíz blanco*, white corn, used for *chicos*, dehydrated corn, in the horno or adobe oven, which we cooked with pinto beans for flavor. He also planted a few plants of *maíz piquiní* used for popcorn. Grandpa Lolo even planted a couple of plants of so-called Indian corn; the yield consisted of multicolored (yellow, blue, red, and white) corncobs that he hung on the wall or porch for decoration.

As a rule Grandpa Lolo reserved the first row of corn for these special varieties, whose yield he shared with my father and uncle. Planted among some rows of corn were watermelons and *melones roñosos*, cantaloupes, but pinto beans enjoyed a tract of land all to themselves. The calabazas (pumpkins) and calabacitas (zucchini) were also planted separately and apart from the rest of the crops. By the time late August or early September was upon us, the pumpkin patches added a special glow to the fields.

Grandma Lale had set aside a large plot of land north of the cornfields, behind a small hill adjoining El Camino de la Cañada; there she planted *chilecayotes* that she used in making *jalea*, jelly. To my knowledge, she was the only person in our village, and perhaps in the entire Río Puerco Valley, who planted these small watermelon look-alikes. The flesh was white, and she added sugar to it, boiled it, put it into small mason jars, and covered it with paraffin wax to keep the jelly from growing mold. This is something housewives did with other jellies as well.

Grandpa Lolo loved jellies. He was particularly fond of chilecayote jelly. He forever delighted in preparing the soil for Grandma to plant chi-lacayotes. My father also enjoyed the jelly from this unique and intriguing crop. Like father, like son!

Dad was home for the weekend, and it was time to head for the fields to begin planting corn. We got up early Saturday morning and ate breakfast. While he ambled to the corral for his horse to hitch to the plow, Mom and I washed dishes before I joined him. The plow he used for planting was called an *arao de mancera*, literally, plow handle. He owned one, and so did Grandpa Lolo. The sharp, pointed blade could cut through the dirt like cold lard being sliced with a hot knife.

Once Dad had hitched the horse to the plow and had the reins knotted and securely draped around his neck and under his left armpit, he held onto the plow's handles. He used both hands (that was the reason for the reins around the neck and armpit), for balance and for effective plowing. The plow cut furrows about six to eight inches deep from one end of the field to the other as my mother followed right behind with a ten-pound can full of corn seeds. I walked alongside her for observation.

Her undertaking appeared to be easy, but in reality walking on loose soil and dropping about four to six corn seeds into the furrow at each step was hard and tiring on her legs. When my father came to the end of a furrow, he would turn around and go back in the reverse direction, using the plow to cover the seeds Mom had just deposited in the ground.

From time to time Mom allowed me to dip my little hand into the can. I would hand her a few seeds of corn. In that way, I could learn and as a consequence eventually assume her role. I was now eight years old and no doubt was ready for the challenge. She cautioned me, though, never to drop more than a few kernels of corn at a time into the furrow. Her warning was tempered by saying, "Hijito, remember one thing, corn doesn't lie. It's like the truth; sooner or later it comes out." Many times on hot days after I took her place, I was anxious to get rid of the corn fast, but her words of caution rang loud and clear, and I therefore resisted the temptation.

Dad and I repeated the process of going up and down each furrow countless times until we finished. The sequence was simple, but it was hard work for him behind the plow, as it was for the horse that was pulling it.

The animal could work up a good lather, as could the plowman and the sower.

The only relief from the heat for both Dad, Mom, and me was water from a canvas-covered canteen. There were no soft drinks, lemonade, or cold water, but the fruits of our labor rested in the plentiful crops we would harvest in August and September, provided the benevolent skies showered our cornfields with ample rain. That's what dry farming and working the land was all about for farming families like Grandpa's, Dad's, and Uncle Antonio's.

Sunbonnets, Straw Hats, and
Praying for Rain

BY MID-APRIL THE FIRST unexpected light showers came and visible signs of corn were evident. The corn, having germinated, broke through the dry, tilled soil like magic, as if to say, "Here I am. Now take care of me." And care we did, because corn was one of our principal staples and crucial for our livelihood.

Grandpa's glee from the gentle rains was infectious. The next day the bright sun peered over the Mesa Prieta, and the raindrops on the young and delicate corn leaves sparkled as he walked through the fields. The rubber boots that he wore whenever he redirected the arroyo waters from the Cañada del Camino into the cornfields made a squashy sound of contentment. He looked forward to a good harvest in late summer and early fall should the rains continue.

Between now and then, work galore loomed on the horizon for young and old people alike, including grandmas, mothers, and daughters. The work of weeding and harvesting corn knew no gender barriers. They were imaginary lines at best, and most had been traversed long ago among farming families of the Río Puerco Valley. When the time came to put food on the kitchen table, every helping hand left its fingerprints on what we planted, harvested, and ate.

THE HOE

The job of sharpening the hoes in preparation to do battle against the un-invited and invasive weeds by and large fell on one man's shoulders—Grandpa Lolo's. Most of the time it was he who sharpened everybody's hoe. He was quick at using the two-sided *lima*, file, with rough and smooth edges. He used the file on hoes and sometimes on horses' hooves to smooth rough edges when he shod his saddle horses or working horses. By the time he finished sharpening a *cavador*, hoe, you were glad not to be a weed at the receiving end of the blade. You could hold a cocklebur leaf in both hands and run it across the blade with ease. The hoe was as sharp as the old-fashioned hand razor that don José, the barber in my village, sharp-ened on his leather strap.

Grandpa Lolo owned no fancy working table or anvil to get the job done, but he had his own technique for sharpening hoes. He simply sat on the house portal with his legs dangling over the edge. First he would slide the hoe's handle under his left leg until the blade, face up, was up against the inside of his knee. Next he clutched the hoe firmly with his left leg and pointed the blade at a slight downward angle away from him. The trick was to move the file smoothly down the blade but never back and forth, unless it was to get rid of a chip in the hoe. Hence, the blade's edge was sharp on only one side. If the blade turned dull or got chipped by hitting a rock in the cornfields, my grandpa simply sat on the ground, took out the file that he oftentimes carried in his right hip pocket, and repeated the filing process.

Whether sitting on the portal or on the ground, Grandpa Lolo, unlike anyone I had ever seen, was a master at sharpening hoes. Unless one had an interest in or a keen eye for such matters, his skills could go unnoticed. He was a veritable magician with a file. The hoe and file were his musical instruments, and his work with them was music to my ears.

The hoes with wooden handles came in different shapes and forms, although my father owned a one-piece hoe with a thin iron handle that was somewhat difficult to maintain a good grasp on as you hoed. The hands could easily slide up or down the handle. Unlike most wooden han-dles cut from a cottonwood branch tree at the ranch, Dad's handle never broke. Virtually all hoes, except for the handles, were made of iron or steel. They were perfect for weeding, piling the soil up around the base of plants, chopping weeds, or digging furrows for irrigation. A hoe also came in handy when mixing mud for making adobes or mud plastering.

By late evening, after eating supper, Grandpa Lolo had everybody's hoe sharpened, propped up against the north adobe wall to his house, and ready for action early next morning. This was to be our first hoeing exercise of the long spring and summer seasons. Excitement was in the air! And why not? Late afternoon showers had sprinkled the fields during the past two or three days.

I happened by Grandpa's house shortly after he finished with the hoes. I saw the fine metal dust the sharpening had left on the dirt. "Go get the shovel and bury the metal dust so the chickens won't peck at it. Otherwise, you're likely to have scrambled eggs with lead for breakfast," he said to me with a slight grin, thus revealing his two front gold teeth along with his own brand of humor. I always wondered, and never did ask him, where or why he got the two gold teeth.

In addition to the hoe, here are some of the farm tools that Grandpa kept in his arsenal during the planting and harvest seasons:

cavador	hoe
guadaña	scythe
horquilla	pitchfork
hoz	sickle
lima lisa	flat file (metal)
marro/mazo	sledge hammer
pala	shovel
pica	pickaxe
talache/zapapico	mattock

FROM SUNUP TO SUNDOWN

The next morning I heard Grandpa's rooster crowing and at the same time caught a glimpse of the sun that was peering over the Mesa Prieta. It was time for me to get up, light a fire in the woodstove, and start the coffee perking for Mom and Dad. The smell of coffee generally was enough to wake up my mother, above all if she and I were alone while Dad was away on his job. But this was Saturday morning. He was home for the weekend.

While the coffee was brewing, I dashed down the hill with my tin bucket in hand to Grandpa Lolo's corral to milk his newly acquired white-face cow. There was nothing better and more nourishing than fresh milk with my oatmeal (I hated to eat it with Karo corn syrup). Today I would not take the time to skim the foam off the top—my version of a modern-day cappuccino—as I usually did for Mom's coffee. Breakfast would be waiting as I walked back up the hill at a fast pace while being careful not to spill the "white gold," seeing as there was only one milk cow.

I walked into the kitchen, handed Mom the milk, and sat at the table. Dad was already drinking his hot coffee and dabbing a piece of hot tortilla in the sunny-side-up eggs that Mom had fried for him. She had also just flipped over my omelet.

"Come, hijito. *¡Muévete!* Shake a leg! I hear your grandpa and your cousins. They must be ready to go," Dad said to me.

I gobbled my last bite of egg and spoonful of oatmeal, gulped my milk, grabbed my saguaripa, straw hat, kissed mother on the cheek, and dashed out the door. For the time being, only Grandpa Lolo, my male cousins, and I would tackle the hoeing chores early in the growing season. My cousins came up the hill to Grandpa's house, where we all met on the front porch looking out at the fields, with the beautiful Cerro Chivato and Mesa Prieta looming in the east.

"*¿Listos?* Ready?" Grandpa Lolo shouted as he peered into the faces of four eager boys before we headed for the *milpas*, cornfields. Grandpa grabbed his hoe, put it over his right shoulder, gripped it by the handle, and led his small army of hoe-brandishing troopers forward. My cousins and I picked up our hoes in similar fashion and marched behind him in a single file on a man-made trail until we reached the cornfields.

Although hoeing young corn plants was not new to my cousins and me, Grandpa Lolo nevertheless gave us instructions on how to treat and thin out the tender plants. Of the four to six seeds that had been planted approximately every three feet in March, at least half would sprout. If more than three tiny plants were out, we were to carefully pull out the smallest ones, put them in a gunnysack, and take them home to feed my rabbits. Any weeds too close to the plants were to be pulled by hand in order to prevent chopping or injuring the corn. The hoe was then used to pile dirt neatly and gingerly around the plants. Sometimes we did that by hand, as though covering a baby with a blanket.

This was part of the gentle care accorded the young corn plants to enable them to grow and survive until the monsoon season began in earnest come July and August. At times intermittent rain showers came during May and June.

Invariably we had to contend with the pervasive gray and white worms that seemed to pop out of nowhere when we struck the ground with the hoe as the corn grew taller and yearned for rain. To me it was always a mystery—given the dry and oftentimes parched soil—where those wiggly and ugly critters came from. They were no less invasive than the large pumpkin bugs; these seemed to motor their way on the surface of the plants with ease and lots of energy when you least expected them.

NO WINNERS OR LOSERS

Grandpa's cornfield was bordered by a large hill to the south, which is where we started our hoeing. Next in line were Uncle Antonio and Dad's cornfields to the north. Grandpa Lolo assigned each one of us a *carrera*, row, of corn as starters. He took the first row, my cousins got the next, and I was given the last one. A word of caution followed.

"And remember: *Estas carreras no son carreras.* These rows of corn are not races." He played off the double meaning of *carrera*—typical of his subtle humor, but with a serious intent. "Whether you reach the end of your row first or last, there is no such thing as a winner or a loser."

When work was at hand, Grandpa Lolo was like my father—no monkey business—but that didn't preclude anyone in the group from pulling a prank or two. Boys must be boys, and Grandpa knew it. When you came to the end of a row of corn, as a rule you could pause, take off your hat, drape it on the hoe's handle, and wipe your brow, standing up, as the sun beamed down on your head. You could rest for two or three minutes, but only on your feet, before tackling a new row of corn.

The routine was quite simple. You went up and down the field hoeing at your own pace. Some moved faster than others, depending on the number of weeds hugging a plant, the amount of thinning each one required, and how adroit you were at the task. My cousins and I were like little beavers at work.

SNACK TIME

By midmorning, more or less—no one had a pocket watch, let alone a wristwatch (the sun was our clock)—we glanced toward my grandparents' house on the hilltop to see if we could spot Grandma Lale or Mom. It was time for the morning *merienda*, snack, to tide us over until lunchtime. Before I could say boo, I heard Grandma's *cencerro*, cowbell, alerting us that she and Mom were on their way. Both were *estrenando*, trying out, their brand-new *papalinas*, sunbonnets, which they had sewn during the winter. They also had on their working dresses, hand sewn to boot. It was unthinkable and unladylike for women to wear pants, whether they were in the fields or not.

Mom and Grandma Lale's arrival was invariably greeted with great joy because of the goodies they brought with them. My grandma carried the ten-pound can that formerly contained Cudahay's lard, whereas Mom had a small pot of hot coffee and a tin cup for Grandpa. The rest of us drank water from the small aluminum canteens or mason jars that we carried with us.

Smack in the middle of Grandpa's cornfield was a huge cottonwood tree that provided wonderful shade and was the ideal place for a snack as well as a *siestecita*, short nap, during the heat of the day. For now the heat was not a problem; in springtime it was still relatively cool. The tree was special since it was the only one in sight, unless one looked across the Montaño property, but that was far off in the distance. Under Grandpa's tree is where Grandma spread a small dish towel and Mom set the coffee-pot and cup.

"Come, come! Time for a little snack," Grandma Lale hollered as if to tease us, even though we had already started walking—or running— toward the tree after sticking the handles of our hoes in the ground with the blades aiming toward the heavens. Some handles were long, like the one on Grandpa's hoe, and the others varied in length according to our individual heights. As I looked at the hoes stuck in the ground, they resembled *descansos*, the resting places bearing crosses that marked where someone had died and their soul had ascended to Heaven.

Rather than having each one of us dig into the can, Grandma and Mom neatly spread bizcochitos and pastelitos on the dishtowel. The small square pies had been baked that morning from the *tasajos*, strips of pumpkin harvested the previous season and kept in the storage shed. I was pleasantly surprised to see such treats, because the merienda usually consisted of tortillas, cold sopaipillas (which I liked), or bizcochitos. Perhaps noticing the surprised look on my cousins' faces and mine, Grandma beat us to the punch before we could say boo.

"This is the first day of hoeing, with many more to come. Consequently, look upon the pastelitos as a special treat. Next time all you may get is a dry tortilla," she said somewhat sarcastically. Her sense of humor at times was difficult to decipher.

Besides being practical, both Mom and Grandma Lale were smart. Hardly anyone ever pulled the wool over their eyes. No doubt anticipating that one of us boys would prefer pies over bizcochitos or vice versa, Grandma cautioned us that we could each have one bizcochito and one pumpkin pie. That settled matters before we began whining. If either my cousins or I wanted to trade one for the other, which we often did, that was our prerogative.

For the moment, Grandpa Lolo sat peacefully on the ground and drank coffee and ate his pastry. There was no limit to the number of bizcochitos or pastelitos that he could eat, which prompted a comment from Cousin G., who was kind of a cutup.

"How come Grandpa gets to eat as many bizcochitos or pastelitos as he wants?"

"Because he's a grandpa and you're not," my grandma responded mockingly, leaving my cousin speechless.

"*Bueno le dijo la mula al freno. ¡A escardar!*" Grandpa shouted all of sudden as he got up. The words, which I hadn't heard since the previous planting season, sounded familiar. "Okay, back at it. Let's get hoeing" is what they meant, although the first part was also one of Dad's favorite expressions.

Somewhat energized after snacking, we tackled the weeds with vim and vigor. My cousin G. started cutting up, pretending that he had a stomachache, something he did from time to time. Cousin J. followed suit.

"I drank too much water. I have to pee."

"Well, pee, *cabrón*, you shithead," said Cousin G., making sure Grandpa didn't hear us use profanity. "What's to hold you back?"

"I can't open my *bragueta*," complained his little brother J.

"If you can't open your fly pull down your pecheras, *pendejo*," Cousin G. added mockingly while motioning as though he were pulling down his own overalls.

Cousin J. desperately pulled down his pants. Before he could aim in any one direction, he sprinkled the plant in front of him. "¡*Uh, a la chingada!* You've fucked up!" remarked Cousin G., using more foul language. "That's Grandpa's special white corn. Now it's going to turn yellow."

We all burst out laughing. Grandpa heard the laughter and sensed that something fishy was going on but ignored us. Cousin J. quickly pulled up his pants and piled dirt around the wet plant to cover up the evidence, so to speak.

We went back to hoeing, but once the sun beamed directly above us, it was high noon and time for lunch. We all ran up the hill in helter-skelter fashion. This time we didn't tag along behind Grandpa Lolo. In fact, because of his arthritic knees, he was the last one to get home.

LUNCHTIME

Mom was fixing lunch. She was in the process of rolling out the last tortilla. "How did you do, hijito?" she asked. "How many plants did you and your cousins destroy today?" she added laughingly. This last question did not require an answer. I knew Mom liked to kid me.

"Stir the *caldito*, stew. I don't want the potatoes to stick to the pan. Lunch will be ready as soon as I cook this last tortilla, okay? Are you hungry?"

"Yes, I'm ravenous," I responded as I tore a piece of warm tortilla from the one on top of her stack.

Since Mom had fed Beltrán, Juanito, and Julianita before I got home from the cornfields, she and I ate lunch alone. My brothers and sister were already down for a nap. After we finished eating, she and I played a game of cards before I took my siesta under the bed, the coziest and coolest place in the house.

In the late afternoon my cousins and I met at Grandpa's house. It was time once again to resume our hoeing chores. Since we had left our hoes behind, we casually ambled down to the cornfields in haphazard fashion. This time there was no walking behind Grandpa as his foot soldiers.

When we reached the fields, each one of us went about our business without uttering a word. Everyone seemed a tad sluggish, perhaps even groggy, from the short nap. Occasionally, you'd see one of us in the group pause, remove his hat, and wipe his brow. Early in the spring this sequence of movements and action was attributed more to restlessness or fatigue than anything else. Grandpa Lolo was totally oblivious to the scenario. He was the epitome of endless energy, regardless of the task at hand. He hoed and hoed, and the rest of us followed suit—well, sort of.

Suddenly, we were all shaken from our stupors when Cousin T. yelled, "There's Mom!" Everyone except Grandpa looked up and saw Aunt Taida coming down the hill.

My aunt usually brought treats and something to drink in the afternoon. Like Grandma and Mom, she also headed straight for Grandpa's huge cottonwood tree in the middle of the cornfields. Some of us ran, while others walked at a fast pace. Except for Grandpa, we all converged to help my aunt spread a small tarpaulin that she carried rolled up under her left arm; in her right hand she carried a large tin can. She took out a dish towel and a few bizcochitos that were inside the can, along with two jars of drinks.

"Oh, good!" one of my cousins shouted. "I like lemonade."

I had never heard the word *limonada* before, and I did not have the vaguest idea what it was. Aunt Taida, who came from Martíneztown in Albuquerque, was used to introducing new drinks or foods to the rest of us, including her own children. She explained, for my benefit more than anyone else's, how lemonade was made out of a powdery substance mixed with water. Thereafter, she passed the two jars around. Each one of us took a swallow. I liked the tangy taste, but then I took a bite of bizcochito. The two didn't go together.

I tried not to make a face. I didn't want to hurt my aunt's feelings. My cousins evidently were used to mixing the two, because they ate and drank rather nonchalantly, without frowning. As for Grandpa, he had either experienced the two together, or the combination didn't bother him. I had seen him mix jelly and pinto beans like his friend don Juan José did. I thought mixing these two foods was ghastly, but Grandpa was no stranger to outlandish concoctions. I guess that stemmed from getting tired of cooking for himself when Grandma was at their second home in Albuquerque.

In any case, we finished our drinks and bizcochitos and went back to hoeing. In the early evening, before the sun hid behind the San Mateo Mountains, we went home to feed the animals. I had to tend to my rabbits before eating supper.

After supper, I went and sat with my grandparents on their portal as they reflected about not having had any rain since the middle of April. Now we were well into May. For the time being, they both prayed for rain so those delicate plants we had painstakingly taken care of could survive for a good harvest crop. Along with corn and pinto beans, our mainstay crops, we also had peas, pumpkins, cantaloupes, watermelons, and chilecayotes.

NUESTRO SEÑOR DE ESQUIPULA

Sporadic light rains came in late May, but the June showers that sometimes struck before the torrential rainstorms of July and August eluded us. According to Grandma Lale, they were tucked away in some recondite clouds, unwilling to burst forth to quench our thirsty crops. She sensed that this could well be a dry summer and was therefore ready to spring into action with her favorite santo, Nuestro Señor de Esquipula (our local pronunciation). I recall her santo, religious statue, vividly to this day because of one very impressionable characteristic. He was black! A black Christ was unlike any other santos I had witnessed in family or community households.

One morning I dropped by Grandma Lale's house to help her feed the chickens, something I did routinely, and she invited me to accompany her to the bedroom—a rare glimpse at where she and Grandpa slept—to get her santo. Without thinking, I made the mistake of saying he was ugly. By the look on her face, my unwitting remark did not sit well with her, but she ignored her grandson's observation as she fetched the santo from the nicho and carried him like a newborn infant to the kitchen table.

"Go tell your parents and your aunt and uncle and your cousins to come over after they've taken their afternoon nap. I need their help."

"What about me, Grandma? Can I come too?" I asked.

"Of course! Now scoot." And I took off to inform everyone of what Grandma had said.

That afternoon I hardly slept a wink during my nap, wondering what Grandma had in mind. I was the first one to show up at my grandparents' portal. They were both up from their siestas and doing something in the kitchen. I waited outside until everyone else arrived. I could tell by the looks on my aunt, uncle, and parents' faces that they knew what Grandma was up to. The rest of us were in the dark, so curiosity lingered in the air.

Out came Grandma Lale from the kitchen, wearing her *tápalo*. The black shawl was something she only wore to church or for special religious functions. "In a moment," I thought to myself, "something important is about to happen." My curiosity was about to be put to rest as we promenaded down the hill and headed for the cornfields. Grandma led the religious pilgrimage, a new experience for me. Mom, Aunt Taida, and the rest of us followed her, while Grandpa held up the rear.

With Nuestro Señor de Esquipula clutched in her arms, Grandma Lale led us in prayer in the forlorn-looking cornfields. "Our Father, who art in heaven . . ." she said, and we joined in prayer in chorus-like fashion, marching up and down several rows of corn. First came Grandpa's cornfields, then Uncle Antonio's, and, finally, Dad's. From time to time, I'd see Grandma whisper something to her favorite santo, in obvious reference to the thirsty crops that were in dire need of a good soaking.

Though the afternoon heat had passed as Grandma Lale paraded Nuestro Señor de Esquipula throughout the fields, it was still hot enough for perspiration to form on her brow. Her black shawl did not help matters;

it just added to the intolerable heat. Mom was wearing her white sunbonnet and Aunt Taida, a yellow one, so they were able to withstand the heat much better. The rest of us, with our straw hats, perspired just as much as Grandma.

Following the religious trek, which probably lasted no more than half an hour, Grandma Lale marched us up the hill until we reached her house. She walked casually to the bedroom, where she returned her santo to his nicho. Now she would wait to see if Nuestro Señor de Esquipula brought us rain in answer to her prayers.

For days on end nothing happened. Grandma's santo did not respond to her pleas. "When God doesn't wish to act, the santos are helpless," I once heard an old-timer say. The afternoon and evening clouds peppered the heavens, but they were no more than a tease. As night approached and the breezes came, the large popcorn clouds traveled east and dissipated over the Mesa Prieta. Grandma Lale did not take kindly to their teasing, for she recognized that we were in the midst of a genuine drought, and the planted fields were in imminent danger of drying up and dying. What would she do next to break the silence of the heavens?

One day, when I was on my way back after collecting the eggs from the chicken coop, I saw Grandpa Lolo sitting on his portal, looking out at the cornfields. I stopped by to visit with him. I had three or four eggs in the Rex jelly can that I used to carry them in.

"How many eggs do you have in your can? It's so dry I bet even the chickens are refusing to lay eggs," he remarked in a disenchanted tone of voice. His comment was a bit unusual for him. He rarely sounded pessimistic about anything. "Go take your eggs home and then come back. I want you to go with me."

I hurried home, being careful not to break or drop the eggs. I told Mom that Grandpa wanted me to accompany him. "And where are you going?" she queried.

"I don't know. He didn't tell me."

"Fine, but wherever you go or whatever you do, be careful"—familiar words coming from Mom anytime I went somewhere.

As it turned out, Grandpa wanted to go survey the cornfields. As he walked around the gloomy-looking fields in a downcast manner, I could tell that he was truly worried. Why, I even heard him mumble to himself the following words as he kicked the ground: "If rain doesn't come soon, these plants are going to die."

Before we started back up the hill to his house, we paused to rest under the shade of the large cottonwood tree. Immediately he stretched himself on the ground with his hat over his eyes. I did the same thing, but I wasn't tired. I removed my hat and just stared at the sky through the tree's green leaves.

All at once, high up, I saw a snake crawling down one of the branches in the direction of the ground close to where Grandpa Lolo was resting. As my eyes followed the snake, I was taken aback to see Grandma's santo perched on one of the tree branches. Apparently she did this now and again whenever she beckoned her benevolent santo for rain. Either that or she would turn the santo facing the wall in her nicho as punishment for failing to bring rain to the crops. I knew about the santo in the nicho, but what I found unusual this time was the fact that Nuestro Señor de Esquipula was upside-down—on his head—something I had never seen in the past.

Since I was scared that the snake might bite Grandpa Lolo, I nudged him and woke him up. "What, what, what's going on? Why did you wake me up?" he mumbled, for he obviously had fallen into a deep sleep.

"A snake, Grandpa! A snake!" and I pointed to it.

"Ah, don't worry, hijiito. That's a bull snake. It's not like a rattlesnake that can bite you and kill you. Bull snakes are the farmer's best friend. They eat field mice. But they also like to suck the yokes from eggs in the chicken coop. Aside from that, they're good to have around."

When Grandpa and I got back home, I was anxious to tell Grandma about the snake, but I was more curious as to why she had turned Nuestro Señor de Esquipula on his head. As soon as I walked into the kitchen, I asked straight out: "Grandma, why do you have your favorite santo under the tree? And why is he on his head?" *

---

*   See *Grandma's Santo on Its Head: Stories of Days Gone By in Hispanic Villages of New Mexico / El santo patas arriba de mi abuelita: Cuentos de días gloriosos en pueblitos hispanos de Nuevo México.*

"He's been a bad santo, that's why. Until he decides to bring us some much-needed rain, he's going to find himself looking at the heavens upside-down, even if he gets a headache," she explained, adding these last few words with a touch of sarcasm.

"Yes, Grandma, but the snake almost bit your santo." I forgot for one moment what Grandpa had said about the harmless bull snake.

"Good. That's what he gets for not answering my prayers."

Two days later a torrential downpour came late in the afternoon. While it was raining cats and dogs, Grandma walked down to Grandpa's tree. She came back totally drenched, but she brought her santo out of the rain, tucked under her apron. She placed him in his nicho, where he belonged, but instead of facing the wall or standing him on his head, she stood him upright, facing out. She had left the door to the bedroom ajar. While I sat on the porch, I overheard her say, "Thank you for the rains you brought us." She walked out as happy as a lark.

That evening I could hear the frogs and their relentless croaking in the cornfields. They were just as elated as Grandma. The harvest season was no longer in doubt or in jeopardy. Crops would be plentiful for family consumption and animals alike. Grandma's prayers, with a little help from the rest of us, had been answered. The power of prayer had vindicated her harsh treatment of Nuestro Señor de Esquipula. Now I understood her motives and actions much better. After all, grandmas always knew best.

20

Lent and Holy Week

I HAD LEARNED PLENTY from Grandma Lale by witnessing her petitions to Nuestro Señor de Esquipula. Now I could perchance understand a little more perceptibly the significance of Lent (La Cuaresma) and what it conjured up for people in our valley. This was especially true of women like my mother, who was, after all, the torchbearer of religion in my family.

Without doubt the Lenten season was the most solemn time of the year in my household. Mom made sure of that. The same thing held true for many mothers up and down the Río Puerco Valley.

Ash Wednesday was the official beginning of Lent, but it was not always celebrated with a Mass in the placita, unless the priest traveled from Jémez Springs, where he occupied a permanent home. Otherwise, the Penitentes or the locally recognized rezador/a, the prayer leader, recited the rosary in lieu of a Mass to commence the Lenten season. There were no blessed ashes on Ash Wednesday, as was true of other nearby hamlets that did not claim a priest in residence to help honor the holy day. The priest, of course, traveled to our village on Easter Sunday and sometimes even on Palm Sunday, but back-to-back visits were rare.

Lent meant forty days of prayer and abstentions of one sort or another for elders and young children alike. Abstaining from doing something or eating certain foods was strictly an individual's choice, and many times they were difficult to abide by throughout the entire Lenten season. That was true not only for adults but for kids as well. Like any personal vow, some were kept; others went unfulfilled.

Children like me and my cousins were just as culpable as other kids our age. For most of us, vows were a game whose rules were apt to be broken without committing a sin. Adults, especially men, did keep their promises because it was a challenge to see if they could adhere to their vows and hence outlast their friends or compadres for forty days. Here is a brief list of some of the typical kinds of things adults and kids promised to honor personally during Lent:

No candy (children)
No chewing tobacco or snuff (adults)
No cursing (men)
No dances or parties (everyone)
No gum chewing (children)
No liquor (men)
No shaving (men)
No shooting marbles (boys)
No smoking (adults)

Unlike the foregoing list of no-no's, which we sometimes yielded to temptation on, there were tacit agreements among families regarding other, more formal and serious obligations within the Catholic Church. For example, hardly anybody ate meat on Fridays all through Lent, above all during Holy Week, to wit, from Monday to Friday. Some people even included Holy Saturday and Easter Sunday. Between Monday and Wednesday noon of Holy Week, I had to chop and split enough wood to last until Saturday or Sunday. Except on the days when I fed my rabbits and Mom's chickens, my mother had me sit down in a corner of the kitchen floor and pray every afternoon.

For me it was a peaceful time, a moment when I could lock myself within my own world of meditation, seemingly oblivious to all man-made noises beyond the walls of Mom's kitchen. The singing of birds coupled with Chopo barking provided me with the lullaby of music that lulled me to sleep for my afternoon siesta. All this was a reward well earned after chopping piles of wood for Mom's woodstove.

My mother also made sure that we as a family recited the rosary every Friday evening after supper, plus each day for the duration of Holy Week. These were holy days of observation and obligation following Palm Sunday.

LENTEN FOODS

First and foremost, as mentioned above, most people did not eat meat on Fridays all the way through the Lenten season. A few individuals abstained from eating meat during the entire forty days of Lent (the period of Christ's fasting in the desert), beginning with Ash Wednesday. And once Holy Week was upon us, my mother—like so many other women—cooked and baked everyday foods (minus meat, of course), but she also had her repertoire of Lenten foods that she served starting on Ash Wednesday and on Holy Thursday, Good Friday, Holy Saturday, and Easter Sunday. These are some of those typical Lenten foods:

chaquegüe (similar to brel, shepherd's bread, but made with blue cornmeal)

empanaditas de fruta (fruit turnovers)

molletes (small loaves of sweet, anise-flavored bread baked in the adobe oven)

natillas (custard pudding)

pan de horno (bread baked in the adobe oven)

panocha (a delicious pudding made from ground sprouted wheat once upon a time prepared and eaten primarily during Lent)

quelites (cooked canned or wild spinach sprinkled with red chile seeds)

salmón en lata (patties dipped in egg yolk batter and fried)

torrejas al caramelo (egg yolk fritters dipped in homemade caramel sauce)

torta de huevo (egg yolk batter deep fried in fat and dipped in red chile sauce)

tortillas de nixtamal (blue corn tortillas)

Some of the same Lenten delicacies were replicated from time to time when one of my siblings was baptized, when one made his or her First Holy Communion, or when other festive occasions came to pass at our house. The foods were modest but plentiful.

VÍA DOLOROSA

No other day during Holy Week surpassed Good Friday, when Christ's Crucifixion took place, in importance. Led by the local Penitentes (Los Hermanos Cofrados de Nuestro Padre Jesús) following a week of praying in their *oratorio*, people from our placita and outlying areas flocked to the Virgen de Guadalupe Church to recite the stations of the cross, referred to locally as the Vía Dolorosa. The oratorio, similar to a morada, was located across the church. The Penitentes served as the primary spiritual leaders, although a rezador/a assumed the same role—in both cases minus Mass—whenever a priest was not available.

On the afternoon of Good Friday my father hitched the horse wagon, loaded the whole family, and took off for our village to join in the recitation of the stations of the cross. Each one of the fourteen scenes, from Jesus being condemned to death up to and including the resurrection, was reenacted. Except for the sickly or very aged, most Guadalupanos, including children, participated in the religious observance.

When Mom and the rest of the family walked into the church, I noticed that the santos and other images were veiled with purple cloth, but not the prints of stations of the cross.

To a small boy like me, the draped santos looked spooky. I asked Mom why they were covered. Her response was pretty straightforward. "They're covered," she said, "to show the mysteries of *la pasión de Jesucristo*, Christ's Passion" (Christ's sufferings on the cross). The unveiling of the santos to honor the Lord's Passion took place on Good Friday around two o'clock.

Important, too, during the afternoon was the recitation of the so-called Las Siete Palabras (the Seven Words). Though literally not seven words, they were, more appropriately, phrases that Christ articulated on the cross before dying. For the local and nearby residents they were an important and an integral part of the religious ceremony.

The reciting of the stations of the cross was a solemn occasion; it usually ended with an *alabao*, a hymn of praise depicting the Passion. Reproduced here is a hymn (still in my archives) that Grandma Lale had in her book of alabaos; it was sung by a local Penitente.

Despedida del sagrado corazón de Jesús	Farewell to Our Sacred Heart of Jesus
1	**1**
Salve corazón abierto,	Hail, oh, open heart,
santa y dulce habitación.	sweet and holy room.
Adiós Jesús de mi vida,	Farewell my dear Lord,
dame vuestra bendición.	please give me your blessing.
2	**2**
Salve corazón cargado	Hail, oh, heavy heart
con la cruz de la pasión.	with the cross of the Passion.
Adiós Jesús de mi vida,	Farewell, my dear Lord,
dame vuestra bendición.	please give me your blessing.
3	**3**
Salve corazón cruzando	Oh, save us, crossed heart
con nuestro olvido y traición.	from our neglect and deception.
Adiós Jesús de mi vida,	Farewell, my dear Lord,
dame vuestra bendición.	please give me your blessing.
4	**4**
Adiós amante querido,	Farewell, oh, dear lover,
dueño de mi corazón.	possessor of my heart.
Adiós Jesús de mi vida,	Farewell, my dear Lord,
dame vuestra bendición.	please give me your blessing.

The mournful voice of the Penitente brought tears to some of the people's eyes as the celebration of the stations of the cross ended. Some parishioners, including those who lived in the placita, then stayed inside the church to meditate more.

At least on one other occasion that I can recall, the stations of the cross were celebrated at dusk, but not inside the church. The sacristan and his compadres prepared fourteen stacks of wood that were interspaced around the church. Called luminarios (see chapter 17) and similar to those that brightened our placita at Christmastime, each one stood for a station of the cross. Lit one by one, people stopped at each luminario and uttered their prayers as they were led in the procession by a Penitente or the prayer leader. The lighting of the luminarios was a colorful event that signaled the end to the religious activities on Good Friday.

As people left the last luminario, I heard doña Adelita, the local prayer leader, recite the following words: *"Los luminarios son las llamas que alumbran el camino espiritual y físico de nuestras vidas, gracias al Señor que padeció tanto por nosotros."* That is, "The bonfires are the flames that light up the spiritual and physical paths in our lives, thanks to our Lord who suffered so much in our behalf."

Once the recitation of the stations of the cross was over, everyone departed for home and prepared for Holy Saturday, a day on which local villagers and other faithful observed Christ's Passion and death in anticipation of His resurrection from the dead on Easter Sunday. This day, perhaps the most important in Christendom, brought to a close the Lenten Season and the days of praying, fasting, and penance.

To celebrate Easter Sunday, grown-ups and children sometimes wore new clothes (*estrenaban ropa nueva*), some of it made by the mother or grandmother. Other people put on their Sunday best, as if to express happiness without being overly ostentatious in appearance. After all, it was a day to honor Christ's rising from the dead by reaffirming one's faith, which gave assurance to a new life on this earth and beyond. Easter Sunday was—and is to this day—when a spiritual and physical life began anew for all the faithful until the next Lenten season came about a year hence.

21

The Three Cs

Catechism, Confusion, and Communion

RELIGION WITHOUT A DOUBT was the most important beacon that guided our lives, whether you lived in the village proper or in its outlying areas. Translucent and claiming no geographic boundaries, spirituality rose above mesas, ravines, arroyos, and foothills, reached out, and connected with people. Whether you were old or young, rich or poor was inconsequential, because your soul was touched in a number of spiritual and indefinable ways from the time you were an infant clad in diapers until you were called upon to depart this earth.

Like beads on a rosary, baptism was the first celebration in a long line of religious practices and ceremonies that brought families and friends together in small communities like mine. This was certainly true of First Holy Communion, weddings, and *velorios*, religious vigils held when someone died (see chapter 29). Celebrations, both joyful and mournful, were a community affair. Everyone felt the joy as well as the grief.

Religion began at home with the mother and was reinforced by the father, whose tacit role as head of the family was traditional and of fundamental importance in the rearing of children. Grandmothers, both paternal and maternal, as a rule were also strong supporters of the tenets of Catholicism.

Religious upbringing in my home was no different from that in other families in my village of Ojo del Padre. It started with my mother. An outward manifestation of her spirituality, as nearly as my memory allows me to recollect, takes me back to the dinner table when I was about four years old. "*Gracias a Dios, que nos da el pan de cada día. Amén.* Thanks be to God, who gives us our daily bread. Amen" are the first words invoking religion that Mom taught me. Her expression of gratitude at any level, whether religious or secular, has stuck with me like Super Glue all through my adult life. Saying grace at supper was standard, but at times, without Mom leading the chorus of words, I would silently utter the same prayer at lunch. My siblings were to follow suit when they were old enough to grasp the meaning of her words.

When I turned five or six years old, Mom taught me to kneel down beside the bed and to say a prayer before going to sleep. The words were simple and unobtrusive. They went something like this: "*Le doy gracias a mi Tatita Dios por otro día de vida.* I thank Almighty God for another day on this earth." The intent of the prayer was what mattered, not its eloquence or lack thereof. A similar recitation was often repeated in the morning, but I did this of my own volition after observing my mom, not because she insisted on it. She was not fanatical about prayer, but she really believed that you had to show gratitude on this earth, and where better to start than with God?

All the while, what Mom was doing, unbeknownst to me, was laying the groundwork for other rites of passages that occurred in a normal evolutionary manner. They were celebrated—not forced upon you—only if and when the mother felt that you were ready to cross the next religious bridge in your life. As a child I recall all too well that my fate regarding certain religious responsibilities was in my parents' hands, with Mom leading the way.

First Holy Communion is a case in point. Preparations for this rite of passage began with catechism lessons in the summer after the school year had ended. I was eight years old and headed for the second grade. By then Mom had already taught me the Our Father, Hail Mary, and Act of Contrition—all in Spanish, since English was a foreign language to us and virtually nonexistent to all in our community except for the teacher, who tried, seemingly unsuccessfully, to teach her students English.

At bedtime Mom would have me recite each prayer after her until, over time, I was able to repeat them without making a single mistake. By the time I began catechism I was already ahead of the game, so to speak. Listening to the three prayers at Mass once a month, when the priest visited our village, or during the recitation of the rosary at home, plus at my paternal grandmother's house all through Lent, also helped me memorize the words.

The day that school ended in late May, I got off Uncle Antonio's school bus, and there was Mom waiting for me. I ran toward her, happy as a lark, dangling my report card in the air. School was over for the summer. "How did you do, hijito? Did you pass to the second grade?" she asked with a teasing look on her face. She knew better. "Yes, amá, and guess what? Now I don't have to study for a long, long time." "Oh, yes, you do. Monday you have to start catechism with Mrs. G. in the placita."

My face dropped to the floor, but my disappointment was fleeting at best. "Will there be kids there I know?"

"Yes, your friend Loyola will be going with you. He'll stop by on Monday."

"Good," I responded and left it at. "Catechism will certainly be a new learning experience for me," I thought to myself. I had heard older kids talk about catechism and First Holy Communion. Not only that, I knew Mrs. G., who ran a small grocery store this side of the river, across from the placita. My cousin J. and I would stop there from time to time to buy chewing gum or candy.

I decided to ride El Prieto to the Virgen de Guadalupe Church, where catechism was to be held. El Prieto could handle big waves better than Bayito, my other horse, and the current in the Río Puerco was running pretty strong because of heavy rains over the past weekend in the Río Puerco's headwaters in the Nacimiento Mountains north of Cuba. I had been taught never to cross the river in a straight line and certainly not against the current unless the water was shallow. Flowing with the current in a diagonal way, above all when the rolling waves were huge, was less dangerous. The ever-present concern was that one would be swept off the horse, so holding onto the saddle horn was of paramount importance.

Loyola and I rode together but on separate horses. We took our time getting to the placita; it was no more than twenty to twenty-five minutes from my casita. As we got to the riverbed we saw the gushing waters with large waves resembling a giant washboard. I knew that despite the authoritative up-and-down water movement, the real danger was crossing where the water was tranquil. Calmness tended to indicate deep waters with an undercurrent that could wreak havoc with a horse. With Prieto, however, I was not afraid.

Loyola was not accustomed to crossing the Río Puerco near the placita. I told him to wrap the reins around his saddle horn and to hold on tight to his horse's mane. He was to follow me. I could tell he was a bit scared. I had done this many times. I was used to traversing the raging waters. Once I crossed, I turned around and looked. Lo and behold, Loyola was still on the other side of the river. I hollered at him, "What happened? Why didn't you follow me?"

"I'm scared. I thought your horse was going to disappear as he sank into the water," his loud voice echoed amid the sound of the rolling water.

I went back for him, but this time he got on my horse. We left his tethered to a tree in the shade by the riverbed. I told him to climb in the saddle. I sat behind him and held onto the saddle straps (*látigos*) until we found ourselves across the river. This time Prieto showed more confidence. He was a strong steed.

At the placita, I watered him at a trough next to the community well and then tied him under some shady trees a short distance from the church. By the time Loyola and I walked in, Mrs. G. was there, along with her son and a few other kids from the placita and Santa Clara, a tiny hamlet a few miles north of my village. All total, there were about eight to ten kids ready to learn catechism in preparation for our First Holy Communion later in the summer.

Everybody knew Mrs. G., but she introduced herself nonetheless, as well as calling off all the children's names. The group was about equally divided between boys and girls. Just two girls were strangers to me, but I had seen them in church. They belonged to the Ramírez family. The rest of the kids came from the Gonzales, Aragón, Salas, Jaramillo, Montaño, and García families. The parents were all members of the Virgen de Guadalupe Church.

Well respected in the community, Mrs. G. was an excellent prayer leader who could recite the rosary with ease and charisma. Her crystal-clear voice when singing the mournful alabaos, hymns of praise, during Lent or at religious wakes in honor of the departed was legendary. She was the consummate example of spirituality and human decency and the ideal person to teach us catechism.

Her explanations for coming together were straightforward and to the point, which was to learn the fundamentals of catechism with the ultimate aim of celebrating our First Holy Communion. "Catechism," she explained, "revolves around faith based on God's powerful existence, the Ten Commandments, the Seven Sacraments, and the Lord's Prayer." Along the way Mrs. G. taught us that God, day and night, was omnipresent and that He represented good, not evil, with the ability to punish you for your misdeeds or to reward you for your kindness. Some of these things were accepted at face value. Others, like punishment from God, evoked confusion in my mind and I'm sure in the minds of some of the other kids. Later in life I was to learn from our elders that "*Dios no castiga con palos ni azotes.* God doesn't punish people by flogging you." That is to say, He has His way of meting out punishment according to His own self-rule and judgment.

"And what is evil, Mrs. G.?" asked one of the kids, raising his right hand. As if she had anticipated the question, she took out two pieces of cloth, a white and a black one, from a knapsack that she harnessed over her right shoulder. She held up the white cloth in her right hand and the black one in her left hand. "*Mira, hijito.* White means good; it's like sitting at the right hand of God. You can do no wrong. Black symbolizes evil, like the darkness of night when evil spirits [*la cosa mala*] can appear before you."

No sooner had she answered that kid's query when another hand popped up. Before Mrs. G. could acknowledge the waving hand, the boy asked, "Like La Llorona, Mrs. G.?"

"No. La Llorona is not an evil person who goes around hurting people. She is just repenting for having drowned her children. That's why her wailing is heard at night along the riverbanks, the arroyos, or the acequias. That's a different kind of punishment for a different kind of sin."

"So is being a *zurdo*, left-handed, like my Uncle Flavio, bad?" asked the same boy.

"Not at all. Being left-handed has nothing to do with evilness. You're either left-handed or right-handed. That's God's choice to make."

"What are sins, Mrs. G.?" asked one of the Ramírez girls.

"They are things you must not do. For example, never use God's name in vain. Do not tell lies. Do not steal. Do not disobey your father or mother."

"And what happens if you disobey them?" asked someone else in the class.

Before Mrs. G. could answer the question, a kid who had been sitting quietly in a pew behind me blurted out an unexpected pronouncement. "My father says that if you strike one of your parents, your arm will either shrivel up or the earth will part and swallow you up to your waist. Is that true, Mrs. G.?"

"That's right, hijito. That's God's way of punishing you," and she proceeded to tell us the story of the Disobedient Son, who wandered the four corners of the earth minus his legs for his transgression.* She cautioned that the fate of the defiant son or daughter could vary from one offspring to another. "Ballads," she added, "have been composed concerning the Disobedient Son or Daughter."

Mrs. G. digressed momentarily and gave the example—and sang a couple of verses—of "Rosita Alvírez," the popular Mexican ballad of the young lady who went to a dance against her mother's wishes. On the dance floor the daughter rejected a young man's offer to dance, which was against social etiquette, whereupon he shot and killed her.

I had heard Mom sing the same ballad. Therefore, Mrs. G.'s words didn't shock me. However, as I looked around, I noticed some of the other kids seemed to be awestruck, if not frightened. I couldn't tell for sure which symptom fit best.

Unable to resist asking a question, and at the same time unknowingly breaking the silence, I said, "Mrs. G., if black is evil, how come the priest always wears black and not white?"

Whether she was disturbed or annoyed at what must have seemed like something out of the blue or she didn't have a suitable answer, her reaction was swift and uncharacteristic of her demeanor. "Just because," is all she

---

* The story of Gustoso Gustavo, the Disobedient Son, is in my book *Grandma's Santo on Its Head: Stories of Days Gone By in Hispanic Villages of New Mexico / El santo patas arriba de mi abuelita: Cuentos de días gloriosos en pueblitos hispanos de Nuevo México.*

said. A sudden silence descended on the class once again, but her reply left me confused. The other kids expressed surprise as well at Mrs. G's impetuous response. The next words that came out of her mouth were orders for us to memorize the Our Father and Hail Mary for our session two days hence.

We all dispersed in different directions, some within the placita, where a few of the kids resided; others, like me and Loyola, lived farther away. We mounted Prieto and headed for the Río Puerco a short distance from the church. There were two ways to go back across the river. Coming over, Loyola and I had first crossed using the south crossing. This time I decided to take the north bajada, or descent, which was closer; it didn't take as long to reach the riverbed. The river was narrower here than at the south bajada. As a consequence, the water was deeper, but once again the trick was to cross diagonally in a southward direction. The rolling waves, still very much in command, looked more menacing in late afternoon than they had earlier in the day. Perhaps this was because of the straightaway course of this part of the river and the speed of the water.

Just as I was getting ready to prompt Prieto, Loyola heard a horse wagon making a creaky noise down the north bajada behind us. It was Mrs. G. pulling back tight on the reins, applying her right foot to the brake, and hollering commands at the horses until she reached the riverbed. Her son, standing behind her, was holding onto the back of the seat. "¿Qué pasa, muchachos? What's wrong, boys?" she asked in a sympathetic voice.

"Nothing. We were admiring the huge waves before crossing," I responded, trying to sound nonchalant and brave at the same time, but in reality I was petrified at the strong current, even though I had the utmost confidence in Prieto.

"Look," added Mrs. G., "why don't you tie your horse to the back of the wagon and ride across with us?"

Loyola and I didn't blink an eye at her offer. As Mrs. G. navigated the rollicking waves that climbed more than halfway up the wheels, I could tell that she was just as much in command of her team of horses as she was of catechism back at the church.

We thanked Mrs. G. for the ride. Loyola then fetched his horse, and we left for home, where Mom was waiting for me. Loyola still had another ten to fifteen minutes before reaching his house by El Cañoncito. Mom asked about catechism. A conversation ensued. I gave her a blow-by-blow description of what Mrs. G. had talked about, but I didn't mention anything regarding my question about the priest's black attire. I did tell Mom that I had to practice the Our Father and Hail Mary for the next session, something she and I did that evening and the next day.

The next time we met with Mrs. G., I could recite both prayers (in Spanish, of course) practically without making a mistake, despite my nervousness. As it turned out I was ahead of the game, because only one girl was able to say the Our Father and Hail Mary from start to finish. She was really good. The rest of the kids stumbled here and there, but we all laughed together at our mistakes, not at each other. In fact, a couple of kids, the ones from Santa Clara, who were cousins, I believe, added some levity to the class.

While one of the Ramírez girls was struggling with the Hail Mary, the two cousins chimed in—in alternating fashion—from the back of the class with their own rendition. "*Santa María, dame tortillas. Madre de Dios, dame de a dos.* Holy Mary, give me tortillas. Mother of God, make it two at a time."

Even Mrs. G., a serious person for whom religion was no laughing matter, cracked a smile at their dialogue. The rest of the kids, including me, didn't know whether to chuckle or cover our faces. All of a sudden a burst of laughter erupted among all of us, and one of the poor Ramírez girls blushed thinking that the two boys were mocking her. From that moment forward, catechism was less tense and much more enjoyable. The urchins from Santa Clara had broken the ice.

"We can all laugh and have fun, but we must now turn to something that is very serious," Mrs. G advised. "By next week all of you must learn by memory the Ten Commandments. You must do this before you can make your First Holy Communion. *Los mandamientos de la ley de Dios son diez.*" She asked us to repeat each one, whereupon she explained briefly their importance. First of all, she emphasized in simple terms that they were God's laws. Second, she underscored their significance as a moral and religious compass to guide us—men, women, and children—in being good citizens while on this earth. During the course of her explanations, Mrs. G. seemed to dwell on a handful of commandments, some of which she had mentioned previously when we asked her about sins:

No usar el nombre de Dios en vano. (Do not use God's name in vain.)
Honrar a tu padre y madre. (Honor your father and mother.)
No robarás. (Do not steal.)
No dirás mentiras. (You will not tell lies.)
Guardar el domingo como día de descanso y rezo. (Keep Sunday as a day
    of rest and prayer.)

Perhaps Mrs. G. selected these commandments because they were easier
for us to understand than the others. As a matter of fact, I, too, was already
familiar with these five, although my parents didn't present them as man-
dates from God the way Mrs. G. did in her brief presentation. She reiter-
ated, nonetheless, that we would understand each one better as we got
older. For the time being, some of the remaining commandments were
nothing more than esoteric pronouncements that meant nothing to me and
the other kids.

Catechism classes went on for several more weeks, until Mrs. G. felt
that we were ready for First Holy Communion. The day came when each of
us had to recite in front of the group the Our Father, the Hail Mary, and
the Act of Contrition in addition to the Ten Commandments. Some kids
performed just fine; others required a little coaxing. But we all passed the
test and were now ready to take the big plunge.

The second Sunday of the month, which is when the priest was to come
to my village from Cuba or Jémez Springs, was just around the corner. He
traveled either on horseback or by horse carriage. Evidently the date for
celebrating our First Holy Communion was already on the calendar. Now
the only thing the catechism class needed was a few last-minute instructions from Mrs. G. She addressed these in our final session preceding the
big event.

When we met, even some parents showed up. Undaunted by their presence, Mrs. G. proceeded with whatever loose ends had to be taken care of,
most of them having to do with obligations preceding and following our
First Holy Communion: fasting, confession, Communion (the meaning of
the Host), and penance. Mrs. G. explained each one without overburden-
ing us with minutiae or their religious implications. She invariably strove
to keep spiritual matters at an elementary level so that we kids grasped at
least a modicum of their significance.

"*Miren, hijitos.* Listen here, children. Before you go confess your sins at least once a month when the priest comes, you must *ayunar,* fast. What this means is that you cannot eat any food past midnight, although you may drink some water in the morning."

"What about after we take Communion?" asked one of the imps from Santa Clara.

"Then you can eat *hasta que te revientes,* till you blow up!" blurted his sidekick.

Mrs. G. pretended not to hear him and continued her instructions. "When you go to confession, to the right of the altar through that door"— and she pointed—"there's what is called a confessional. You kneel down. The priest will be sitting on a chair with his eyes closed. He won't know who you are, but over time he'll recognize your voice. Before you begin your confession you say these words: 'Bless me, Father, for I have sinned. It's been a month since my last confession. My sins are . . .' He will then give you penance for absolution.

"The penance depends on the severity of your sins. For example, he may ask you to recite five Our Fathers and five Hail Marys before taking Communion. You will also recite the Act of Contrition at your pew. Confession will be prior to Mass, except for kids in the placita, who may come and confess on Saturday afternoon around four or five o'clock, when the priest gets to the placita. When taking Communion you will receive the Host from the priest by opening your mouth and sticking your tongue out. He will then place the Host on your tongue, but you must not chew the host. You have to let it melt. Here's how you do it."

Mrs. G. then asked the girls to line up in a single row, and she took out a tortilla from her knapsack. Playing the role of the priest, Mrs. G. stood in front of the altar, and one by one she placed a small piece of tortilla on each girl's tongue. The boys were next and the routine, the same. Then we all sat down. Mrs. G. immediately noticed that both the girls and the boys, including me, were sitting with their mouths shut.

"The tortilla is only for practice. You may chew and swallow it," she said, whereupon everyone's jaws went to work. "Does anyone have any questions?" Mrs. G. asked.

There being none, she dismissed the catechism class and promised to

The author's First Holy Communion, c. 1944.

see us at the end of the month for the big celebration. And what a big celebration it was! All the families and friends of the celebrants were present. In fact, it looked like the entire community turned out. Even my grandma Cinda from Bernalillo attended.

Everybody, above all the sons and daughters making their First Holy Communion and their parents, dressed up for the occasion. The girls' attire was all white, from the thin veil, hat, and dress down to the shoes. Most of the boys wore dark suits. My parents had bought me a dark blue suit, black shoes, a white shirt, and a tie. In addition, each boy and girl carried a long decorative candle as we marched into the church behind the priest. The girls walked in first, followed by the boys. We occupied the two front pews to the left and right of the altar.

Following the First Holy Communion ceremony, the priest blessed us and then gave every boy and girl a prayer book, a scapular for us to wear around our necks, and a small medal of the Virgin Mary. When my parents, grandparents, the rest of the family, and I got home, the first thing Grandma Cinda did was to ask me to kneel down in front of her. She offered her blessings and congratulations. Mom followed suit, making the sign of the cross on my forehead with her right thumb and forefinger. She was radiant. And I was a proud little boy. After all, being the oldest offspring, I was the first child in the family to make the First Holy Communion. Henceforth my spiritual life would be different, including my role as an altar boy, a so-called *monecilla*.

Up to now I had acted as my cousin J.'s helper, which meant that I could only ring the little bell in church before Communion. I could not handle the wine because I was not a full-fledged altar boy. Nonetheless, Cousin J. had promised that once I made my First Holy Communion we could exchange roles. Fair enough, but I never envisioned what was to happen between him and me after he reneged on his promise.

The next time the priest came to our village, I was ecstatic at the prospect of handing the wine to him. Sure enough! Right before Mass, Cousin J. and I met with the priest and went over the roles each of us would play that morning. When Mass began, Cousin J. knelt to the right of the altar, with the little bell at his side on the floor. I was kneeling to the left of the altar, where my cousin customarily knelt. The priest would always signal my cousin to fetch the wine, but this time it would be me. However, as the priest nodded his head, Cousin J. stood and headed for the wine on top of a small table to the right of the altar. Feeling betrayed, and without thinking, I stood up and tackled him in front of the entire congregation. The parishioners no doubt were stunned. Some must have been embarrassed, especially my dear mom, but I wasn't about to let my cousin break his promise. Equally beside himself was the priest, who tried to separate us as we wrestled on the altar. He finally succeeded, but I won the battle of the wine.

Once home, Mom wanted to know what had precipitated the foregoing affray. She was satisfied with my explanation, and my role as altar boy continued for the next year or so without further incidents. Cousin J. learned to keep promises, and I vowed never again to embarrass my mother in front of churchgoers.

22

Cattle Roundups and Camaraderie

MY FIRST HOLY COMMUNION was behind me, and the late spring roundup loomed just around the corner. This was to be my second roundup, last year having been my first. For me rounding up cattle was one of the most exciting events of the year. Once I came of age and learned the ins and outs of herding cattle, most of them being whitefaces, I could hardly contain my excitement. Seeing the newborn calves tag alongside their mothers was exhilarating. What made the roundup even more special and different from other community events, both secular and religious, was the camaraderie among the cowboys, who came together from communities like mine of Ojo del Padre, Cabezón, and San Luis, as well as from nearby ranches.

Several days of chasing and cutting cattle, of branding and earmarking calves, and of cooking, eating, and sleeping in the open air created picture-perfect scenes that remain lodged in my mind to this day. Listening to grown-ups' stories at night as we huddled around the campfire before going to bed was an added treat for me. I was anxious for the roundup to begin.

But before the hubbub and hobnobbing came into focus, Grandpa Lolo, Uncle Antonio, and Dad undertook a series of preparations. In my own household I assisted my father in gathering everything he needed except for food. Mom took care of that. The ultimate aim was to meet the rest of the cowboys at La Laguna Número Dos, situated several miles east of Cabezón Peak in the Ojo del Espíritu Santo Land Grant, called a *merced*.

This grant encompassed part of the grazing area ranchers leased from the government west of San Ysidro; it wasn't far from the highway leading to Cuba (formerly Highway 44; today, 550).

The list of items required of all *vaqueros* for a roundup, most of which they owned, seemed endless but necessary. Here's an inventory of what accompanied my father.

bedroll (blankets, tarp, and small bedsheet)
bridle
chaps of steer hide for protection against thick brush or cacti
cigarette rolling papers (OCB brand)
cowboy boots and socks
cowboy hat, pants, and shirts
horse hobble with cuffs and swivel
jacket and raincoat
kerchief or bandanna
leather gloves
leather saddlebags
pocketknife and sharpening stone
rope and quirt
saddle and cinch
saddle blanket (Navajo wool)
scabbard or other covering for a saddle gun
smoking and/or chewing tobacco
toe guards (*tapaderas*)
toiletries (razor, shaving brush, soap, comb, towels, and baking soda for
    cleaning teeth)
working spurs

Since I was to ride with Grandpa Lolo in his wagon to La Laguna Número Dos, I helped him load his equipment the night before our departure. Grandma Lale, who was at the ranch this time of the year for the hoeing season and not in Albuquerque, would be the one packing his provisions and other items necessary for preparing meals. Grandpa Lolo was a very good *cocinero*. He would be cooking for himself, my dad and me, and my uncle and his two sons. His setup at the campsite was not exactly a chuck wagon per se; it was more of a ragtag arrangement, but efficient and practical nonetheless.

Beyond Grandpa Lolo's personal effects, the foodstuff and other items that he would need at camp are on the following lists; they came from all three families.

Foodstuff

baking powder (*espauda*)
beef jerky
blue corn flour (for atole and chaquegüe)
canned goods (i.e., sardines, Vienna sausages, potted meat)
dried fruit (e.g., apples, pumpkins)
dried pinto beans
dry onions
eggs
home-canned foods (e.g., corned beef, corn, peas)
homemade biscuits (galletas)
jelly (jalea)
lard (*manteca*)
oatmeal
potatoes
raisins
rice
roasted coffee beans and grinder
salt
salt pork
sugar
white corn flour

Equipment and Accessories

ax
axle grease
bedding (bedsheets, blankets, and pillows)
branding irons
cast iron cauldron
cast iron skillet (comal)

cotton or wool
dehorning clippers and paste
dish rags
dish towels
dishes (tin plates, bowls, and cups)
firewood and kitchen matches
grinding stone (metate)
hand and face towels
horseshoeing items (pliers, nails)
kerosene lantern (*farol*) and oil
kitchen utensils (carving knives, forks, rolling pin, and spoons)
mentholatem
mercurochrome
needle and thread
pots, pans, and skillets
Rosebud salve
rubbing alcohol
shovel
tent, poles, and pegs/stakes
tin dipper
two small wooden barrels of drinking water
wooden mallet or hammer

Mom spent all day Sunday baking galletas, bizcochitos, and pastelitos—fruit pies made with dried peaches, apricots, or tasajos (strips of dried pumpkin)—which she put in separate tin cans for freshness. The cans' interior wax coating also kept the pastry from developing mold. These were little tricks people learned in the hinterland. The rest of the food that Mom packed was fairly standard and useful for roundups.

Dad was home for a few days from his job with the rinches, forest rangers, to join the rest of the ranchers in the roundup. It was now Monday morning, and Grandpa Lolo, Dad, Uncle Antonio, Cousins J. and G., and I met at my grandparents' house before departing for La Laguna Número Dos. I knew I would be riding with Grandpa and his dog Ligero in the horse wagon. My horse Bayito and Grandpa's Colorao, both saddled, were to ride behind us, fastened to the back of the wagon that he and I would ride. The rest of the group was to go ahead of Grandpa and me, rounding up cattle along the way to take to our campsite.

Mom, Grandma Lale, and Aunt Taida were present to bid us good-bye. Before climbing on the wagon, Mom hugged and blessed me. "*Con muncho cuidadito, hijito.* Be very, very careful, my son" were her last words, which hardly registered in my anticipation of hitting the road. The rest of the farewells were rather perfunctory, especially between grown-ups. They simply said, "Adiós," and we were on our way.

La Laguna Número Dos was six to eight miles away; it took Grandpa and me about an hour and a half to get there. Traveling on a winding dirt road, we passed through La Cañada del Camino, where the ubiquitous prairie dog colonies were located, went by El Aguaje, and then stopped at El Ojo de Esquipula to water the horses. Thereafter we headed up toward El Bordo before beginning our descent toward our final destination. The entire trip was slow going, but not boring. Ligero kept barking at whatever moved. He was quite wary of rattlesnakes.

Grandpa Lolo was a quiet, gentle, and patient man, the perfect traveling companion. He took the time to explain things to his grandsons regarding the region's topography, which he was acquainted with like the palm of his hand, having lived there since the age of about eight. You could learn a lot from him, if you listened to his soft-spoken words.

Along the way, besides picking up dry firewood close to the road, he told me a story or two on one subject or another. Some were based on his personal experiences; others involved friends or acquaintances of his. Needless to say, this was a good way to while the time away as his team of horses, Camastrón and Magué, trotted along at a slow but steady pace.

"Would you like some gum?" he asked out of blue as the wagon wheels churned the dirt on the road we were climbing toward El Bordo.

"Sure!" I responded, all excited, whereupon he pulled on the reins and stopped the horses in their tracks. He pushed the brake lever forward, tied the reins to it, and climbed down from the wagon. "Come, jump!"

Feeling a bit curious, if not confused, I walked behind him as he headed for a pine tree. There he found a big glob of pine sap, *trementina*. He reached and tore off a chunk of the sticky stuff. "Here! This is your chewing gum." I stuck it in my mouth and began chewing. It was hardly gum like what we bought from time to time at our local general store, but I was not going to look a gift horse in the mouth. After a few minutes of chewing, my jaws were ready to protest.

When we reached El Bordo, the highest point on our journey, I knew we were not far from La Laguna Número Dos, perhaps a couple of miles at best. Grandpa stopped the horses. He removed his hat, placed it on his kneecap, and let out a deep sigh. "Hijito, those are the Jémez Mountains in the distance," he signaled, pointing to the east. "Aren't they beautiful? *La belleza y la hermosura poco duran.* Beauty is here today and gone tomorrow" unless we take care of our terrain, he said. I just listened. Grandpa was known for his words of wisdom and concern for the environment and animals.

As we approached La Laguna Número Dos, where we would set up camp, I saw at least two or three cowboys driving small herds of cattle not far from the road. They removed their hats and waved them at Grandpa Lolo. He waved back. Not much more activity was evident, but that would change in the ensuing days. We came to the gate that led to the corral and the lagoon; it was locked.

"*¡Ándale!* Shake a leg. Unlock the gate," uttered my grandpa, at which point I stood up, planted my left foot on the front wheel, and took aim for the ground. I hit it pretty hard as I tumbled over. "Are you okay?" he asked. I nodded my head yes and proceeded to open the gate. "Just follow me" were the next words that came out of Grandpa's mouth. He went around to the east end of the man-made lagoon and stopped. He climbed down from the wagon. Ligero followed us. "This is where we're going to set up camp, but first unsaddle your horse and go water him. I'll do the same with Colorao."

I untied Bayito from the wagon and took off the saddle. Lather had already formed around the edges of the saddle blanket. The sun was beaming almost directly above us. It was practically noon and getting hot. I walked behind Grandpa as he led Colorao to the shallow edge of the lagoon, where the horses began drinking water. Bayito waded in until the water was up to his belly. I held onto the rope that I had draped around his neck. I had only been to La Laguna Número Dos once, but that was last year. I was now eight years old. The lagoon looked huge to me, filled with lots of water. There were a few heads of cattle to the east end, where the water was a little deeper, but not enough for them to get stuck in the mud. Cows purportedly are not very bright, or they have a tendency to be careless. Several times we'd had to rescue one or two of them from the muddy waters of the Río Puerco near my home.

When Colorao and Bayito finished drinking water, we hobbled them and turned them loose. There was a fence that encircled the lagoon and extended to the west for about a quarter of a mile; the horses couldn't wander off too far. I then helped Grandpa with Camastrón and Magué. They drank water before he turned them loose to pasture. He didn't hobble them. They weren't apt to wander off like the other horses.

"Are you very hungry?" Grandpa Lolo asked. "*Ya se comen las grandes a las chiquitas, ¿eh?*" he added with smile. I knew what he meant, for I had heard my father use the same expression, which in essence meant to be famished. "If you're hungry, we could eat a little before setting up camp. What do you think?" I sure was glad he asked. I was starved. Because of the excitement of getting on the road, I hadn't eaten very much for breakfast.

He unpacked a can of sardines, a can of potted meat, and a few biscuits. In his bedroll he always carried a small piece of tarp, which he spread on the ground beneath the wagon to use as a tablecloth. Eating underneath the wagon would also protect us from the shimmering sun. First he opened the potted meat with the key that came attached to the can. He tried to do the same thing with the sardines, but the key bent and almost broke, whereupon he got out his pocketknife and cut around the lid and pried it open. The lunch was simple but fun.

"Do you want some onion to go with the sardines?" Grandpa asked as he put a sardine and a slice of onion inside a biscuit. I had eaten such a combination when Dad and I came to the monte nearby for firewood. I liked onions. Boy, did they change the flavor and texture of the sardines! No wonder Grandpa consumed his sardines with gusto. I had heard my father employ the expression "*A la boca pan y cebolla y no a la olla.* Bread and onion should go directly in the mouth and not in the pan."

After we finished eating, Grandpa suggested we take a little snooze, a siestecita, under the wagon before pitching the tent. "And watch out for the rattlesnakes!" he cautioned with a slight grin. This was a constant worry around ranchers and farmers. "The hot days draw them out from their winter hibernation. They are cold-blooded, you know. That's why they seek warmth," Grandpa added.

I was petrified at the sound of their *cascabeles*, rattles. My hearing was pretty good, but the rattlesnakes made noise only if you startled them. That's when they coiled up and hissed. But the thought of having one slither across my neck while I slept was very unsettling.

Grandpa must have detected my discomfort. "But listen. Don't worry about the rattlesnakes. Here's what you do to protect yourself against them. Draw a circle around you, make the sign of the cross, and they won't bother you." This was something Dad had learned from him. I drew a circle. I noticed that he didn't draw a circle for himself.

"What about you, Grandpa? Why don't you draw a circle? Aren't you afraid of rattlesnakes?"

"Nah," he responded in a casual sort of way. "Snakes don't bother a viejo *bombo*, an old goat like me. They just go after little boys like you. Now, say no more; it's time for a siestecita."

His last words were hardly a consolation, but I knew he was kidding. Drawing a circle related more to catching witches in flight at night out in the open range, a story I had heard from my father.

I looked over at Grandpa, but he already had his hands interlocked behind his neck and his hat over his face. I curled up inside my circle and fell asleep. I woke up a few minutes later to the whoopin' and hollerin' of a couple of cowboys who were approaching the lagoon with a herd of cattle. Cowboys and cow handlers always made noises while driving cattle. *Epa* and *jeya* were common words. Whistling punctuated their verbal chorus.

Special Spanish Roundup Lingo

Amarrarle las patas (to tie its legs; referring to a calf)

Arrastrando un becerro terco en la tierra (pulling a stubborn calf along the ground)

Arrímalo a la lumbre (get him—the calf—close to the branding fire)

Atajar (to head off)

Bramar (to low; referring to cows)

Capar (to castrate)

Comerse la tierra (to eat the dirt; said of a horse that was fast)

Cortar los becerros (to cut off the calves, to separate them from their mothers)

Dale güelta al cabestro (twirl the rope; to wrap the rope around the saddle horn)

Desátalo (untie it; untie him; said of a calf)

Descornar (to clip the horns; to dehorn)

¡Epa! (Heads up! That's enough!)

Encerrar el ganao pa la noche (to bed the herd down for the night)

¡Jeya!, ¡Jeya! (Get a move on! Move it!)

Lázale las manos (rope it by the forelegs; referring to a calf)

Lázalo de las patas (rope it by the hind legs; referring to a calf)

Marcar (to brand)

Ponerle cabestro en el pescuezo (slipping a rope around the neck; said of a horse)

Renegando (cussing; saying bad words)

Renegón (said of a man who has a foul mouth)

Señalar (to earmark)

Tumbar (to knock or throw down)

Un fregal de vacas (a whole bunch of cows)

Un penco (a runt or a dogie, disowned by its mother)

Una palabrota (a big, bad word)

Una vaca brava (a mean cow)

Una vaca preñada (a pregnant cow)

Grandpa already had the tent and other accessories spread out on the ground when I got up from my nap. He was ready to pitch the tent, a luxury among some of the cowboys; most of them just slept on the ground in the open air. It was their way of roughing it. Grandpa drove the first two wooden corner stakes into the dirt and hooked the tent's metal rings to them. He did the same thing on both sides of the tent. Next he fetched a long pole and stuck it through a hole at the middle of the tent. With a big huff and puff from him, up went a wobbly tent. I held onto the pole while he dug a deep hole to secure it in; otherwise a gust of wind could easily topple the tent. Now we had to secure the last two corners of the tent. As a precaution against rain, Grandpa also dug a trench all around the tent. In this way the water would not get inside.

All along Grandpa Lolo cautioned me to watch him carefully. He was giving me a lesson on how to pitch a large tent. I had put up a small one for myself during the fall roundup of the previous year, but the spring gathering was much more elaborate, educational, and picturesque in comparison. The huge tent—at least it seemed so to me—is where Grandpa, Dad, Uncle Antonio, and I would be sleeping for the next few nights. We would be protected from the elements. Thanks to Grandpa, we were able to enjoy a comfort not afforded other cowboys. Cousins G. and J. slept in their small tents adjacent to ours.

From the covered wagon, Grandpa and I unloaded our bedding, which we put in the tent, plus a folding cot that he had brought along for himself. We also put the nonperishable food items inside so they'd be well protected from the sun and rain, if it came. From foodstuff to pots and pans, Grandpa knew where everything was for easy access. The frying pan that he used to scramble eggs and the jumate, dipper, for drinking water hung from the center pole inside, along with the farol, kerosene lantern.

Late that afternoon he and I walked over to the corral, which would soon be the hub of activity. From roping, branding, and dehorning to earmarking, the corral was the place to be. We took the branding irons and the dehorning clippers and hung them on the wooden fence. The cowboys would use them later.

Meanwhile, Dad, my uncle, and my cousins were still out on the range. They would be headed for our campsite by sunset. By that time Grandpa would have a warm meal fixed for all of us. Over the years, in Grandma's absence, he fended for himself; as a result, he had become a very good cook.

I carried the cast iron cauldron, the so-called Dutch oven, from the wagon and helped Grandpa Lolo peel potatoes for one of his delicious stews, which every cowboy who was acquainted with his cooking longed to taste. Other ingredients for the stew included home-canned beef (in a large mason jar) from the latest steer that had been butchered, Mom's home-canned peas, and dry onions. He also put in a couple of red chile pods for added flavor. He filled the cauldron almost to the brim with water. Everything was ready for the fire pit that Grandpa had built and into which he had placed a few rocks. He set the cauldron on top and huddled it with firewood that we had gathered on our trip here. The wood would

Nasario P. García, the author's father. Photo by Isabel A. Rodríguez, 1980.

last for a while, but he and I went scavenging for more in the nearby arroyos and wooded area to replenish the woodpile.

By the time we returned to the campsite, Dad and the rest of the gang were waiting for us. They had driven what cattle they found beyond the confines of the lagoon but well within the Ojo del Espíritu Santo Land Grant. Each one unsaddled and watered his horse, hobbled it, and set it to pasture for the night. I could tell by the looks on their faces that they were all dead beat from combing the open range for cattle. They were not in a very talkative mood, which was fine with me—and I'm sure with Grandpa, too—because he and I were tired as well.

Everyone grabbed a plate and utensils and filled his plate with stew. All of them plunked themselves on the ground to eat supper. Grandpa then passed the can of homemade biscuits around. The coffee had been brewing on top of the coals in a blue tin coffeepot dotted with white. He poured Dad and Uncle Antonio each a cup to accompany the meal. The rest of us drank water from the wooden barrels wrapped in burlap.

My first day of spring roundup on the open range was history. It had been tiring, but I had learned a lot from my grandpa. Except for the cows mooing in the corral, a stone's throw from our campsite, and the coyotes howling in the distance, the night was peaceful and restful. The oil lantern, which Grandpa had strung from the tent's center pole to provide us with light, flickered as if to lull me to sleep. I thought of Mom as I rested in my makeshift bed and said my bedtime prayer.

The next morning I got up as soon as I heard Grandpa Lolo stirring about. He was the first one up. Everybody else got up soon thereafter. By that time Grandpa had a large coffeepot going on top of the coals and a Hills Bros. coffee can full of water heating for the oatmeal. He placed a washbasin half-full of water at the back end of the horse wagon for us to wash our hands and faces. For Grandpa Lolo, a splash of cold water on his face came first. He truly believed that washing your face with cold water in the morning added extra years to your life. To this day I still wash my face with cold water as a matter of habit, not superstition. Next he scrubbed his hands with P&G soap and water.

Breakfast was nothing fancy, but food plentiful. Besides coffee and oatmeal, Grandpa whipped up a batch of scrambled eggs. He also sliced and

fried two strips of salt pork bacon for each one of us. A special treat from
him was when he warmed up the biscuits on a comal that Grandma Lale
had packed. He didn't do this very often, as it turned out, but this was the
first morning on the range. Maybe that had something to do with his kind
gesture.

The day ahead of us was packed with excitement, as it turned out. Dad,
Uncle Antonio, and Cousins J. and G. had gathered enough cattle and
their offspring the day before to earmark and brand, provided the calves
were old enough. A month-old calf was deemed too young for branding;
therefore, calves that age were only earmarked in this roundup but would
be branded later in the summer, when cowboys usually traveled in pairs
combing the range for newborns. A cowboy always carried a branding
iron with him for that purpose.

That first morning, I found Bayito not far from our campsite. I saddled
him and was ready to join Grandpa Lolo and the rest of the group at the
corral, a scant couple of hundred feet from our tent. That's where the excitement was to take place. Many of the cattle within the fenced area
around the lagoon were herded into the corral. This included not only the
Garcías' cows but also those of the cowboys Grandpa and I had seen the
day before on the way to our camping site. The corral was practically full
of cows and calves; the latter were two or three months old. The cows and
calves were mooing and mooing as though they knew something was
amiss.

Buried deep in the ground in the middle of the corral was a *bramadero*,
hitching post. Toward one corner of the corral a fire was popping and
crackling. Several branding irons immersed in the fire had turned glowing
red. Suddenly Grandpa, the elder statesman among the group, gave the
word: "*¡Güeno, muchachos, listos!* Okay, boys, ready!" It reminded me of
when he took charge of the matanza at home.

As soon as he gave the word, Cousins G. and J. started twirling their
ropes over their heads. They had been to a spring roundup before; consequently, they knew the routine. Both of them worked as a team in cutting
the first calf to make sure that the calves belonged to the right mother, one
bearing one of the three García brands. Doing so was of overriding importance. The three brands in question were 99 (Grandpa Lolo's), 3 (Uncle

Antonio's, with a quarter moon above the 3), and Dad's NP (also with a quarter moon above the letters).

Cousin G., the older cousin, immediately roped a calf by his forelegs and dragged him close to the branding fire. There Dad, who was young and strong, picked up the calf by the neck and the pubic region and tossed him to the ground. He put his right knee to the neck and held him down while Cousin G.'s horse was rearing to keep the rope tight and the calf from getting up. The calf was too young to brand, but my uncle earmarked him; it was his.

My Grandpa, meanwhile, castrated the calf and handed Cousin J. the *huevitos*, testicles (nowadays restaurants call them Rocky Mountain oysters). He put them on top of a fence post, where they would accumulate throughout the morning until there were enough to roast over the hot coals. The huevitos, a delicacy indeed, were our midmorning merienda, but we had to keep an eye on the birds, who would peck at them, and the hawks, who would whisk them away.

Thereafter came a heifer or steer that was bigger than a calf. Cousin J. roped a steer's hind legs and Cousin G. lassoed it around the neck. Each pulled in opposite directions until the steer was on its side on the ground. Uncle Antonio, wearing leather gloves, grabbed a hot branding iron and affixed Grandpa Lolo's brand on the left hip. He was careful not to burn through the hide and into the flesh. The smell of hair was unmistakable. As soon as my uncle finished, he brushed the burned hair away, and Grandpa's brand stood out. The number 99, which he also used on his horses, was one of the oldest brands in the Río Puerco Valley. The brand had been his since the end of the nineteenth century.

After seeing my cousins doing all the roping, I knew I could do it, too, because all of us at one time or another had roped calves out in the open range just for fun. I itched to show off my own skills with the rope when, without warning, I heard Dad yell at me. "¡*Ándale*! ¡*Métete*! Come now! Get in there!" he hollered in a forceful voice amid all the cow mooing and the hue and cry taking place.

I knew Bayito's capabilities and weaknesses, but roping is something he and I had practiced numerous times. My horse was aware of what to do and how. I unfurled my rope from around the saddle horn and twirled it over my head several times. "That one!" my uncle Antonio shouted, and I promptly roped a small calf by its hind legs on my first throw and pulled him close to the branding fire. The mother was having fits—lowing and lowering her head as though she were ready to charge any moment. Dad picked up the calf, swung him to the ground, and tied one front leg and the two hind ones together while keeping an eye on the fuming mother. My uncle Antonio took out his pocketknife and in a jiffy earmarked the young calf. This one also belonged to him.

You could tell that Dad and Uncle Antonio had worked as a team many times. Everything they did was in one swift motion. Dad untied the calf's legs and patted him on the ribcage, and up he went while I retrieved my rope. I had passed the test and was now geared up for the next heifer or steer.

No sooner had I finished than Cousin G. lassoed a *torito*, a small bull, like the one he was bucked off of one Sunday morning after Mass. The steer was several months old and proved to be strong as all get out. After Cousin G. roped his hind legs and Cousin J., its forelegs, my father put his right knee on his neck and I sat on his stomach while my uncle branded him. Afterward, Grandpa Lolo castrated and dehorned him; both procedures were specialties of his. Earmarking was not necessary; that had been done a couple of months earlier, in the early spring.

Castrating, branding, earmarking, and dehorning were repeated throughout the morning. By noon we had tended to more than twenty calves, notwithstanding the startled and oftentimes angry mother cows. With rare exception, most of the offspring in the first round of activity belonged to the Garcías. Our cattle, locked in the corral the previous day, were sort of the vanguard for the present lockup, but the livestock population was to change come evening.

Cows belonging to the Luceros, Valdezes, Lovatos, Tachías, Montaños, and Gonzaleses were destined to alter the bovine mosaic for the next day as well as the overall cattle roundup. Their cattle had begun to trickle in, and by late afternoon the pace picked up because of darkening skies. One would have thought that rounding up cattle and locking them in one corral was an invitation to mayhem, but like magicians with their wands—and like the mother cows—the cowboys knew which offspring belonged to whom. The roundup was hardly chaotic. Everybody pitched in; camaraderie among ranchers was marvelous. Everybody referred to one another as primo (see chapter 1). "Primo" here and "primo" there was quite evident and an expression of friendship. The concept of primorazgo came alive, even though most cowboys were not cousins, per se, or even blood related at all.

By evening, as the sun faded away behind the imposing Cabezón Peak, spring showers commenced to dampen the parched brown ground. The cowboys from Cabezón and San Luis scurried around setting up camp. Most of them pitched their one-man tents in a circle, within an ear's shot of one another, with a place in the middle for building a fire. Their tents were not far from Grandpa Lolo's large one. Following supper, some of them, if not too exhausted from a rough day on the range, mingled with friends or compadres from other ranches.

Twice ranchers ambled to Grandpa's campsite. This gave me an opportunity to sit around the bonfire to watch and listen. They rolled and smoked their cigarettes and talked. The chatter focused on an array of topics. Most of the talk dealt with personal experiences, to wit, breaking a bronco, coming face to face with a bobcat, brushes with death in the roaring waters of the Río Puerco, or quibbles with ruthless Bureau of Land Management (BLM) officials over grazing rights. Listening to grown men was rather educational for a young boy like me.

Once in a while the cowboys got off on a tangent and talked about things like witches and the supernatural, much to my delight. This is when I heard Dad talk about the woman in the dead of night who could walk on water, like the lagoon next to our campsite. I had heard his story before at home; it still commanded an aura of spookiness. Grandpa also chimed in with his tales related to witches and clues on how to wrest them from the sky while they were in flight, no doubt headed to inflict harm on some hapless victim.

Other wranglers had their own stories to tell, like those from San Luis who spoke of the enchanted mesa near their village. The telling of tales of all types was one aspect of the roundup that I thoroughly enjoyed. Much to my regret, exchanging stories at these rendezvous was rare, since cowboys by and large were tired by the end of the day. Cattle roundups were not something easily done. They demanded hard work.

The fire had begun to flicker unsteadily, and one by one the cowboys got up and left to retire for the night. I did the same thing, but my cousins remained. I was tired from the second straight day of steady work and excitement. As I lay quietly on my makeshift bed on the ground, trying to assimilate everything that had transpired, the lowing of cattle in the corral got uncharacteristically louder. Grandpa came inside the tent about that time.

"Why are the cows in such a mooing mood?"

"It's the weather, hijito. I think it's going to rain tonight. The cows sense that. It's like the story about the little donkey that frolicked about one evening, a sure sign that it was going to rain. And it did!"

Off in the distance, I could hear the coyotes howling for the second straight night. It was strange because there was no moon, but Grandpa assured me that they were reacting to the elements as well, in particular the lightning that occasionally traversed the dark blue skies. He gave me a couple of pieces of wool to put in my ears—something he used himself for earplugs—and I dozed off.

The thunderbolts cracked the skies with such fury that I woke up in the middle of the night despite the wool. They startled me to death. The raindrops loudly pelting the tent sounded like huge balls of hail. The only thing I could think of was to invoke Mom's words: "*¡Santísimo sacramento del altar!* Holy Mother of God!" The thunder subsided, and I finally fell back asleep until morning, when I heard Grandpa and Dad milling around. My uncle and cousins were still dead to the world, and, as best as I could ascertain, they had slept through the night without waking up. But now the sun had begun to peek over the Jémez Mountains. It was a cheerful beginning of a new dawn in the countryside, although trudging through the morning's mud was hardly a picnic.

Thank goodness Grandpa had dug small trenches around the tent for the water to drain into. Otherwise, it would have run right through our tent, possibly even toppling and ruining everything.

After breakfast Grandpa heated water in a pan to wash the dishes. I helped him while everyone else went after the horses, including mine. When they returned, I saddled Bayito and all of us, except Grandpa Lolo, left to round up more of the family cattle. Because of his advancing years (he was in his seventies), he didn't participate very much in gathering cattle; rather, he stayed back to tidy up the campsite and to help the other cowboys from Cabezón and San Luis who were branding and earmarking in the corral.

I was anxious to join Dad and the rest of the entourage. I packed in my saddlebags a modest lunch of biscuits, potted meat, jerky, some dried fruit, and a small fruit pie that Mom had baked. I also carried a canteen full of drinking water. Our destination today, according to Dad, was the eastern part of El Ojo del Espíritu Santo Land Grant. The idea was to reach an area called El Arroyo Piedra Parada (today this region belongs to Zía Pueblo), reconnoitering along the way for cattle belonging to us and to the other fellow cowboys from San Luis and Cabezón. We would round up the cattle and drive them back to the campsite.

At the periphery of the land grant, landscape that was new to me, there were several *ojitos de agua*, springs of water. But between La Laguna del Número Dos and Piedra Parada, there was water for livestock only after it rained. Perhaps that explained why there were so few cattle in that area. A string of small arroyos that emptied into a quasi valley formed watering holes following rainstorms.

After we watered our horses, we found a nice shady tree under which to eat lunch. I asked my father in between bites if he was acquainted with that territory. My question jogged his memories. "Look. I traveled this road with your grandpa on many occasions on the way to Albuquerque via Corrales to buy family provisions to bring back to the ranch. That's before I married your mother. I was still a boy, a little older than you. Your grandpa had been a *fletero*, freight hauler, for don Ricardo Heller from Cabezón, who had large flocks of sheep. That's when your grandpa was a young man; he hauled wagons full of wool to Albuquerque. In fact, thanks to don Ricardo and the partido system, your grandpa became an independent rancher. So you see, this area is not strange to me, but it is not a favorite of mine because it is far removed from the Cabezón and Ojo del Padre regions. Those are much more familiar to me."

I listened attentively but didn't ask any more questions. I had enough information to absorb, in addition to enjoying the surroundings, which I found interesting because they were different from the Río Puerco Valley.

To me the multicolored shapes in the landscape were perhaps more picturesque than the sandstone and lava-type formations close to Cabezón Peak
and Los Cerros Cuates to the south, near our family ranch.

On our way back to camp, my dad, uncle, and cousins ran across a number of cattle, but they all had strange and unrecognizable brands. With the
exception of the ones we saw earlier in the day, we found very few cows and
their calves with familiar or family brands that we could round up. There
were probably no more than fifteen cows, with half as many calves, which
we earmarked. This was something we would not have to perform once we
got back to our campsite.

The return trip was slow and uneventful, except for one thing: I spotted
a long skeleton on the ground that was virtually intact. The bones looked
like kitchen matchsticks glued together. I halted my horse. My father wondered what I was looking at. He quickly spurred his horse and went back to
where I had stopped.

"What's wrong?" he asked with a worried look on his face as I stared at
the ground. "¡Híjole!" he remarked. "That was a big one."

"A big what, Dad?"

"A rattlesnake. It must have died of old age right on the spot. That's why
it's still in one piece." I had never seen any rattler that big. It had to measure
about six feet long.

I thought my excitement for the day was over, but as we approached the
camping area I saw from the distance a cloud of dust. At first it looked like
a dust devil or whirlwind kicking up dirt, a typical sight in the open range.
The *llano* was known for this kind of hurly-burly. But the closer we got,
the more I was able to discern what was going on. I saw two huge bulls
fighting and raising clouds of dust. Right away Uncle Antonio cautioned
us to keep our distance, lest the bulls charge one of us instead of each
other. Time and again they lowered their heads, kicked back dirt with
their front legs, and charged each other. The loud cracking sound of horns
as they smacked together was the most frightening thing I had ever heard.
At times they would interlock horns as though they were never going to
get untangled. What was equally terrifying was the agonizing groan each
one made every time they collided.

The bulls, according to my father, weighed way over one thousand pounds each. Surely he knew, since one of the bulls, as it turned out, belonged to my grandpa; the other one belonged to Eduardo Valdez, from our placita. It goes without saying that the more I observed, the more fascinated I became with the two brawny creatures. After fighting for about twenty to thirty minutes, their tongues sticking out from exhaustion and bathed in dirt, they walked away and went their separate ways. It was a classic draw between two very powerful animals. But no one ever told Grandpa that his bull had been in a fierce fight. What would have been the point?

Grandpa Lolo had been cooking pinto beans all afternoon and had added home-canned beef for flavor. What's more, he had prepared red chile with jerky that he had pounded gently and softened with a hammer on top of the metate that he brought with him. One of the cowboys, a close friend of his from Santa Clara, north of our placita, had shot a couple of cottontail rabbits with his .22 rifle. He gave one to Grandpa to fry. That was an added treat for my cousins and my uncle, but not so much for Dad and me, since I raised *conejitos*, and rabbit meat is something Mom shared often with Grandpa back home. He had also fixed rice pudding with raisins for dessert.

After we enjoyed Grandpa Lolo's delicious supper, Cousins G. and J. and I helped him with the dishes. Dad and Uncle Antonio sat on the ground, with their backs up against the wagon wheels, smoking their rolled cigarettes. My uncle smoked canned Prince Albert tobacco, while my dad enjoyed Golden Grain, which he carried in a little sack in his shirt pocket.

As soon as we finished the dishes, I hit the sack. I was dog tired. I slept like a log in spite of occasionally dreaming about the rattler's skeleton and the fighting bulls. In fact, I didn't even hear Grandpa the next morning until he banged a *cucharón*, large spoon, on a frying pan as a signal for us to shake a leg.

"*¡Arriba, arriba! ¡El que no se levante se le encoje la barriga!* Up, up! If you don't rise your belly's going to shrink!" shouted my grandpa. During a brief discussion at breakfast, speculation was that today could well be our last day on the range. Most of the cattle were accounted for, although quite a few calves needed to be branded and earmarked. They had spent the night in the corral. The routine, as in previous days, did not vary much, except that I got acquainted with new brands that were unfamiliar to me. By noon or so the corral was practically empty, and the word got around that no more cattle or calves would be making their way to the corral.

Once the corral was deserted, all the cowboys congregated around the hitching post to exchange good-byes before returning to their homes. There were only a couple of old-timers, my Grandpa being one of them. The other gentleman was don Bernardino, a good friend of his from Cabezón. They proposed a *brindis*, toast, a kind of tradition in honor of a successful roundup. Each one grabbed a bottle of *aguardiente*, whiskey, from his knapsack, took a sip, and passed it around. There was all kinds of chatter until the "fiery water" made the rounds.

My cousins and I just watched. Some day, when we were old enough, we would be doing the same thing. The cowboys, including my dad and uncle, not to mention my Grandpa, were a happy bunch and in high spirits. By now everybody was ready to head home.

The cowboys would all meet again in late October or early November. That's when they would round up the cattle and drive them to a huge corral across from where the CCC camp had been located long ago at El Rito de Semilla, near the highway south of Cuba, where Dad's sleeping quarters were once located. It was there that buyers came hauling their trailers behind huge semi trucks from Albuquerque and elsewhere. Cowboys negotiated the best price on the hoof and sold their precious stock. The occasion was both happy and sad, because ranchers left for home afterward with money in their pockets, but accompanied only by their steeds.

After Grandpa Lolo and the rest of us snacked for lunch on what little food was left, we helped him collapse the tent and break camp. Dismantling things was a lot easier than putting them up, not to mention the fact that there were more helping hands now than when Grandpa and I had set up camp. The last chore was to cover the glowing coals with dirt before leaving. I got a shovel and tossed dirt on the smoldering coals to make sure they did not reignite and cause a fire. Grandpa asked me to fetch two or three buckets of water from the lagoon to douse the coals.

As I did this, it dawned on me that the roundup had ended. For a fleeting moment I reflected on the events of the past few days. They had truly been enjoyable and a learning experience. Through the sum total of things that happened, especially during the roping and branding in the corral, when tensions ran high, I even learned some *palabrotas*. These were bad words and expressions that cowboys used on the range. Over time I was able to absorb most of them. Here is a list of the ones I can recall.

¡A la chingada! (Fuck it! To hell with it!)

Cuidao que no te dé un chingazo. (Don't let it [the calf] give you a good whack.)

Es una chinga. (It's a pain in the ass.)

Esa vaca cabrona. (That damn cow.)

Esa vaca tiene el culo caliente. (That cow's horny.)

Ese pinche toro. (That damn bull.)

Ese toro no vale madre. (That bull isn't worth shit.)*

Hijo de su madre que lo parió. (Son of a whore.)

Le dio una patada en la mera rosca. (He got kicked right smack in the ass.)

No andes ahi con el pedo atorao. (Get the lead out of your ass.)

No seigas pendejo. (Don't be an idiot.)

No vale una mierda. (It isn't worth a pile of shit.)

No vale verga. (It isn't worth a fuck.)

No vales maceta pa nada. (You aren't worth a shit for anything.)

Sunavabiche. (Son of a bitch.)

Ya la jodites. (You've fucked it all up.)

¡Ya metió la pata pal carajo! (He fucked up!)

Ya se lo llevó la chingada. (He's gone all to hell.)

Ya se zurró en los calzones. (He's crapped in his pants.)

Cowboys, including my uncle and father, were not stuffy individuals, and what better testimony than hearing them cuss (*renegar*)? Using cuss-words was a way of life and constituted an integral part of the wrangler's personality. The colorful and at times earthy words and expressions came naturally. This was more than ever true in the corral during branding and dehorning. The use of bad language was not intended to be crude or to show the cowboy's bravado; far from it. Nor did the cowboy refrain from using bad words in front of us children. It was all part of the growing up

---

* I knew, for example, a cowboy who swore his bull was gay.

and learning experience we were given among our elders during cattle roundups. Much of their profanity conjured up a laugh or two. I never knew a cowboy worth his salt who didn't curse.

With the roundup officially over and the cattle free to roam once again, everybody hit the road by midafternoon. There would be no siesta today. Dad, Uncle Antonio, and my cousins J. and G. rode ahead of me and Grandpa Lolo in case they spotted strays along the way. But this time, instead of accompanying him in the wagon, I rode Bayito alongside the horse wagon, while Ligero sat in the front seat with Grandpa. Riding Bayito seemed to quicken the pace. Even Grandpa's large team of Camastrón and Magué moved at a pretty good clip, as though they too were anxious to get home. There was no one more eager than me. I was dying to see Mom. I missed her. Moreover, I would have a lot to share with her after Dad returned to doing manual labor with the government. I would wait till then to share with Mom the scoop and particulars of the roundup.

We passed by El Ojo Esquipula, but this time we didn't stop to water the horses. Just as Grandpa and I began to descend the slope at El Aguaje, I could see my casita a short distance away. La Cañada del Camino, where even the prairie dogs seemed to welcome us with their wagging tails, began to unfold before my eyes.

Unable to wait any longer, I spurred my horse and galloped home, leaving Grandpa and Ligero behind. I quickly dismounted Bayito and dashed inside the kitchen. It was a touching moment, even more so as Mom hugged me. There were times when Mom didn't say much. Her facial expression and hand gestures conveyed her feelings. I was thrilled to see her—and she was happy to have me home again.

23

Fiestas, Food, and Fun

EL DÍA DE SAN Juan, Saint John's Day, on June 24 was indisputably the most popular holiday in Ojo del Padre. Local villagers, including those from neighboring villages, as well as visitors from Albuquerque and other communities along the Río Grande Valley, partook in the festivities.

Members of my immediate and extended families never failed to attend the local fiesta. It was a day of jubilation packed with an array of activities. Nobody, regardless of age, was spared from the merriment. By late evening, the village's dance hall, like the stars in the sky, trembled as residents danced to the scratchy music of local musicians whose instruments at times were hardly in tune. It was excitement at its best, but first things first.

"On to bed, on to bed, hijito!" my mother shouted the night before. "Tomorrow is Saint John's Day, and the priest is coming to celebrate Mass. You must get a good night's rest so you can rise early." She blessed me and tucked me under the bedsheet to discourage the mosquitoes from having their nightly feast at my expense. It was barely summer, but the nights were already hot, and the little devils loved to buzz around my ears, as if to remind me of their presence, much to my irritation. I hated them, but the tiny vampires enjoyed my flesh and sweet blood.

I loved Saint John's Day, but trying to sleep while looking forward to all the hustle and bustle, fending off the mosquitoes, and coping with the heat was not easy. Throughout the night I tossed and turned. The pillow, generally my friend, became my nemesis. I placed it under and over my head, under my tummy, and beneath my feet, but all this movement and

231

accompanying gyrations were to no avail. Finally, in the wee hours of the morning, I managed to steal a few winks of sleep, but I woke up groggy and dragging my feet. It would be a long, though joyous, day.

Mom didn't need to wake me up. I got up with the crowing of Grandpa's rooster, before Mom and Dad even awoke. As usual, I lit the fire in the wood-stove and got the coffee going before splashing cold water on my face from the bandeja, washbasin, that Mom kept in the kitchen on a small table.

Mom was just as excited about the day ahead as I was. Why, she didn't even wait for me to bring her coffee in bed! She hopped out of bed almost immediately after hearing my footsteps in the kitchen. She fixed a quick breakfast for Dad, because he rarely fasted. As for me, I had already made my First Holy Communion, so I, like Mom, would fast. We would not eat until we got home from church. Once in a while she tucked a tortilla in her purse for me to eat on the way home in case I was too hungry to wait.

While Dad went to hitch up the horses to the wagon, I helped Mom wash the dishes. I then got ready myself and helped my little brothers put on their clothes and tie their shoes while Mom dressed Julianita. Mom looked at her Westclox. We had to be at church by nine o'clock. She was almost dressed. As for Dad, it didn't take him long to put on his clothes before we took off for our placita.

Dad drove the horse wagon. This time, unlike previous occasions when I had ridden with my parents, Mom allowed me to ride my horse Bayito, as long as I followed behind them. This new experience would add to the thrills that were yet to come during the day. Bayito was my pride and joy when it came to showing off one's steed in public. Once we got to the village, we left the horses under the tall trees adjacent to the church, where they could enjoy the shade until Mass was over.

There was nothing extraordinary about the church services. Some people were already inside; others were still going in as the sacristan tolled the church bell (el solo diente) to warn potential latecomers that Mass was about to begin. When my parents and I walked in, the scene was quite predictable. Those families with reserved pews, namely, the mayordomos and old-timers, occupied the first few rows, followed by mothers and their children. Mom and Dad sat about ten to twelve rows from the altar.

Except for those men who were up in years, most of them leaned with one foot against the back wall of the church. The scuttlebutt was that they stood clutching their hats while pretending to be the veritable gentlemen when, in reality, it was to get a better glimpse of the young girls as they walked in. True or not, they were quite a sight. The men were also the first to exit the church once Mass had ended; thus they also got a good view of people greeting their compadres, comadres, and friends as they came outside.

Mass as a rule lasted around an hour, and today was no different. People who didn't go to confession on Saturday afternoon, particularly those who were not from the village proper, did so on Sunday morning prior to Mass. For most kids, myself included, the Mass was rather boring. The best part of the service was the singing of the choir.

But seeing the priest pass the collection plate up and down each pew (he was an eyewitness to each donation) was also kind of fun, because I got to catch sight of the money he collected. Since cash was scarce, that's the most money a few people saw at any given time. Some families donated a dollar, but the majority sprinkled a few coins on the plate, hardly ever more than a fifty-cent piece. In and of themselves, the coins' soft and loud sounds on the large white china plate told a story. On the other hand, most families fulfilled their charitable donations to the church through the yearly diezmos y primicias, tithes and first fruits from harvest season. Several times I saw Grandpa Lolo load one or two barrels of corn off the cob after harvest season to take to the priest on behalf of the García clan.

Once the Mass had ended, the priest led the procession to the outside of the church and waited in front to bid people good-bye as they came out. He generally commingled with parishioners until he ate lunch at the mayordomos' home, if they resided in the village. Otherwise, he was invited to somebody's home in or near the village before he returned to Jémez Springs or Cuba.

This was true as well of people who did not live in Ojo del Padre. Friends or relatives invited them to lunch, whereas those who came from nearby homes went home to eat or ate at friends' homes before returning to participate in the afternoon's festivities.

As for us, we went home. It was probably midmorning or so when we reached our house. Mom rushed inside and scurried around while she munched on a piece of tortilla or whatever else she could put her hands on. "People are coming to join us for lunch," she exclaimed. "Hijito, go bring some wood so we can light a fire. I have to make some fresh tortillas"— Mom thought you should never serve your guests warmed-over tortillas— "before the Montaños get here," as if she were racing against time. She wanted to make sure everything was picture-perfect when they arrived. In that regard, Mom never failed to be meticulous.

The Montaños, Fernando and Virginia, were good friends of my parents, so the luncheon was quite informal. Still, Mom wanted her guests to be treated right. When they arrived, the table in our tiny kitchen was set. The food was simmering on the stove, along with the ever-present coffeepot, and her fresh tortillas were wrapped in a dish towel to keep them warm.

Following the usual leisurely talk that preceded a good, hearty meal, the grown-ups sat down to eat first. Then the two Montaño kids, my siblings and I would take our turn at the table. Meanwhile, we played outside until Mom called us. What follows is a typical, albeit modest, menu for lunch at my house.

   agua (water)
   alverjones (fresh or home-canned peas)
   arroz con leche (rice pudding)
   bizcochitos (cinnamon and anise cookies)
   café (coffee)
   caldito (stew made with shredded beef jerky and fried or boiled
      potatoes)
   chile colorado (red chile sauce)
   frijoles (pinto beans)
   frijoles verdes (fresh string beans)
   galletas (biscuits)
   natillas (custard pudding)
   pollo (fried chicken) or *conejito* (rabbit)
   tortillas (made from corn flour)

By the time the adults finished eating and chatting, which seemed like an eternity, I was hungry, despite my having sneaked a bizcochito (with Mom's help, of course) to tide me over. There were times when Mom fed us kids first to keep us from prancing at the kitchen door or peering through the window. In that way, adults could enjoy a much more relaxing lunch. Once they finished, and we kids did too, it was time to return to the village for the afternoon's sporting activities.

Long ago, according to my parents and grandparents, the males, both young and old, had engaged in a variety of games and sporting events that now were no longer practiced. These included running footraces, chasing and catching (or trying to catch) greased pigs, climbing greased poles, and running gunnysack races.

From time to time the Navajos from Torreón, northwest of the village of Cabezón, came to my placita to challenge the young boys to a game of softball. These softball games I did see as a small boy. They were hilarious. First of all, there were no catcher's mitts; the players caught the ball bare-handed. To swing at the ball they used a makeshift bat cut from a thick branch of a cottonwood tree. As for the ball, the Navajos brought their own; it was crafted from a bundle of old rags covered with cowhide and stitched together with baling wire. Home runs were rare.

But without a shred of doubt the most popular sport was the *corrida del gallo*, a misnomer at best, since it was not a rooster race at all.[*] A better categorization—and more to the point—was to call the sport, *sacar el gallo*, "rooster pull."

A description of the sporting event using a live rooster—as I learned from Grandpa Lolo and my father, since this was before my time—could well vary from village to village, but in the main, the object of the game was identical. That is, the principal test of the *galleros* (riders) from two competing teams was to pluck a live rooster from a mound of dirt where he was buried with his head showing. Other times the live rooster was buried with his head in the ground and its legs sticking up.

As the first gallero took his turn and galloped by at full speed, he held onto the saddle horn with his right hand and leaned way down to his left. If he was lucky, like a hawk swooping downward, he grabbed the rooster

[*]   My story "Rooster Racing," in *Grandma's Santo on Its Head: Stories of Days Gone By in Hispanic Villages of New Mexico / El santo patas arriba de mi abuelita: Cuentos de días gloriosos en pueblitos hispanos de Nuevo México*, is about this sport.

by the neck or legs and took off for a marked spot designated by the gentleman in charge of the so-called race. As the gallero galloped, he tried to fend off his challengers from the opposing team. Often, by the time he reached the mark, there was nothing left of the poor fowl except its legs or neck. If the gallero crossed the mark without having a member of the opposing team wrest the rooster from him, then the gentleman in charge of the sport declared him and his fellow team members winners.

Though the sport was part of the fun of Saint John's Day, the losers were obligated to sponsor the evening's dance at the local dance hall. This meant either paying the musicians or paying the dance hall owner for use of the hall.

Once upon a time—again, according to Grandpa Lolo and my father— the gallero wore a white dress shirt, a red kerchief, Levi's (lonas), cowboy boots, and a hat. By the time the event was over, the riders were soaked in blood from whacking one another with the rooster. Because the women labored to wash the stained shirts on Mondays, combined with their revulsion at the cruelty heaped upon the poor fowl, a number of women began to protest. At some point their complaints were heeded, and the galleros discontinued using a rooster. But reference to the sport as a rooster pull remained even as the sport changed.

During my youth, a hodgepodge of shirt colors, including white ones, was more common. Empty beer bottles had also replaced the live rooster. Even so, the sport did not lose its glitter and appeal, although its popularity following World War II began to wane for several reasons. Chief among them was the exodus of families out of the Río Puerco Valley, above all to Albuquerque and its environs. The young men's refusal to return to village life after being discharged from the military, mostly the U.S. Army, further exacerbated the sport's demise. There being no heirs apparent to rooster racing, the once-popular event eventually petered out.

At the height of its glory, rooster racing reigned supreme among other events on Saint John's Day. By late afternoon, as the heat of the day dropped, people began to congregate under the large trees near the Virgen de Guadalupe Church, where Dad had tied his horses in the morning before Mass. The word had spread throughout the day that the corrida del gallo was to start around four o'clock.

This was a sport for the young men and the hardy. There were enough galleros from Ojo del Padre to challenge a group from Casa Salazar, a neighboring village to the south along the Río Puerco. But an older man, looked upon as the elder statesman in my placita, suggested that to kick off the event, it should be every man for himself instead of team competition.

Someone in Ojo del Padre had donated some empty beer bottles: an amber-colored one, a green one, and a clear bottle. Evidently they were bottles from a previous fiesta. To be sure, bottles were never in short supply; there were plenty of beer drinkers, above all the younger men who shunned hard liquor due to its debilitating effects.

In the corrida del gallo the rider worked in unison with his steed. Having a good horse that reacted to the horseman's moves was paramount. Those from Casa Salazar had the reputation of owning superb horses. They were fast and rarely lost a race against those from my village. In fact, they had a history of trouncing us.

But when it came to the rooster pull, they danced to a different tune (*otro gallo les cantaba*). True, they had fast horses, but the riders apparently lacked finesse and dexterity in plucking the hapless bird buried in the ground. During my time, when bottles were used instead of a living rooster, the story was no different.

One of the riders from Casa Salazar, in collusion with his fellow galleros, concocted a scheme to ensure victory. But unbeknownst to them, a young boy my age, whose name I don't recall, overheard their conversation about what they planned to do to win the corrida del gallo. Not predisposed to questioning the boy's veracity, the Guadalupe riders took his word to heart and kept an eye on the gallero from Casa Salazar.

Born—or cursed, some averred—with long legs and a short torso, the gallero rode a small mount, which gave him an added advantage over his competitors in plucking the beer bottle because he didn't have to reach as far. For an even further edge, he decided to lower the left stirrup, so that it practically touched the ground. That proved to be his downfall.

Unaware that the Guadalupanos were keeping an eye on him, someone loosened the cinch, so that when his turn came to gallop at full speed to scoop up the bottle, the saddle swiftly slid down to the horse's stomach. The *bottler* from Salazar, instead of aiming for the goal line, found himself bouncing upside-down underneath his galloping mount, looking at the horse's belly, no doubt a strange and different world. Everyone present, including his own countrymen, burst out laughing. In their eyes what had just happened was hilarious. Kids like me joined the chorus of laughter. The young gallero had learned a bitter lesson, and neither he nor his companions ever again tried to outwit their Guadalupano opponents by resorting to subterfuge. An elderly man was overhead to say, "*Lo que se aprende bien, no se olvida de un día pa otro.* What is learned well won't soon be forgotten."

The incident was hardly heroic, but it did bring an end to the day's activities, and earlier than anticipated, before the evening dance commenced and kicked into high gear. In the meantime, families like mine from nearby locales returned home. Others stayed to visit friends in the village until the dance started.

Most of the time Saint John's Day did not coincide with a Sunday; that's why there was no Mass. But even if the holiday didn't fall on a Sunday, the duties of feeding the farm animals and tending to household chores before engaging in the day's activities did not abate one iota. Everyone performed his or her normal tasks until two or three hours before getting ready for the *bolote*, shindig, as the locals called it.

From my perspective, waiting for the evening dance to begin created both excitement and anxiety among older women and young girls, like my two cousins, Catalina and Eremita, who were teenagers and interested in boys. Their mother had passed away when they were small, and now they were being reared by Grandpa Lolo and Grandma Lale. Sometimes before a dance they would skip supper and not even have a snack, and if they did eat, they gobbled their food down so they could start getting ready . . . but under the watchful eye of my grandmother, a disciplinarian in her own way. At times when my cousins were getting ready for a dance, I would drop by their home next door to witness what struck me as nothing short of bedlam.

The tug-of-war between teenage sisters scrambling for this dress or that one (no pants were allowed under any circumstances!) or that blouse and this pair of shoes constituted part of the mayhem. "Last time I had to wear the blouse with the blue pigeon on the back, while you wore the one with the red rose—and you got all the boys to dance with you. So for tonight's dance, I want the one with the red rose," one of the sisters argued over the blouses homemade from flour sacks.

"Fine, but I get to put on the black shoes with the gold buckles," the rivaling sister countered.

Both sisters got along well and hardly ever bickered except over apparel for the village dances. The words *"Me toca a mí"* (It's my turn) and *"No te toca a ti"* (It's not your turn) exchanged between them sounded more like musical tunes than bickering.

My grandma's intrusion and admonishments added to the mini-comedy. "And go easy on the face powder. And don't go put on too much rouge! I don't want you looking like you've got two red apples sticking out from your cheekbones."

"¡Güeno, güeno! All right, all right!" the sisters responded in unison. They bowed their heads submissively, a sign of respect, but they had smirks on their transformed faces. "And not too much of that black stuff around your eyes," Grandma added, referring to the *hollín*, soot from the potbelly stove or the stovepipe that women used for eye shadow.

This time I could hardly contain myself, and I burst out laughing because I knew what my grandma was talking about. I had seen females at dances, young girls in particular, with the black goo dripping down their faces during hot summer nights. "And what are you looking at, *entremetido*, busybody?" muttered Eremita, while Catalina glared daggers at me.

"Yeah. You're nothing but a little *chucho*," Catalina said as she winked at me, because she knew that I was no nosy parker. What is more, being a tattletale was not something my parents tolerated. My cousins teased me just to get me rattled.

"Come, hijito. Go on home. Your cousins need to get ready," Grandma Lale said to me.

At home I found Mom ironing a pleated white skirt and a soft-colored pink blouse. Pink was her favorite color. Loud clothes among the women for any festive occasion, including local dances, were frowned upon and deemed out of character. There was a saying among older women that went something like this: "A woman's character can be judged from the waist up," which meant, among other things, not to overdo the makeup or show too much cleavage.

In contrast, the males' apparel was generally less glitzy and therefore not a burning issue among parents or guardians. In fact, the older males looked more like a bunch of clones because, with rare exception, they all wore Levi's, cowboy boots, and tan, blue, maroon, or green gabardine shirts. The three-button cuffs and pearl stud buttons matched the shirts and added a touch of elegance. The young boys wore dress shirts, not gabardine, and Levi's and nonbrand hats, whereas the older men customarily sported Stetsons in different styles and shades of black or brown. They included El Vaquero, La Mesa, La Fiesta, and don José, the latter the quintessence of elegance.

"Come, hijito. Get dressed," Mom said. "I need you to go ask your grandma for some face powder. Tell her I'm almost out."

I put on my brand-new Levi's, which Dad had bought me at don Ricardo's General Store in Cabezón, and walked over to Grandma's. My off-white shirt and dark brown boots complemented my pants. I hated new Levi's because they were stiff and rubbed your inner thighs. And worst of all, the copper rivets on the hip pockets created a rash when you rode on horseback. Thank goodness for Rosebud salve; it alleviated the discomfort.

"¡Ay, qué pantera! Boy, you look dapper!" said my grandma, who was in the kitchen ironing a pair of skirts for her granddaughters. "What can I do for you?" she added inquisitively.

"Mom sent me for some face powder. Hers is almost gone."

Grandma walked out the kitchen and across the portal to her bedroom. I followed right behind her. When I entered, I saw quite a sight, something I had never witnessed before. My cousins had just finished putting up their hair in so-called curlers, but they weren't rubber like the ones Mom used. Rather, their hair was rolled up in lids from sardine cans (the metal curled up when you opened the cans). I had to contain myself from laughing. I could clearly see the inside of the shiny-yellow lids as well as the blue letters on the outside that showed the brand of sardines. Evidently, as I was to find out much later, sardine can lids were commonly used in lieu of commercial curlers among many women in my placita back in the 1940s.

Thanks to my father, who had discovered *rizos*, curlers, at don Ricardo's store in Cabezón, my mother never had to curl her hair using the lids of

sardine cans. He thought it was gross for a woman to attend a dance smelling of sardines, although in fact most women were meticulous enough to
boil the lids in hot water to get rid of the lingering fishy smell.

I returned home with the pink face powder. When I walked in the
kitchen, Mom was warming up leftovers for supper. Dad and I sat down to
eat. He was dressed and ready for the big fandango. As nearly as I could
tell from previous dances, Dad wasn't the greatest dancer, but he enjoyed
the hoopla. The chance to chat and down a shot or two of whiskey with his
friends and fellow farmers and ranchers was frosting on the cake.

It would be just a brief time before we departed. While Mom dressed, I
strolled down the hill to Aunt Taida's house to see if Cousin J. was ready to
go. I walked in, and lo and behold, there was my cousin S. with sardine can
lids on her head! This time I dared not even feign a snicker for fear that I
might get in trouble with my aunt. As a result, I didn't dilly-dally. I went
back up the hill to wait until we departed for don Porfirio's dance hall in
my placita.

The ride on horse wagon was slow but pleasant as the sun played peek-
a-boo in the western foothills before it disappeared behind the San
Mateo Mountains. I had made the trip dozens of times and was therefore
used to the ride from my casita to the village. I have no idea how long it
took, but it was not long. Since I was not old enough to partake in the
dancing jubilee, getting there quickly was the least of my worries. I enjoyed listening to the sound of the wagon wheels as they stirred up the
dirt on the road and played their own brand of music.

At community dances children were observers at most, but from time
to time kids, regardless of gender, danced with their mothers or grandmothers just to have fun. After all, a dance was a place of gaiety—without
inhibitions—irrespective of age. Once kids got sleepy they were tucked to
bed under the tarimas, wooden benches, where we slept until the dance
was over and returned home.

When my parents, my little siblings, and I reached the dance hall, a
few local women flushed with excitement were making certain they got
the prime seats close to the musicians. The players, as usual, consisted of
a violinist and a guitarist, both of whom were local villagers already up
in years, or so it seemed to me. They always occupied a makeshift stage

Juan Córdova's house, store, and dance hall, Ojo del Padre (Guadalupe), built c. 1905.
Photo taken in 2004.

up against the back wall, with a small table in one corner where they placed their instruments when they took a break. Other times they put them on top of the two chairs that they sat on to play whenever they got tired of standing.

The women and children occupied the wooden benches alongside both side walls, whereas the men generally shuffled in and out of the hall once the dance kicked into high gear. The front wall to the entrance was where young men stood guard, as it were, to keep an eye on their favorite girls and to make a mad dash when the musicians struck a tune to their liking. The boys usually assumed a kind of a cocky posture by standing with their right feet raised up against the wall, leaving black shoe marks on the whitewashed walls—much to the dismay of the dance hall owner, who had to clean them the next day.

By the time it got dark, the dance hall was pretty packed with Ojo del Padre villagers and those who came from the outlying areas. Some folks hailed from villages a few miles away, like Casa Salazar and Cabezón. Others came from as far away as San Luis or Cuba. But this was invariably true on Saint John's Day. It was indeed a celebratory occasion and an opportunity to whoop for joy regardless of the long distances people traveled either by horse wagon or on horseback; few people had automobiles.

Darkness having set in, people were seated, including my Grandma Lale and my cousins Catalina and Eremita. Mom and I and my two little brothers and sister sat next to them.

As the musicians made their grand entry down the middle of the hall, they played the marcha, often referred to as *la gran marcha* by some old-timers. This march—different from the wedding march—was the first musical number (*pieza*), and it engaged everyone from small kids to the very old. No one was excluded. The marcha, a tradition in most small villages like mine, was led by the church mayordomos; it was a preamble to the dance itself.

After the marcha was over, it was customary for the sons to dance with their mothers and sisters before they asked local girls to dance. Similarly, the husband was expected to dance with his wife. At times he forgot to follow the rules set forth by the elders in years past and as a result found himself in the chicken coop, in a manner of speaking. "*A dormir con las gallinas.* Now he'll have to sleep with the chickens" was an utterance that echoed throughout the dance hall. "One time a fool; second time an idiot," people said of lackadaisical husbands who time and again ignored or simply forgot the rules of etiquette and tradition.

Additional traditions unfolded on the dance floor whose significance I didn't quite grasp at first glance, but which over time I came to understand and appreciate for their meaning and purpose. Observing the older folks and listening to what they did and said was a great way to learn about the customs of one's community. That's why I always made an effort to stay awake as long as feasible. It also paid not to be bashful about asking questions of either your mother or your grandmothers. In my case, they were receptive and good providers of information. I learned a lot, in particular from Mom and Grandma Cinda, both of whom were infinitely patient in answering my queries.

For me dances were a great source of information. A case in point was the presence of an elder statesman dressed in a dark suit who roamed the dance hall collecting a nickel or two or a few pennies here and there to pay the musicians, who charged on occasion. The gentleman was known as the *bastonero*, a kind of floor manager who kept men with plenty of nickels in their coin purses from monopolizing the small dance floor. He was also responsible for maintaining peace, since rivalries existed and arguments or fisticuffs broke out time and again between men from my placita and those from other villages. The bastonero was in fact a well-respected citizen whose reputation transcended my community. His words, whether of warning or rebuke, were considered gospel and thus heeded; failure to obey them could result in banishment for the evening from the dance floor. If a scuffle erupted and *moquetes*, fists, started flying, the bastonero immediately told the musicians to stop playing, and the dance ended on the spot. Such was his clout.

Apart from fisticuffs, there were several other things the bastonero did not tolerate on the dance floor. For example, it was deemed disrespectful for a man sporting a hat to ask a lady to dance. Worse yet was for him to be wearing and clanging spurs, as if to show his machismo. Though women knew wearing a hat and/or spurs was frowned upon, they did not reject the offer to dance, because ladies were taught from a young age never to *desaigrar*, snub, a man under any circumstances. Even if he was drunk! Doing so was considered the height of impoliteness and not ladylike.

I recall vividly a man from a neighboring settlement who was inebriated and made the unforgivable mistake of not taking off his hat. As soon as he hit the dance floor with his dancing partner, the bastonero swiftly told him to remove it. The poor fellow was bald as a cue ball! Wearing a hat proved just as embarrassing as having no hair at all. People laughed just the same at the unfortunate soul. Perhaps he learned his lesson.

Men had the reputation of imbibing, but never in the presence of women, not if you were a true *caballero*. For that reason, any liquor consumption was done outside the dance hall. Since there was no bar in my village, a vendor, a veritable entrepreneur, showed up at dusk from Cuba, Bernalillo, or Albuquerque the day of the dance and sold liquor from the bed of his small truck. Hard liquor, like whiskey (aguardiente), and wine were the most popular drinks, although beer was coming into its own among the young men.

At one time during Prohibition, *mula*, white lightning made from corn, was in high demand in the Río Puerco Valley because of its potency. According to my father, it took only a few shots of corn liquor for one to feel tipsy and one or two more to become intoxicated. What is more, according to him, you could sprinkle a few drops of white lightning on the ground, light a match to it, and watch as a small explosion erupted.

A couple of rather audacious men customarily liked to buy their own half pints in what was called a *flate*, flat, with whiskey or wine in it, which they tucked into a hip pocket of their Levi's. Sporting liquor in that fashion was a way of putting on airs. People called these men *facetos*, show-offs. But the flates were also convenient because every time they stepped outside the dance hall for a sip or two, they didn't have to stumble around searching in the dark for the bottles of liquor they had stashed away in the bushes or sagebrush for safekeeping. Besides being tagged "facetos," men looked upon carrying a flask in their hip pocket as a macho thing, not to mention the fact that it was also a means of keeping young boys from stealing or hiding the liquor.

One of those cocky individuals was none other than an uncle of mine in Ojo del Padre. Considered a so-called rooster (gallo) in the community, a cock-of-the-walk of sorts, he was also a supreme waltz dancer who enjoyed flaunting his dancing prowess. Women admired him and were in awe of the ladies who danced with him. But in addition to being a supreme dancer, he liked his wine and enjoyed showing off the flate tucked in his Levi's as he whirled and spun his dancing partners (not my aunt).

The straw broke the camel's back on Saint John's Day after my uncle had imbibed one drink too many. Everyone was dancing up a storm and having a grand old time when he entered the dance hall. Perhaps feeling a sense of guilt for not having danced with my aunt, he headed straight to where she was sitting to ask her to dance. From the look on her face, she appeared to feel somewhat bemused, because she lacked the flair for waltzes. Unbeknownst to her—or to him—he evidently had fallen on his flate out in the bushes, and by now his pants were dark and soaked, but it wasn't just wine. Clearly, he had cut himself, and blood was oozing from his right buttock.

Unexpectedly, amid an array of oohs and ahs, one of the women hollered to my aunt as she and my uncle danced, "Comadre, your husband is bleeding!" At that very moment my aunt stopped my uncle in his tracks and gave him a quick look. Sure enough, by now the right seat of his pants was saturated with blood. "You're bleeding!" she said to him in astonishment while my grandma and Mom gathered around him along with a few other onlookers.

"Yeah, he's bleeding from the *fundillo*, his butt," muttered a rather uncouth voice close to the musicians.

"Nah," my uncle responded matter-of-factly, "it's only red wine," as though nothing had happened. The rest of the women put their hands over their mouths and giggled.

Sensing maybe that the mood for a change of pace was just right, the bastonero asked the musicians to take a short break. This gave the people, the majority of them women, an opportunity to congregate and to catch up on the latest hearsay. Though the last dance before the break ended was a waltz, I learned later from Grandma Cinda that other musical pieces once popular on special days like Saint John's Day included old folk dances whose titles were *La cuna*, *El rechumbé*, and *La escoba*. None of these rang a bell with me. But of more recent vintage were dances like *El chote* (also called *El chotis*) and *La Varsoviana* ("Put Your Little Foot" dance); these were familiar to me.

Mexican songs like "*Allá en el rancho grande*," the ballad "Adelita," the fast-moving "*Échele nicle al piano*," the nostalgic "*Tú, sólo tú*," and of course the loving "*Mi chaparrita*" were beginning to make their way into the Río Puerco Valley and my placita. This repertoire of dances was changing the complexity of the music that musicians played and that old-timers in Ojo del Padre and their neighbors to the north and south danced and listened to.

By now the musicians were back from their break and possibly feeling no pain. No doubt but what they had had their good *pajuelazos*, whiskey shots, compliments of a few of their compadres and fellow villagers who huddled around a bonfire in front of don Porfirio's dance hall, chatting and chewing the fat throughout the night instead of dancing. The early summer night was warm, and the fire was more for show than anything else.

Some jokers claimed the fire was to light up the place for a better view of the young girls when they left the dance hall headed for the outhouse. If the mothers or grandmothers allowed them to go unaccompanied, it was also the perfect opportunity for the girls to flirt openly with the boys who were waiting behind the bushes in the dark. Young people had their clever ways, signals, and messengers.

But what followed next was a surprise to me and to the rest of the kids who were still awake and not tucked under the wooden benches. "Ladies and gentlemen," boomed the bastonero's voice. "Now we will have the *chiquiao* in honor of our guests from the neighboring villages. As some of you may recall, this dance has not been performed here in Ojo del Padre in a long spell. Music, please!"

"*¡Todos a tirar chancla!* Let's dance, everyone!" These words came from a commanding male voice near the entrance to the dance hall. "*¡A arrastrar suela!* Let's burn shoe leather!" another gentleman hollered. No sooner said than done, dancing couples, young and old, packed the floor.

After a few minutes the music stopped and the bastonero went from couple to couple collecting his nickels and dimes from the men. While he did this, I could hear a constant chatter, more than the normal level of conversation, between male and female dancing partners. I wasn't quite sure what the prattle was all about. The man, as nearly as I could ascertain, would utter something, and his partner would respond in kind. The scene was new to me.

The chiquiao dance came and went with dancing couples exchanging partners. Even Mom and Grandma Lale got into the act. Laughter erupted from time to time among the couples. Everybody was having a good old time. As for me, I was both amused and confused by the chiquiao dance. I wondered what was behind the hilarity.

I was to find out later from Grandma Cinda, who was well versed on many aspects of Hispanic folklore in New Mexico. She was a book of knowledge and predisposed to teaching her grandson the intricacies of the chiquiao as she knew them.

"Look, hijito, the chiquiao is a beautiful dance, not because of the movements. It's because of what dancing partners say to one another. You see, chiquiao comes from *chiquiarse*," a term that was not foreign to me. On occasion, when spending the summers with her in Bernalillo, I would pout if I didn't get my way. That's when she would invoke the following expression or something akin to it: "*Ah, ya se chiquió mi hijito.* Ah, my grandson needs a little sweet-talking."

She continued. "You see, a chiquiao is something an older man recites to a woman—not his wife—or a young man to a girl as a means of flirting or flattery. A chiquiao is especially important if a boy wants to impress a girl in hopes of marrying her. She can play coy, begging to be coaxed. That's what chiquiarse means. It's a fun game between couples. Do you understand what I'm saying?"

"I think so," I responded, and she proceeded to give me some examples of chiquiaos, poetic quatrains. Some convey love or affection, the kind of poetry a boy might recite to a girl. Here's one that my grandma taught me as a child and that I still remember fondly to this day:

De la pera no comí,	From the pear I did not eat,
del vino bebí una gota.	from the wine I took a few sips.
Del besito que te di,	From the short kiss I gave you,
dulce me quedó la boca.	my mouth turned sweet like your lips.

In another quatrain that I also learned from Grandma Cinda, a young man hints at marriage. It is straightforward and to the point.

Que bonita vas creciendo,	My, but you're turning pretty,
como la espiga del trigo.	like the tassel of the wheat plant.
Ya me voy apreviniendo,	I'm getting all primed up,
pa casarme contigo.	so that I can marry you.

The girl's response (or rejection), rooted in the popular New Mexican expression of "*dar calabazas*" (to hand out the pumpkin treatment), was swift and not at all subtle.

Que bonito vas creciendo,	My, but you're getting handsome,
del tamaña d'esta casa.	like this great big house.
Ya me voy apreviniendo,	I'm getting all pumped up,
pa darte calabazas.	to toss you out like a mouse.*

---

* For more chiquiaos, consult my book *Más antes: Hispanic Folklore of the Río Puerco Valley.*

The quatrains exchanged between grown-ups, many of which were composed right on the dance floor, were done in jest. From time to time, liquor impeded a man's judgment, and out spewed an indiscretion that landed him in hot water. Such a situation was rare but not unheard of, according to Grandma Cinda.

Some men were not necessarily bold; they were just dimwitted in what they said. Provoking or insulting a woman—a legitimate excuse for the lady to retaliate—could well earn him *un buen revés*, a good slap in the face, also called a *cachetada*. The husband was not far behind in getting into the fray. That's when the bastonero intervened and ended the dance in short order.

The ensuing quatrain, the kind that could get a man in trouble, unless the woman was keen on the idea of being stirred up, is something I recall from my elementary school days in Rincón del Cochino. Other boys and I used it sheepishly in flirting with the girls. It goes like this:

En una mesa te puse	I placed on a table just for you,
un plato con elolotes.	a plate full of ears of sweet corn.
No lo hago porque me quieras,	I don't do it so you'll like me,
sino porque te alborotes.	but to get you all excited.

The chiquiao dance must have lasted longer than most dances, because next thing I knew Mom was waking me up to go home. By now it was late, and many of the children were sound asleep under the long wooden benches and totally oblivious to the last discordant sounds of the violinist and the guitarist.

I could tell that fatigue had also caught up with Mom and Grandma Lale. They were both yawning. Even the kerosene lanterns on the wall, perhaps running low on oil, flickered with more frequency as if to suggest that they, too, were heavy eyed. Tired people and musicians were a tip-off to the bastonero that the time had come for the fandango to end.

Saint John's Day had been packed with activities and excitement. And, unlike other holiday dances I had witnessed, there had been no serious altercations, much to the delight of the bastonero.

It was now very late, conceivably past midnight, and the last dance of the night was imminent. Hence the word spread quickly. I don't recall if it was traditional or not, but on this given night the last dance announced by the bastonero was *"Adiós mi chaparrita,"* a slow-moving Mexican song. It was also the perfect time for men to make amends if they had spent more time throughout the night drinking with their buddies (cuates) than dancing with their wives. I recognized the sentimental words to the beautiful song, because Mom sang it often (see chapter 9).

The bastonero's pronouncement "*¡Se acabó el baile!* The dance has ended!" signaled the conclusion of a long and joyous day typical in Ojo del Padre. People now looked forward to the next bolote, or celebration. Then the lids of sardines cans would shine once again in my cousins' hair.

24

Harvest Time and Field Mice

HORSE WAGONS AND GRINDING WHEELS

THE SWELTERING SUMMER HEAT waves had begun to dissipate, and the cool fall evenings and breezes loomed not far in the future. Harvest time was virtually upon us. Having enjoyed fresh vegetables like sweet corn, peas, and zucchini during the summer, we also took pleasure in eating cantaloupe, watermelon, and Grandma Lale's jelly (jalea) made from boiling the meat of the chilecayotes.

But now the corn for livestock and full-grown orange pumpkins were ready for harvesting. One by one Grandpa, Uncle Antonio, and Dad took stock of the crops and the time it would take to pick the three perennial ones, that is, corn, pinto beans, and pumpkins, before transporting them to their respective storage spaces. The grinding of the wheels of wagons loaded with crops was music to my ears. The harvest season was about to begin for most farmers in the Río Puerco Valley. From there on, the number and kinds of vegetables grown depended on what families (including the three García families) preferred and what the soil was conducive to growing, since the land varied somewhat throughout the valley and even on Grandpa's ranch.

My parents, especially Mom, liked to plant peas, cucumbers, yellow squash, zucchini, chickpeas (garbanzos), radishes, and, on occasion, turnips, whereas my father enjoyed planting cantaloupes. Both had small tracts of land adjacent to the cornfields reserved for these vegetables (cantaloupe is a vegetable though many people mistake it for a fruit). Grandpa Lolo and

251

Uncle Antonio, on the other hand, planted watermelons and cantaloupe among the rows of corn plants rather than separately.

All three families helped each other harvest crops, especially pinto beans, which required threshing, a team effort among Grandpa, Uncle Antonio, and Dad. In contrast, harvesting, shucking, and grinding corn involved virtually all the members of the three families.

The end of the summer months meant that my father was back to work with the government. He never mentioned the specific agency, but the CCC camps and WPA program were now history, gone with the end of the Great Depression. The nature of his work, building fences and the like, remained unchanged, as did his Monday-through-Friday working schedule.

Saturdays in September were particularly busy for Dad and Mom. First, he would hitch up his team of horses—El Moro and another blue roan horse. To my knowledge, Dad owned the only wagon in my village—possibly the entire valley—with iron wheels three-quarters the size of the wooden spoke wheels normally found on most horse wagons. The wagon was also lower to the ground than a typical wagon, but the loading capacity was just as great, if not greater, because of the sideboards (barandales) that Dad had built for it.

PUMPKINS BIGGER THAN THE SUN

To a kid, everything looked large. One's perspective of things, to wit, people, animals, and the terrain, defied reality. That was true, too, of pumpkins, which to me looked bigger than the orange sun on a scorching day at sunset.

It was Friday, which meant that Dad would be home for the weekend in time for supper. Mom had spent part of the afternoon getting ready for his arrival while I took my siesta. Once I got up from my nap, I helped sweep the kitchen and brought in wood for the stove. "Hijito, go get me a chicken. That's what I'm fixing your dad for supper."

Chicken and rice, a specialty of hers, was also one of Dad's favorite dishes. She cooked it in a red earthen clay pot she had brought back from Jémez Pueblo. For the past two years, 1943–1944, we had gone to the pueblo to exchange some of our crops for fruit that the Indians raised but that were virtually unheard of throughout my valley, such as mission grapes, peaches, and apricots.

"Which one do you want?" I asked with a smirk, since the chickens gave me fits before I could catch one.

"It doesn't matter. Just get me one of the big chickens," she responded as she opened a can of tomatoes I had bought at the local general store and post office in our placita a day earlier.

I took a shortcut by hopping over the wooden gate to Dad's corral and walked across to get to the chicken coop on the opposite side. After a few fruitless attempts at trapping a chicken, I finally pounced on one, grabbed the unhappy and startled creature by its legs, and took it to Mom.

I walked into the kitchen somewhat exhausted from running after the critter. I handed Mom the hapless chicken as it flapped its wings while I struggled to hold onto it by the legs.

"Here you are, Mom! This is the biggest one I could catch. It was also the slowest moving," I said proudly, but Mom crushed my spirits in a split second.

"No, no, hijito. That's the one that lays the most eggs! Not that one. Go get me a different one."

"But you said to get a big one. This is the biggest I could find," I responded, then I slowly returned, a bit downcast, to the chicken coop with the fowl as it relentlessly flapped its wings.

The meal that evening, as usual, was mouthwatering. Dad licked his fingers even as he held and ate a drumstick with both hands. Mom watched him knowing full well that he was enjoying her home-cooked meal instead of the concoctions he and the other men fixed at El Rito de Semilla's government quarters during the week.

A short time later, after it got dark, Mom put Beltrán, Juanito, and Julianita to bed. Mom let me stay up a little later for my food to settle. During the week she and Beltrán and I ate a light meal for supper. Our main meal traditionally was at noon.

"Okay. It's time for bed," Mom said. "Tomorrow we have to go pick pumpkins," she added, her voice rising in excitement.

I went into the bedroom, undressed, set down my clothing on top of my shoes, and tucked them under the bed, as I usually did. I knelt and said my prayers. Mom joined me before saying goodnight. "Sleep well. Tomorrow is a big day," and she left the room to join Dad in the kitchen.

The next morning, after an early breakfast, Mom and I accompanied him to the pumpkin patches, where we started gathering the golden globes. One by one they went in the wagon with the iron wheels. This was one crop I thought was really fun to harvest. Dad would tear off the pumpkins from the vine and load them at the back end of the wagon, and Mom and I would roll each one toward the front before we stacked them two or three high. By the time the wagon was fully loaded, you could see the pumpkins rise above the sideboards.

By then we were ready to head home. As a rule we made two or three trips and then shared some of the pumpkins with my grandparents and my aunt's family, since we usually had a large crop. But more often than not we kept the largest pumpkin for us; it usually weighed twenty-five to thirty pounds. Mom cooked that one to make pumpkin pies.

At home we unloaded all the pumpkins in front of our house. In that way, they'd be easily accessible for Mom to use or for my aunt and uncle and grandparents to take for their share. "Be very careful not to break the *calabazota*!" warned my dad with a smile, as though I could really lift the giant pumpkin.

Mom had two ways of preparing the pumpkins. First, she would cut a pumpkin in half (usually the larger ones) from the stem end to the bottom along the ribbed area, remove the mushy strings and seeds, and cook its meat in the oven. The cooked pumpkin could be eaten for dessert with sugar (preferably brown sugar, if available). This is something we did whenever we found a ripe pumpkin prior to the actual harvesting. Second, the smaller pumpkins were cut into short strips called tasajos; these we spread on top of a tarpaulin on the ground for them to sun dry. While drying, they were covered with large pieces of cheesecloth to protect them against the flies. Some families who had a slanted front portal, like my grandparents, dried the strips of pumpkin on top of the porch's tin roof. Later on—above all during the winter months—these tasajos were boiled in hot water and used in pie fillings or for making empanaditas, deep-fried turnovers.

Some women throughout the Río Puerco Valley cut the pumpkins' meat into small pieces and canned them, whereas other women liked to peel the smaller pumpkins, cut them in half, and drape them like small hats on fence posts near their homes. There they dried like the tasajos, but they took much longer because the meat part was exposed only to the wind's undercurrents and not the sun. It was another way of drying the pumpkin flesh without cutting it into strips.

I remember seeing, close to my village, a string of peeled pumpkins propped on top of fence posts; they looked like a bunch of bald-headed men standing erect a few feet from one another. It was quite a sight. Kids like me were not at a loss for a joke or two concerning these bald creatures. Sometimes my cousins and I even dared to use the pumpkins on fence posts for targets when we practiced shooting our slingshots. The pumpkins were also prime candidates for the daring crows or large birds that liked to peck at them.

DIRTY MELONS

One of the crops that Mom and I harvested as a team after school during Dad's absence was cantaloupes (melones roñosos). We called them "dirty melons" in the Río Puerco Valley. Depending on the June and July rainfalls, coupled with the heat of the July summer days, some cantaloupes tended to ripen early, and we ate those. For the others we waited until mid-August or so.

Once the cantaloupes were ripe, Mom and I headed for the cantaloupe patch. We looked for those that were yellowish in color or cracked around the stem that was attached to the vine. Either sign meant the cantaloupe was ripe and ready to eat. These were tricks that I learned from my parents and paternal grandparents growing up on the ranch.

My father had sewn together a contraption from three pieces of canvas—one large piece and two pouches resembling saddlebags—that we draped over the horse's bare back. That's how Mom and I hauled the melons, but it was important to balance the load on both sides with equal weight in each pouch. If not, the cantaloupes went tumbling down on the ground and cracked. Depending on the size, Mom and I could easily put at least five cantaloupes inside either pouch and head home. At any given time, we probably made two or three trips at most, but we never picked all the cantaloupes in a single day, because once we were home Mom had to prepare them for safekeeping for the winter months.

In retrospect, what she and other women did to prevent spoilage was practical and wise. Mom would peel (*mondar*) the cantaloupes and cut them into little wheels (*rueditas*) by starting where the vine was detached from the cantaloupe and cutting round slices perpendicular to the stem, one strip at a time. These wheels, different from the pumpkin strips mentioned earlier, were also sun dried and put into empty flour bags. Thereafter, they were hung from a beam in Grandpa Lolo's adobe shed, or dispensa, which was designed and built especially for perishables, since refrigerators were nonexistent. The temperature inside kept perishables cool until the colder days of late October and November greeted us.

The cantaloupe seeds were also fully sun dried and saved in jars until the next planting season. Seeds from the same generation of melons were never used for more than two planting seasons. Otherwise, the cantaloupes conceivably could become smaller and smaller and the yield reduced as well. This kind of knowledge was passed on from my paternal grandfather to his sons and from my father to my siblings and me.

As was true with countless other farming enterprises, reaping the benefits from cantaloupes was a delight for a young boy like me. Mom relished seeing me smile from ear to ear when I picked a ripe melon and loaded it into the horse contraption Dad had sewn for Mom and me. A snack or dessert was not far behind.

CORN AND CUT HANDS

Harvesting corn was, plain and simple, hard work. By now—late August or early September—the cornstalks were dry and the corn ripened. Because insecticides were unheard of, a black fungus called *mojo* (or *moho*) invariably infested some ears of corn. Whenever the dark, silky smut rubbed off on your hands, it was like ink or black soot from inside the pipe of a woodburning stove. Those ears of corn we tossed and left on the fields for Grandma Lale's hogs to eat. For some reason, the crows liked the fungusinfested corn as well. Were they aware of something we didn't know?

Everybody, including women and young boys, plus girls if needed, got into the act of picking corn by hand. We yanked it from the stalks with our bare hands—work gloves for kids were a luxury—by pulling each ear of corn downward and tossing it into a horse wagon with sideboards. (Sometimes my father called these sideboards *humentos* instead of barandales; see chapter 12.) Given that the leaves on the plants were dry and sharp, oftentimes one's fingers got painful, razor-type cuts. We would stick our index fingers in the wagon's axle for grease to rub on the cuts, or I applied Rosebud salve when I got home to prevent infection, though the pain did not abate one iota.

Once a horse wagon was fully loaded and transported to Grandpa's large corral, a rake was used to unload the corn through the back end of the wagon. The process of picking, loading, and unloading ripe corn was repeated over and over again until the cornfields were cleared of everything but the cornstalks.

They were then cut at the root with a sickle, gathered in bunches of three to five stalks (depending on their size), and held together with baling wire. Several of these bundles were stacked upright, like teepees, in bunches of three for equal balance. In late September or early October, we loaded the cornstalks on a horse wagon and piled them on a special place called a *tapeiste*; this was a makeshift loft situated above the horse stalls, or caballeriza, adjacent to Grandpa Lolo's corral. Keeping the stalks off the ground and exposed to the open air protected them against rotting due to wetness from rain or snow. The stalks, together with homegrown hay, were used to feed the horses during the winter months.

After the cornstalks were cut at ground level, nothing was left but rastrojos, stubbles. These made perfect fodder for Grandma Lale's hogs when she turned them loose in the cornfields. Come planting season in the spring, what remained of the stubbles was gathered with a horse-drawn harvester dump rake, stacked, and burned, making the soil easier to plow. At that stage the fields were free of nearly all debris and ready to be plowed in preparation for planting new crops.

SHUCKING CORN AND STORYTELLING

Soon after cutting, stacking, and storing the cornstalks on top of the ta-peiste, all three García families began shucking corn. This chore was always carried out in early evening after supper. It was truly a family affair. Everyone from grandparents and parents to children sat on the ground facing the huge mountain of corn.

In pulling the leaves back (by hand, of course) and breaking them off at the corn stub, my cousins and I were instructed to save the very thin and soft leaves for Dad and my uncle to use in rolling their cigarettes. We were also told to set aside a bit thicker leaves, not the outer ones, for Grandma to use in making and steaming her Christmas tamales. She had a special wo-ven Indian basket for her grandchildren to deposit those leaves in for safe-keeping. Suddenly and out of the blue, we heard the magical words coming from somewhere near the horse stables: "The Bogeyman (El Coco) is on his way. It's storytelling time. Come, come if you wish to have a little fun."

Quickly we moved our working area so we could listen to Grandma Lale. She encouraged her grandchildren to gather around her if we were interested in hearing some of her favorite stories. A few tales were based on legends like La Llorona; others were lodged in witchcraft of the Río Puerco Valley (see chapter 5). One of her favorite stories concerned the magical colt that kept nagging Grandpa's mare in the dead of night as he and Grandma were on their way home by horse wagon from a village dance. Trouble is, Grandpa's mare did not have a colt. Like any typical grandma, her stories at times left you mesmerized and yearning for more. Other times you were left to ponder the outcome. Listening to her made husking corn an adventure, a happening, as you might say, and not a hum-drum affair.

By the time she finished her storytelling, the pile of shucked yellow corn had grown higher. My cousins and I had also gotten tired and were ready for bed; the following evening we would renew our work of shucking more corn. The task was enjoyable, but by the end of two weeks, all of us, grown-ups and grandchildren alike, had grown weary and were anxious for it to end until next year.

BINS, BARRELS, AND MENACING MICE

As the heaps of shucked corn grew, we started the process of removing the kernels from the ears, called "grinding." Except for Uncle Antonio, who had a hand-grinding machine that he bought with money earned from driving the local school bus, the rest of us removed the corn from the cob by hand.

The trick was to hold an ear of corn firmly in your left hand, with the sharp part pointed in upward and away from you, or in between your legs for a steady grip. You held a second ear of corn in your right hand; that ear of corn became the "grinder," so to speak. This ear of corn, too, had to be pointed straight up or else slanted slightly downward, depending on the position of the corn in your left hand. Then you rubbed the ear of corn in your right hand against the corn in your left hand in a clockwise, left-right motion; the corn chipped off the cob into a tin bucket or tub in front of you. The grinding process was done in swift repetitive motions until you reached the bottom, or fat end, of the ear of corn. By that time the corncob was free of any kernels.

Each time you finished an ear of corn, the corncob (*elote* or *elolote*) was tossed into a special pile that grew higher and higher. These corncobs were burned in the potbelly stove during the winter months; they were for warming up homes. The cobs turned red-hot and generated a tremendous amount of heat. Corncobs, along with dry cow chips (*buñigas*), another excellent source of heat, enormously helped us economize on firewood during the cold months. I also rejoiced at not having to chop and split as much wood.

After we ground the corn, it went into bins or fifty-gallon open-mouth wooden barrels that my uncle used for storage in a special room in his house. Everybody's corn was stored there and marked accordingly. Two problems usually arose with corn in barrels: mice and snout weevils (*gorgojos*). The covers to the barrels had to be well secured to protect the corn against the mice. To find mice droppings in the corn intended for horses, chickens, and hogs was less than desirable. Regarding the snout weevils, they were a nuisance but not a serious problem. You simply had to separate the weevils from the corn before feeding the animals; horses and hogs generally consumed most of the corn.

HARVESTING PINTO BEANS

Our second major crop was pinto beans. They were as important as corn, albeit for different reasons. Every family up and down the Río Puerco Valley, including the three García families, ate pinto beans. Most families, including us, even ate them at breakfast. Mom without fail cooked beans on Tuesdays, which is when she ironed clothes (see chapter 9). Eating beans at least once a week was as natural as having tortillas every day with all three meals. But in the hot summer days cooked beans could spoil very quickly. There was nothing worse than sour (*chocoque*) beans. They were ghastly and inedible.

Pinto beans thrived in dry soil and for that reason were ideal for dry farming. Harvesting them was not as complicated and difficult as picking corn. All three García families participated in the process. After planting them in mid-April or early May, we harvested the beans in September. Once the plants had dried in the fields, it was a matter of uprooting them by hand, something that was easy in dry soil. We made small stacks—all in a row—before loading them on a horse wagon. Like corn, the dry beans required sideboards, but the loads were bulky rather than heavy.

Grandpa Lolo, Uncle Antonio, and Dad then hauled the pinto beans to a threshing floor called an *era*, no more than a hop, skip, and a jump from Grandpa's house. He had built the threshing floor around 1924. It stood between two small hills, where the wind currents from the west were perfect for threshing and cleaning the beans. My grandfather's era was round, fenced, and the size of a small corral. The ground was hard, compacted, and suitable for threshing beans when horses or goats walked on the pods. A soft or sandy surface was not conducive for separating the beans from the shells.

The pinto beans were unloaded from the horse wagon onto the threshing area and scattered in a circle; an open space was left in the middle, like a hole in a donut. Grandpa, who was in charge of the entire threshing process, placed a wooden pitchfork, a flat wooden shovel, a sieve, and a large, folded piece of canvas in the "donut hole."

Teodoro García and family threshing pinto beans, c. 1921–1922.
The author's father is standing on the fence, Uncle Antonio is on horseback, and
Uncle Ramón is in the foreground holding a stick.

My uncle owned a team of sorrel horses that was properly trained for threshing beans. They, unlike other teams I had witnessed, did not require blinders, *tapaojos*, to discourage them from taking an occasional bite of the dry bean plants. Moreover, the horses were small and suitable for stepping on the plants to separate the pods from the shell without ruining the crop. Larger horses tended to crack or split open the pinto beans, which housewives didn't like to find when cooking beans. A self-contained bean retained the flavor better than a cracked one when cooked in hot water.

In addition to hogs, Grandma Lale raised goats. In fact, she had a large herd of the pesky creatures. Sometimes Grandpa Lolo used the goats for threshing, rather than my uncle's horses, especially if the bean crop was modest. It spared the beans from being smashed by the heavy pounding of the horses' hooves. Goats were ideal for threshing pinto beans, albeit they could be somewhat unruly since they disliked going round and round in a circle. Trying to keep them together without their scattering was a challenge, indeed. Besides, unlike some horses, you didn't put blinders on goats.

Home-crafted *criba* (sieve) for removing the hulls from pinto beans.

Once Grandpa had decided the beans were trampled enough, it was time to "air" them (aigrar). This entailed tossing the beans up in the air with the wooden pitchfork so that the wind could separate the dense beans from the lighter hulls—the outer covering or shell. The propitious time was at dusk, when the sun disappeared behind the San Mateo Mountains to the west and the breezes from the nearby buttes became active. Grandpa, Uncle Antonio, and Dad took turns tossing them in the air until the only thing that remained was the beans and a few hulls.

At that point, the large canvas was spread in the middle of the threshing area and, using the flat wooden shovel, the men stacked the beans in a pile. This was the penultimate step in threshing. Using this same shovel, Grandpa, my uncle, and my father, with the wind at their backs, took turns tossing the beans up in the air so the wind could blow away whatever hulls remained.

The final step in harvesting the pinto beans was to clean small quantities of beans in a sieve, *criba*. This was a homemade contraption that Grandpa had built. It was a simple but practical apparatus consisting of four boards joined together to form a rectangle. The area in the middle contained a fine screen that was used to sift the beans. Whatever residue (e.g., straws) remained disappeared in the sifting process. Then they put the clean beans in gunnysacks, again using the wooden shovel, which was softer than one with a metal blade.

Most of the beans were stored in the shed the three families shared, although there were times when we used a sack or two to barter for fruit with the Indians at Jémez Pueblo. Fruit of any kind, as mentioned earlier, was unheard of when I was growing up in the Río Puerco Valley. Chile fell into the same category. Only one or two families near the village proper planted and harvested chile, but the chile was for their exclusive use.

Here's a list of vegetables (watermelons, a fruit, are also included), both homegrown and those gathered in the wild, that families typically consumed.

alverjones	peas
calabazas	pumpkins
calabacitas amarillas	yellow squash
calabacitas verdes	zucchini
chilecayotes *	chilecayotes
frijoles	pinto beans
frijoles verdes	green beans, string beans
garbanzos	chickpeas
habas	broad (lima) beans
maíz	corn
maíz pininí	popcorn
melones roñosos	cantaloupes
pepinos	cucumbers
quelites †	wild spinach
rabanitos	radishes
sandías	watermelons
verdolagas ‡	purslane

....

* A chilecayote resembles a watermelon with white meat; it is boiled in water and used for making jelly. It is also spelled *chilacayotes* outside of New Mexico.

† These greens grew in the wild and were picked for home cooking.

‡ These greens grew in the wild and were picked for home cooking.

With the harvest season effectively over and the cool nights just around the corner, canning time was not far off. But first a trip to Jémez Pueblo was looming; there we would barter for fruit with the Indians in preparation for Mom's yearly canning of fruits and vegetables, a process that I truly enjoyed.

25

Canning Time

THE CANNING SEASON FOR me was one of the highlights at home. If people were to ask me why, my answer would be simple and to the point: because the fruits of our backbreaking labor began to show up in jars, subsequently in the dispensa, and ultimately on the dinner table. Though Mom canned a few garden vegetables in late summer, the climax to the canning season occurred in mid-October. At that point I looked back with delight, and more than a modicum of relief, at the planting, hoeing, and harvesting cycles we had completed.

Canning was a time to congregate around the kitchen table and help Mom sterilize jars, lids, and rings. The tinkling of jars and their accessories, as well as the hissing from the pressure cooker, was music to my ears. I was ready for the canning fandango—and what better dancing partner than my mother? So let the party begin!

JARS, LIDS, AND METAL RINGS

Before the first vegetables appeared in the small garden plot Mom and Dad had planted, she took stock of what she would need for canning. Then we traveled to Bernalillo, to go shopping at the Bernalillo Mercantile Company. In addition to foodstuff, my mother bought several cases of mason jars to supplement what she had left over from the previous year. The jars came in quart and pint sizes, both with the same size mouth, and could be used over and over without fear of contamination, provided they were sterilized properly in boiling water. Both size jars fit inside the pressure cooker without any trouble.

Mom also purchased enough boxes of jar lids and metal rings to complement the jars. The lids had round rubber bands glued to the inside of the rim. Once they were screwed on a jar full of food and placed inside the pressure cooker, the lids became sealed and sterilized. After the jars were taken out, the lids were checked to make sure they were tight, as sometimes they became loose while in the pressure cooker. This was a precaution to ensure that the canned food did not spoil.

To this day I recollect that when Mom or Dad opened a jar of fruit or vegetables, they would listen for air to escape. If they heard a sound like a valve releasing air, something was amiss, and they took no chances, fearful of contracting food poisoning. Defective jars of canned food did not occur very often. In fact, it was rare, but if it came to pass, Mom and Dad disposed of the food or fed it to Grandma Lale's hogs.

From time to time throughout the summer Mom and I would venture to the fields to pick fresh peas, green beans, or yellow squash for her to cook. I also ate my fair share of shelled raw peas on the way back home. I liked them better than cooked.

At the height of the growing season, toward mid-August, when these three vegetables were plentiful and ready to can, Mom and I would pick a small tin tub full of peas, green beans, or squash to carry back to the house. This was the beginning of the canning experience that would reach its apogee in October. Unlike green beans, which you snapped in half, or yellow squash, which Mom cut into small pieces, fresh grown peas had to be shelled before canning, a time-consuming process. Filling even a pint-size jar took a lot of peas.

By the end of August and early September, Mom had a good number of canned vegetables stored away in a makeshift wooden cupboard in our small kitchen, all ready for the winter months. Soon we would move them to our dispensa, where perishables were stored for the winter. The main canning episodes, which included fruit, were yet to come.

A TRIP TO JÉMEZ PUEBLO

Every year in the early fall, my parents made their annual trek to Jémez Pueblo, located at the foot of the Jémez Mountains, northeast of the Río Puerco Valley, to trade corn and pinto beans with the Indians for grapes, peaches, apricots, and apples. As mentioned in chapter 2, fruit was unheard of in my valley. In fact, I only remember seeing one lonely apricot tree adjacent to a home that had been abandoned many years earlier when the owners, Jesús and Perfilia Córdova, left for Bernalillo. Through some miracle, the apricot tree kept surviving and bearing tiny apricots, which some of us kids ate, until the tree finally died.

I recall vividly to this day my first trip to Jémez Pueblo because of an unforgettable experience (more on this later). I was riding with my little brothers in the back seat of my dad's Chevrolet. My brothers and I were flanked by a sack of ground yellow corn on one side and a second one of pinto beans on the other. Julianita was in the front seat between Mom and Dad.

The journey from my house over winding dirt roads and through the villages of Cabezón and San Luis was slow, but traveling on unpaved roads always left me with the sensation that Dad was really driving fast. This was true above all when the car hit, bounced, and skidded a tad on stretches of road that felt like a washboard. Mom made a comment about the jarring conditions of the road, at which point Dad, whose humorous side came across only infrequently, remarked, "If you want to, I can go faster so you won't feel the bumps," which probably meant going twenty-five miles per hour instead of twenty.

Mom didn't utter a word. She just smiled at him. She knew Dad was kidding. Besides, the dark blue Chevrolet sedan from the 1930s, an old jalopy (*un carrito viejo*), according to him, probably couldn't have gone much faster.

Once we reached the paved road, about twenty-plus miles south of Cuba, the highway felt smooth as ice. Still, I doubt that Dad drove more than thirty miles per hour as we headed south toward Albuquerque. At the San Ysidro junction, we turned north to Jémez Pueblo.

From San Ysidro to the pueblo took a while. Along the way, I looked out the window and was captivated by the beauty of the landscape, above all the red soil, which was not common back home in the Río Puerco Valley.

"Hijito, did you fall asleep?" my mother asked, without turning her head to see if I had dozed off or not. "What about your little brothers?"

"No, Mom. We're awake," I answered as my eyes continued to be glued to the beautiful hillsides and the multitude of trees along the road. The terrain certainly was different from all the volcanic plugs and buttes near my casita.

Dad was quiet as a mouse. He didn't utter a word. With both hands firmly on the steering wheel, he seemed to be in deep concentration. I also thought he was going fast. Once upon a time I had seen some numbers on the dashboard while I pretended to drive in the carved-out shed near the house where my father kept the car, but I couldn't figure out what they were. (Later I learned that I was looking at the speedometer.) In any case, I peered over Dad's shoulder and saw the needle of the speedometer bouncing from left to right and back again.

"Look, Dad!" I said to him, all excited. "The needle is going crazy. You're going too fast."

"Sit back in your seat. We're almost to the pueblo," were his only words.

All of a sudden, there was a horrible whiny noise. I sat up to take a look. Dad looked at Mom, and she looked at him. Both appeared startled.

"Look, Dad!" I blurted out. "The needle isn't jumping anymore," upon which I saw a look of relief on Dad's face.

"Hija," he said to Mom. "it's just the cable or chain. There's nothing wrong with the car," he added to reassure her. He no doubt was thinking of being stranded on the road. The silvery coiled cable to the speedometer evidently had worn out, which didn't matter, since it hadn't been working properly anyway.

Coming and going from my little house to Jémez Pueblo was an all-day trip. It took between three to four hours each way, depending on the wide-ranging road conditions through our valley following the summer monsoon season. By the time we reached the pueblo, the sun was not quite above our heads. This meant that lunch was still a spell away.

Mom and Dad had been to the pueblo before. Dad knew the routine once we set foot on Indian land, as he had made numerous trips there on covered wagon with his parents long before he married Mom. He parked, got out of the car, went inside a house, and came back out with a piece of paper in his hand.

From there we drove to a nearby home. Dad knocked on the screen door, and a man came out. There was a brief exchange of words between them before Dad walked back to the car. Apparently, the paper Dad had in his possession gave him permission to conduct business in the pueblo.

"He's got just what we want," he said to Mom, so Dad and I followed the Indian host while Mom stayed in the car with my little brothers and sister. In the back porch to his home, the Indian had several flat wooden crates full of peaches and apricots, as well as baskets full of apples. After a few minutes of talking and bartering, the score was settled. Dad unloaded the sacks of corn and pinto beans from our car in exchange for two crates of peaches, one of apricots, and a large and a small basket of red apples.

As a consolation prize, as it were, the Indian, a very hospitable gentleman with two front eyeteeth missing, told Dad he could have a free crate full of mission grapes, but we would have to pick them ourselves. Since Dad was not one to look a gift horse in the mouth ("*A caballo regalado no hay que verle el colmillo*"), he said yes, much to Mom's delight. As for me, I was in the dark, because the round, dark grapes that looked like playing marbles were totally foreign to me. The Indian handed Dad a wooden crate, and he directed us to the vineyard that stretched for quite a ways behind his house. A ditch—an acequia, part of the watering system—flanked his vineyard.

I accompanied Dad. Without question this was not his first time picking grapes. He knew how to treat the vines without manhandling them. Before you could say boo, he had filled the crate to the top. I just observed. As he put the last bunch of grapes on top, he handed me a small cluster (*un racimo*). "Here," he said. "You'll like them, but don't go get drunk," he added with a wry smile.

I ran back to the car as fast as my little legs could carry me to show Mom the grapes. "Look, Mom. Look at what Dad gave me, but he told me not to get drunk. What did he mean?"

"Oh, your father was just kidding. He said that because wine comes from grapes. Have you tried them? Let me have one. Here's how you eat them," and Mom grabbed a grape, put it in her mouth, and chewed the grape before swallowing it. "Don't go swallow the grapes whole, or you can choke," she warned.

I tried one grape, then another, until the little bunch was gone. I liked them. By now Dad was on his way back to the car with the crate of grapes hoisted on his right shoulder. He put it in the middle of the back seat, between my brothers and me. I sat on the right side of the car, behind Mom and Julianita, just as I had coming over. My brothers were behind Dad. The crates of peaches and apricots and the baskets of apples, one on top of the other, were on the floor behind Mom and Dad.

Dad shook hands with the Indian and bid him good-bye. The old fellow had a happy look on his face. My parents bore the same expression . . . and I was fascinated with the pueblo. While there I was awestruck by what I saw. To begin with, the Indian with whom Dad conducted business was wearing a *chongo*, a braid. That struck me as odd, because I thought only women tied their hair into ponytails. As for the Indian women, they wore leggings and carried pots on their heads. This was also new to me. I was an enchanted little boy.

On the way home, I asked Mom about those things, and she patiently explained that the Indian people had their own customs and that, in some cases, they were different from ours, including the clothes they wore. This trip was turning out to be a good learning experience for me. I yearned to return to the pueblo.

My first introduction to Indian culture piqued my curiosity. I was excited to learn more about Indians and their way of life. My opportunity came on subsequent visits not only to Jémez Pueblo with my parents but a few years later with Grandma Cinda on her trips to the pueblos of Zía, Sandía, and Tesuque, where she had several Indian friends.

On the way home from Jémez Pueblo, Dad stopped at the junction in San Ysidro called the Y to have a beer at the Triangle Bar. According to Mom, that is something he did without fail whenever he passed through San Ysidro. Mom and my siblings and I stayed in the car. By now, I was getting pretty hungry. I asked Mom when we were going to eat lunch.

"Wait till your father comes back. Then we'll ask him. For now, here's a galleta [biscuit] to tide you over until we stop along the road. I'm sure it won't be long."

Dad returned a few minutes later. When he got in the car the first thing Mom said to him was, "Junie is hungry. *Está con la tripa clara.* He's dying of hunger."

"We're going to stop in just a little bit, not far from here. There's a place that your mom and I have enjoyed in the past. Just hold onto your stomach. Don't let it go away. We'll be there in a jiffy," Dad said to me as he gripped the steering wheel with both hands.

Sure enough! It didn't take long before Dad turned onto a side dirt road and drove toward the foothills not far from the highway. He came to an area where the road ended. He turned the car around to face the highway. My little brothers and sister were asleep. Mom unloaded a ten-pound tin can holding our lunch and put it on a canvas that Dad had spread on the ground. No sooner had Mom sat down than she screamed.

"*¡Jesús, María y José! ¡Una víbora!*" she hollered at the top of her lungs. She had nearly sat on top of a rattlesnake; unbeknownst to her, it had evidently crawled onto the canvas from a nearby bush or sagebrush.

"What, what, what is it?" Dad said, startled but not knowing quite what to make of Mom's screams. He obviously did not hear Mom utter the word *víbora*. It was not uncommon for rattlesnakes to linger until September or early October, if the weather was still warm, before they went into hibernation for the winter.

The word *rattlesnake* had not escaped me. I ran quickly and hopped back in the car, scared out of my wits. Mom was right behind me. She refused to eat at this place. Consequently, Dad loaded up the canvas and the can with our lunch. We stopped not far from there at some hot springs where people like Grandma Cinda went to bathe to alleviate their arthritic pains. That's where we had a tranquil meal before leaving for home.

But, alas, another delay awaited us. Upon hopping in the car, I noticed that it was tilted to the right side, which made it easier for me to get in, of course, but there was definitely something wrong. I told Dad and much to his dismay, the right rear tire was flat as a tortilla. This was also something new to me. I didn't realize that there was such a thing as a flat tire.

For some reason, I thought that tires were made of solid rubber, but Dad explained that tires contained air. That surprised me!

He didn't carry a spare tire (he couldn't afford one), so he had no choice but to fix the tire. The first thing Mom and Dad did was to gather several moderately large rocks to keep the car from moving forward, since it was on an incline. One rock went in front of the right front tire and two more in front and back of the left rear tire.

Next Dad got out the jack, put it under the right rear bumper, jacked up the car, removed the tire, and took out the inner tube. To determine where the tube was punctured, he used his hand pump to fill it with air. He then dipped it in a creek near the hot springs. By submerging and rotating the tire in the water, he was able to see if air escaped by the oozing of tiny bubbles. That way, he knew where the leak was.

He got a rubber patch with an adhesive substance and clamped it to the tube, securing it with a contraption that he carried among his tire accessories. Once he did that, he took out his pocketknife, scraped a few small holes in the cork, and lit a match it. I watched while the cork smoked and burned slowly until the red little sparks disappeared, thus sealing the patch to the tube.

He pumped the tube half-full of air and dipped it again in the water nearby to make sure no bubbles oozed out of the leak. Then he inserted the tube back inside the tire and pumped it full of air. Judging from the number of patches on the tube, I'd say Dad evidently had had a few flat tires. Once he secured the tire back on the car and lowered the jack, he cranked up the engine (there were no automatic ignitions back then), got it started, and took off. Dad was concerned that it would get dark before we arrived home.

He hated to drive after dark on dirt roads because of wandering livestock, especially cows, but he also thought using headlights shortened the life span of the car's battery. In fact, a few ranchers who had vehicles believed the same thing. Often they drove after dark without their lights on, particularly if there was a full moon. One thing for sure, if the tiny fuses that kept the lights lit at night burned out, which happened on occasion, Dad knew how to fix them: he wrapped tinfoil from Juicy Fruit chewing gum around the fuses to create an electrical contact so the lights would come back on again. I remember doing this a number of times when night fell, coming to Bernalillo and Albuquerque or vice versa. That's why I always saved the tinfoil from my chewing gum.

In spite of the flat tire and what had happened to Mom with the rattlesnake, the day for me had been exciting and adventurous. When we got home it was almost evening. I had slept in the car; therefore, I wasn't sleepy. Besides, I was still excited from the trip to Jémez Pueblo. While Mom put my little sister to bed, Dad unloaded the fruit. There was only one thing wrong. When he went to bring in the crate of grapes, I heard him holler at Mom: "Hija, what happened to the grapes? They're practically all gone!" Mom clearly did not hear him, because there was no response. I dashed to the bedroom and hid under the bed.

On the way home after the rattlesnake episode, I had started to eat grapes one at a time. That was my dessert. By the time we got home, I had eaten almost half of the crate. It wasn't long before Mom came into the bedroom to question me about the grapes, although there wasn't much to explain because it was quite obvious I had consumed lots of them.

Mom, forever the consummate mother who worried about her children's well-being, asked if I had a stomachache and if that's why I was under the bed. I wasn't about to tell her the whole truth, of course, even though the grapes were itching to find a way out of my system.

I finally emerged from under the bed, but I wasn't feeling too sprightly, to say the least. As nighttime approached, I felt really sick to my stomach. The night turned into a veritable nightmare, with grapes rumbling around in my stomach like marbles in a soup bowl. By morning, I had been so sick I vowed never to eat grapes again, and, indeed, I didn't consume a single grape for years to come. I had not gotten drunk, as Dad suggested, but boy, did I learn a lesson about those dark grapes. (Many years later my friend Joe Sando from Jémez Pueblo informed me that they were mission grapes.)

Notwithstanding my episode with grapes, the trip to Jémez Pueblo was great fun. I could hardly wait for the next journey. But for now, it was time to get serious, because the task of canning the peaches and apricots awaited Mom and me once Dad departed for his job with the Rangers come Monday morning.

Late that Monday evening my aunt Taida came to our house to team up with my mother to can the fruit; part of it was hers. She and Mom always got together at our house during the canning season. Their partnership had become a family tradition.

OCTOBER NIGHTS—CANNING MARATHONS

The canning routine was simple but exhaustive. No matter how hot and sweaty the kitchen got during the cool October nights, Mom and Aunt Taida truly loved to can fruits and vegetables in their pressure cookers. They were a perfect team at the ranch, and over time they built an unbreakable bond between them. Through thick and thin they remained the best of friends for the rest of their lives. They were like sisters.

Aunt Taida usually arrived right after dusk, walking up the hill to our home with her jars and accessories. By that time my little brothers and sister were already tucked in bed. Canning season was one of few times when Mom allowed me to stay up late when I didn't have school the following day. As a consequence, I was able to observe the canning routine from beginning to end. Canning at times took three or four nights—and sometimes lasted until the wee hours of the morning.

The first thing that Mom and Aunt Taida did was to wash the jars, lids, and rings in hot, soapy water. Then they put them in boiling water to sterilize them. Afterward, they filled the jars with fruit, added water and sugar, and sealed the jars with lids and rings before placing them in the pressure cooker. They always started with the apricots.

I don't know, nor do I recall, where Mom's pressure cooker came from, whether Dad bought it for her or not. Word has it that pressure cookers were donated to housewives after they learned the canning process from a government food consultant or demonstrator during the Great Depression. Be that as it may, Mom and Aunt Taida were masters at home canning. By the time they finished their canning marathon, the kitchen table and another small table nearby were covered with dozens of jars of fruit ready for the two families to enjoy during the winter months.

26

Polite Politicians

I GOT UP EARLY, as usual, just as Grandpa Lolo's rooster began to crow. His timely crowing had a habit of waking me up every morning. Today was Friday, and Dad would soon be home for two days. The week had gone by rather quickly, which elated me because he would bring me my little brown paper sack of hard candy from don Ricardo Heller's General Store in Cabezón. And my sweet-craving molars would rejoice.

Unlike other mornings when I lit the fire in the woodstove and got the coffee going for Mom, today was different. She got up soon after me.

"Is something wrong, amá? How come you're up so early?" I asked, somewhat concerned.

"Nothing's wrong, hijito. I guess I forgot to close the window last night before going to bed and got too much of a draft. Here I am with a droopy eye (*un ojo gacho*). What's your dad going to think?"

"It looks like a mosquito bite, but it doesn't look bad. By the way, will you be fixing chicken and rice or fried rabbit for Dad?" I asked as I ate my oatmeal. It was a foregone conclusion that she'd prepare one of his two favorite dishes.

"I don't know yet. Either way, you'll have to chase down a chicken or a rabbit, but I'll tell you this afternoon after you wake up from your siesta, what do you say?"

"Okay, amá."

As soon as I finished my breakfast, I took off to feed my rabbits and the chickens. Since most of the rabbits ran loose, I scattered alfalfa for them along with some pellets. I also filled their little pans with water. A couple of mother rabbits were in their hutches (*conejeras*). They were expecting little rabbits soon.

Feeding the chickens was easy, too. I had already used Mom's hand grinder to grind some corn, which I scattered on the ground for them to eat. Chickens have no teeth, so the corn prepared in this fashion was perfect, but, then again, they pecked at just about anything. They had their own large pans of water that they loved to flap their wings in. I enjoyed their frolicsome antics, but refilling the pans was not to my liking.

The chicken coop was next to Dad's corral, where he locked his livestock for the night. Overlooking the corral, practically hovering over it, was the huge butte mentioned in chapter 1. The butte provided protection from the westward winds in the spring and shade at dusk during the summer; it also served as a buffer during inclement weather, above all in January and February. These undoubtedly were the coldest months of the year.

As I locked the gate to the chicken coop, I heard the sound of a vehicle roaring up the hill, headed for Grandpa's house. It was a long black car, the biggest automobile I had ever seen. I ran home and reached the kitchen door at about the same time that the car stopped next to the water tank that my grandparents had on the north side of their house. A stout-looking man wearing a light tan Stetson hat got down from the car. He looked distinguished, as though he were somebody important. He went around to the front of the house, climbed the two or three stone steps to the portal, and disappeared from sight.

"Amá, amá, there's a man at Grandpa's house! He's in *un carro grandototote*, a really huge car!"

"¡Híjole! It must be quite a car, the way you describe it. Let's take a look," she said, curious enough herself to look out the kitchen door.

"Ah," she commented rather nonchalantly. "That's don Bernardino. He's a good friend of your Grandpa's. He's a politician. He always comes around right before election to get people to vote for him and his political friends."

That was all gibberish to me. I didn't understand a thing about election and votes. My curiosity begged answers to a question or two, however.

"Amá, what's an election? What's a vote? What's a politician?" I asked in rapid succession.

"I tell you what, when don Bernardino leaves, you go ask your Grandpa.

He'll explain everything to you. He knows all about that sort of thing. He's a politico himself. But don't go interrupt him now. Wait until don Bernardino leaves."

I waited and waited and waited. I looked, I spied, and I peeked from behind the kitchen screen door. I wondered what they were doing, what they were discussing.

"Your neck's going to look like your aunt's *gansos*, geese, if you don't quit stretching it," Mom said in a jovial tone of voice.

Finally, the waiting game ended. Don Bernardino and Grandpa emerged from their hideout. They stepped down from the portal, first don Bernardino, then Grandpa; both were in a jolly mood and smoking cigars. There was no doubt in my mind but what they were puffing on was White Owl cigars; that was one of Grandpa's favorite brands. I had seen him smoke White Owls on Sunday mornings after breakfast. Sitting in his rocker on the porch, looking out toward his cornfields during the summer, admiring the fruits of his labor while blowing smoke from his cigar—this was his weekly ritual, except when the priest came to our placita to celebrate monthly Mass.

Just before don Bernardino climbed into his jet-black car, he put his cigar in his mouth and shook Grandpa's right hand, then patted him on the back and took off. The car's luminous sparkle reminded me of Prieto, my horse, whenever the sun shone on him.

As soon as don Bernardino departed, I dashed over to my grandfather's house. I walked in the kitchen, where they had been talking. Grandpa Lolo was picking up the coffee cups from the table and somewhat oblivious to my presence. He was in a pensive mood. Resting on an empty sardine can that he used for an ashtray was the cigar he had been smoking, but lo and behold, it did not bear the shiny White Owl logo! Upon looking more closely, I could see it was the photo of a man—King Edward—in a dark suit. I had a vague idea from school what the English word *king* meant, so in my mind the logo confirmed what Mom had said about don Bernardino. If he was smoking a cigar named after a king, he indeed had to be an important person. I was to learn later that he was a political kingpin, a juggernaut in the Republican Party.

But for now it was time for me to pick my grandfather's brains. I thought whatever questions were apt to spew out of my mouth would not render Grandpa Lolo speechless. He was an exceedingly patient person, forever predisposed to teaching his grandchildren something new.

"Ah, hijito, when did you come in?" he said, finally acknowledging my presence. "Grab that dish towel that's on the chair and dry these cups for me."

As I was drying the cups and the spoons, I said to him, "Grandpa Lolo, who was that man? He must be rich, driving a big car like that, huh?"

"He's not rich, but he's a good man (*güen hombre*), a dear friend, and an important person, too."

"If he's not rich, how come he left this stack (*pila*) of money on the table?"

"Boy, you sure are full of questions this morning! That money is not his; it belongs to the Republican Party. I'll use that money to get people out to vote on election day in a week or so."

My grandfather noticed that I was scratching my head as though I were baffled at what I had just heard. Needless to say, he was right. Instead of things becoming clearer, they were getting more and more confusing.

"What do you mean by 'to vote'?" I asked, hoping to get a simple answer to my question.

"Listen, to vote"—he pronounced the *v* like a *b*—"is when people go vote (*botar*)."

"And how do they do that? What do they do?" was my first reaction, since I knew that *botar* meant "to bounce."

"It's simple. People go to the old schoolhouse in the placita. There they are given a piece of paper called a ballot, and then they run fast as all get out and bounce up against the back wall inside the school, fall back, and pick themselves up. That's what voting is all about! You'll see when you go with me on election day," and he looked me straight in the eye with a slight grin.

"And do women and kids vote too?"

"Only men and women, because you have to be an adult to vote. Okay. That's enough questions for now. Tomorrow night there's a political dance in the village, and you'll see the schoolhouse where people vote. Now go on home in case your mother needs you."

Sure enough! No sooner did I walk in and Mom put me to work. "Okay. Go fetch me a rabbit. By this evening we'll have fried rabbit prepared for your dad when he comes home."

Dad got home by dusk from his weekly job in El Rito de Semilla. My mom had everything ready: rabbit, warm tortillas, fried potatoes, canned corn and zucchini (calabacitas), plus rice pudding with raisins for dessert.

For the longest time, I wondered why Mom didn't sit at the table to eat with Dad. One day it dawned on me why. My parents only had two place settings, and Mom and I shared the second one. (My little brothers and sister shared a small cup and bowl that at one time had belonged to me.) Mom and Dad did have a complete set of dishes for six people (a pink crystal-type set), a wedding present that Mom used on Sundays or for special occasions when guests came to the house.

While Dad ate, Mom reminded him of the political dance that Grandpa had mentioned earlier in the day.

"Don't forget there's a dance tomorrow night at the placita. We have to go."

"Uh, I had forgotten all about it. Don Ricardo told me about it this evening on my way home."

"You don't sound too excited" was Mom's response to Dad's lukewarm reaction.

"You know me and politicians who show up to sweet-talk the people. *Vienen con sus bienes y se van con sus malas intenciones.* They come with their highfalutin' promises and leave with bad intentions."

My mom listened to Dad's words. She could tell he wasn't very fond of politicians. "But how can you say that when your father's a politician, a *patrón*!" Mom remarked.

"True, but he's not a candidate for office. Besides, he's an honest politician. He doesn't pocket the money they give him to bribe people to vote, including those who are six feet under in the *camposanto*."

I listened to their brief conversation as I chewed on my hard candy. I was getting a different perspective on politics, even if I didn't quite grasp Dad's less-than-flattering words. As a rule, he was very discreet in talking negatively about people. Doing so, in his opinion, was tantamount to spreading mitote, gossip, something he disliked immensely.

Saturday was a busy day on the farm for Dad before we started getting ready for the dance. Mom fixed a quick supper of caldito (a stew of potatoes, cubed beef from the storage shed, and canned corn), spinach (as a side dish, sprinkled with red chile seeds), and hot biscuits. As usual, we ate in shifts, and then I helped Mom dry the dishes before I got dressed.

The political dance was not a special dance like a bolote, a shindig, except for the presence of the political candidates who basked in their oratory and dressed the part: a suit and tie, a white shirt complemented by a vest, cowboy boots, and a brown or off-white cowboy hat.

As for us, we dressed pretty much as we usually did for other dances. Dad put on his Levi's, gabardine shirt (some ranchers wore Pendleton shirts, which they jokingly pronounced "Pedoten"), boots, and his beige Stetson hat. Mom wore a white blouse and long blue skirt and black dress shoes. I had on a white shirt, Levi's, and low-top brown shoes. The entire family looked elegant. Mom wouldn't have it any other way when we went out in public.

Dad hitched up the team of horses, and we hopped on the horse wagon. He and Mom sat on the front bench with Julianita. Beltrán, Juanito, and I sat on a blanket in the bed of the wagon. The sun had already disappeared behind the San Mateo Mountains. Consequently, by the time we reached the placita, where the dance was to take place, darkness had begun to set in as October came to an end.

We were not the first ones to arrive. A couple of families were already there. Greeting people at the schoolhouse were two gentlemen, one on either side of the entrance. They were obviously candidates running for public office. Politely introducing themselves as people entered, they saluted the women one by one by tipping their hats or shaking their hands.

Mom and I went inside and sat on one of the wooden benches (tarimas) that lined both the left and right walls and were reserved for women, their daughters, and the rest of the children. The space toward the back wall was where the musicians, a violinist and a guitarist, played, once in a while accompanied by an accordionist. The guitarist, named don José, was also the local barber. The violin player was not from my village; therefore his name was not familiar to me.

I noticed that the setup in the schoolhouse was no different from that of the dances held in don Porfirio's dance hall, next to the church. But the atmosphere was much more subdued, maybe because tonight's dance was a political affair.

As more and more people arrived, the men congregated outside, in front of the school. Since the night had begun to cool off, someone had started a small fire, whose glow I could see from inside the school. I asked Mom if I could go outside to watch. There were several other kids horsing around in the semidarkness, including Cousin J., who had just arrived with Aunt Taida and Uncle Antonio.

"Hey, when did you get here?" he shouted at me from behind the sagebrush where he was hiding with some friends. "You want to come with us?"

"Where you going?"

"Just around."

After Cousin J. and I got tired of running around and hiding in the sagebrush, pretending to be ghosts and scaring the other kids, I noticed a man at the bonfire passing around a bottle of liquor for everyone to take a swig. Cousin J. and I decided to eavesdrop.

Standing around the fire were my dad, Uncle Antonio, and some other men whom I didn't recognize except for Dad's compadre Salvador. My padrino (godfather) Higinio was also among the group. They were talking politics, of course, and the more I listened, the more animated the discussion became. I overheard one man say to the others, "Listen, *todos están cortados con la misma tijera*. Politicians are all cut from the same cloth. They promise the sun and the moon."

A gentleman wearing a black hat agreed. "That's right. *Se embarran con una mano y se limpian con lotra*. They soil themselves with one hand, and they clean up the mess with the other."

Another man, who sported a huge mustachio and whom I had seen at the local post office, was even blunter. "*No son más que puro pedo y poca caca*. They're all nothing but farts and a little shit." They all burst out laughing at his earthy expression. I got the impression that they, like Dad, weren't too fond of politicians but somehow felt obligated to attend the dance.

At about that moment one of men spotted my cousin J. and me behind the sagebrush. "*¡Epa, chamacos!* Scoot!" And we disappeared in the dark.

I heard the music start, and Cousin J. and I ran inside the dance hall.

The musicians were playing waltzes and other slow numbers. The dance floor was about half-full. People were beginning to have a good time. This went on for a while. Suddenly, one of the musicians, I believe it was don José, rang a cowbell to get people's attention.

Grandpa Lolo stepped forward and welcomed everyone. He introduced a member of the Republican Party from Bernalillo, the seat for Sandoval County. The gentleman in turn introduced the two candidates who were running for office. One got up and gave a short speech promising to build more lagoons for holding water for livestock, better country roads, and new bridges. The other candidate spoke briefly and asked people for their votes. He, too, made a number of promises, above all that he would fight for more money to support the two local schools, the one in our village and the other across the river in Rincón del Cochino, about three miles away, where I attended.

Once their speeches were over, dancing resumed, but this time with more aplomb. The people were now scampering and stomping all over the dirt floor to fast polkas. Some couples were really good dancers, particularly a bowlegged man who had one leg shorter than the other. He lived not too far from our house. He hailed from the Montaño clan.

Political dances, unlike fiesta dances, did not last long. By midnight the schoolhouse emptied and everybody went home, which was just as well because kids like me got bored being bystanders.

The day before the election, Grandpa Lolo told me to be ready the next morning. I was to accompany him to the placita; I got up early, as usual, at the crowing of his rooster, but with an air of anticipation and interest about what people actually did on election day. I got the fire started in the stove, put on the coffee for Mom, and heated a small pan of water for my oatmeal. In the rush of things and clanging of dishes, I woke her up.

"Hijito, what are you doing? What's all the noise for? You're going to wake up the chickens!" she said in a playful tone.

"I've got to go with Grandpa to the placita. He's waiting for me. Amá, are you going to vote?"

"Yes, hijito, but I'll go with your aunt Taida and her family. And you be careful."

"Yes, amá," and I rushed out the kitchen door.

When I walked into Grandpa's kitchen, he had just sat down to eat his breakfast and was in the process of cooling off his coffee. Unlike other coffee drinkers, who simply drank their hot coffee straight from the cup, he had a different routine—a ritual, in fact. He used two cups. First he would fill a cup with hot coffee. Then he'd pour the steaming coffee into an empty cup and repeat that gesture, pouring from one cup into the other, back and forth, until the coffee was cool enough to drink. I never quite understood why he just didn't let the coffee sit until it cooled off.

While Grandpa finished eating breakfast, I went out and saddled Bayito. I thought if I was to accompany him to an important event like voting, I should ride my beautiful and elegant horse for the occasion. By the time I saddled Bayito, Grandpa emerged from the kitchen, stood on the portal, and hollered at me.

"Bring me Colorao so I can saddle him up, but be careful he doesn't kick you"—a cautious reminder, since his horse was mean-spirited. Colorao was notorious for kicking if you made the mistake of going around behind him, something you didn't do unless you were daring or stupid. Colorao also liked to bite when you mounted him, but that's something I didn't have to worry about.

I brought Grandpa his horse without incident. His saddle, blanket, and bridle were on the portal. Grandpa took little time to get Colorao ready. He pulled the right rein to the right and wrapped it around the saddle horn, then he put his left foot in the stirrup and mounted without getting bitten.

Our trip to the placita didn't take long. When we got to the Río Puerco, there were a couple of men watering their horses. Grandpa Lolo greeted them before we crossed the river and headed for the schoolhouse, where voting was to take place. It was located toward the back of the village, near a flat mesa not far from the river. Because there was no shade around the school, we tied our horses under some trees near the church. From there it was a short walk.

The hustle and bustle of activity was beginning to kick up both outside and inside the school building (there were no classes on election day). Some men were arriving on horseback; others rode in with their wives, mothers, or mothers-in-law on their horse wagons. I tagged along behind

Grandpa as we made our way inside the one-room schoolhouse. I looked around; the building wasn't any different than my school, La Mesa.

Once inside, Grandpa headed for two small wooden tables. One person was sitting at each table. A man stood close by. He was the judge in charge of voting, whereas the two persons, a man and a woman—a Republican and a Democrat—made sure the voters affixed their signatures in a rule-lined book. Either that or they put an X next to their names.

Many of the old folks didn't know how to sign their names. Thus one of the people at the table or a relative cosigned, provided the judge witnessed the signature. A paper ballot was handed to the voter and the judge read to him or her the candidates' names and their political affiliations. Then the voter marked an X in a small square next to the chosen candidate's name and deposited the ballot in a cardboard box on top of a third table. The ballot box was watched over by another person. He acted as a judge.

All this time, I observed and waited and waited for the moment when people would run and bounce off the wall, but that never happened. I was anxious to ask Grandpa why not. However, he was too busy handing out money to people and shaking their hands as they emerged from the schoolhouse after voting. Each time a voter came out, he handed him or her a dollar bill from the wad of money don Bernardino had left with him. I noticed that he gave money to certain voters, but not to everyone. This went on all day long, until there were no more people left to vote.

On the way home I was still curious about people bouncing off the wall. Unable to resist any longer, I asked Grandpa Lolo about it. "Grandpa, I never saw people run and bounce off the wall like you said. Why not?"

"Oh, hijito. That's just a silly thing, a *tontería*. You see, *votar* and *botar* are pronounced the same way, but the first word means to vote, and the second means to bounce. Do you understand?"

"Yes, I get it. So, when people say they've already voted (*botaron*), they're kidding, because they actually haven't bounced off the wall like a ball."

"You're right. It's like a game with words—you say one thing but mean another."

Next I asked him how come he didn't give money to everybody. That's when I learned about party affiliation and loyalty and the fact that he, like most farmers, was a staunch Republican. I also learned that family members toed the line and voted like the father or grandfather. Grandpa's family was no exception; everyone eligible to vote did so along party lines, although in later years my father and other of Grandpa's offspring became Democrats.

The comings and goings on election day left my head buzzing. The goings-on certainly were interesting, but I still didn't have a handle on the total scope of things. There was a lot to assimilate. For the moment, I was happy to be home and thankful that Grandpa Lolo took me along for the experience. Some day I would be able to vote just like him. One thing for sure, I'll always remember his comment about voters bouncing off the wall. I thought that was funny and typical of Grandpa's wit.

27

Humor Comes in a Variety of Ways

HUMOR WAS NEVER IN short supply in my household. Nor was it absent beyond the walls of my home and throughout the community. There was always something to chuckle over, but telling jokes as such, unlike storytelling, was not popular. Jokes were more a matter of happenstance. Most of the laughter stemmed from unexpected incidents and real-life situations that I witnessed or participated in as a small boy. At best, they could be categorized as farcical. My childhood was not dull; if anything at all, it was replete with laughter and excitement. The ensuing episodes comprise humorous snapshots from growing up in the Río Puerco Valley that to this day remain richly fixed in my mind.

CALF RIDING

Young boys were forever having fun above and beyond such normal outdoor activities as shooting marbles, target practice with slingshots, kicking the can (Mom hated this game because I scuffed my shoes), arm wrestling on stilts, or La Clavadita, played with a pocketknife. Using your forefinger to gingerly press the sharp point of the knife against different parts of the body (for example, the shoulder), you then flipped the knife into the ground with the forefinger. If the blade stuck in the dirt, you scored points. As we grew older, we sought—and concocted—other ways of entertaining ourselves, sometimes with success, other times with embarrassment.

One Sunday morning following Mass, Cousin G. and two older boys decided that it would be fun to ride Grandpa Lolo's young bulls (toritos). He had been fattening them up at La Vega, his favorite pasturing place on his ranch. He was to sell the young bulls to prospective buyers in late October or early November, following the fall roundup. The September morning was sunny but crisp. Fall was definitely in the air, perfect for riding young bulls; this was a new adventure for some of the other kids, including me. About five or six of us headed for La Vega, located about a mile from Grandpa's regular home. The summer grass was still quite tall but burned and brown from the scorching heat.

Of the group, Cousin G. had the reputation in the community of being most fearless whatever the undertaking. He was the most courageous of anyone (*tenía huevos*), regardless of the risk at hand. But he refused to be the first one to ride the young bulls. He convinced everyone that he had ridden the toritos countless times in the past, but none of the boys, including me, had ever seen him show off his bull-riding skills. We just took him at his word. I had seen him ride goats and pigs, but these domesticated animals were hardly a fair comparison with toritos.

The bulls, born in March and April, were now about five or six months old. To an eight-year-old like me, they looked huge. Cousin G. finally coaxed one of his buddies (cuates), Celso—who hailed from Santa Clara, north of my village—into riding the first young bull, but before doing so they had to lasso him by his hind legs. As the calf fell to the ground, Celso wrapped a rope around the animal's midsection to hold onto, made the sign of the cross to avoid injury, and quickly hopped on the animal. Upon feeling the weight on his back the young bull sprang to his feet and started mooing, kicking, twisting, and turning furiously, as though to shake off his unwelcome guest. Everybody was egging Celso on, but he didn't last long. Before he could say "*Jesús, María y José*," he landed hard on his fundillo, his butt. He got up slowly, holding his *nalgas*, buttocks, one in each hand. Everybody burst out laughing, but at least he had broken the ice, as it were, and not a bone.

A fat kid from Casa Salazar stepped forward. "I'll take the next one," he announced in a self-assured manner. He was a Romero. They were known for being real facetos, show-offs; they also had the reputation of being superb horse riders. He, too, was no match for the young bull. No sooner

had he hopped on the calf than plunk, he landed on top of a large sage
bush. We couldn't see any sign of him. We all held our breaths and then
ran toward where he had disappeared. Because of his weight, the fall had
thrust him not only smack in the middle of the bush but also deep into it.
He was grimacing and holding his right arm. Cousin G., who felt responsible, pulled him out gingerly. We were all horrified thinking that he had
broken his arm, but suddenly he yelled out, waving both arms up in the
air. "Hey, that was fun! Let's do it again! I now know how to fly and crash
into bushes."

Everyone cracked up laughing. "Okay, who's next?" shouted Cousin G.,
relieved that the fat kid from Casa Salazar was safe and sound.

After the last scary episode, everybody was reluctant to ride the young
bulls. I certainly wasn't about to try it, because I had neglected to tell Mom
where I was going after Mass. What is more, I was still wearing my church
clothes, as were the rest of the kids. Most of us had on Levi's, white shirts,
boots, and cowboy hats.

"Okay, you chickens," said Cousin G. "I'll show you how to ride those
toritos. There's nothing to it. Pick me the largest one."

"The black and white one!" hollered one of the boys. "He's not the biggest, but he looks like a nasty bull. Look at those horns. Looks like he could
give you a good *cornada*, whack with his horns, right in the *rosca*, ass."
Everybody laughed, which didn't please Cousin G. in the least. In fact, he
was furious and ready to mount the young bull.

A buddy of his took off after the bull, twirling his rope in the air until he
roped him. The rest of us ran and pounced on the beast. Meantime,
Cousin G. had put on his spurs, and he refused a rope around the young
bull's belly to hold onto. He thought that by digging in his spurs he could
last longer, but he was mistaken. He got on without any trouble, dug his
spurs into the bull's underbelly, held onto the young bull's hide with his left
hand, and waved his right hand in the air while hollering, "Whoopee!
Whoopee!" He lasted longer than anyone else, but before he could say
"whoopee" the third time, he flew into the air and landed smack on top of a
pastel, cow chip, that was no more than a day or two old and still semiwet.
When he got up he looked like he had crapped in his pants. All of us were
busting a gut. It was the most hilarious thing I had seen happen to him.

Cousin G. learned that even the bravest and most boisterous can be humiliated. To add insult to his stinking pants, he had to take them off so he could ride his horse—it was either that or walk. He tied a rope to his pants' legs and dragged them all the way home. The rest of us made sure he rode behind us with his soiled trousers. It was quite a sight. Besides, no one had ever seen anybody at the ranch, least of all Cousin G., riding on horseback in his underwear. He was not a happy rider.

COUSIN G.'S TUMBLE

But Cousin G.'s humiliation extended beyond landing on a wet cow chip. On another occasion, he was thrown off a bucking horse that Dad was trying to train. It was late afternoon on a summer day. Dad, who was then a young man in his early thirties but of course older than my cousin, was having a hard time mounting his unruly horse. Every time he tried to put his left foot in the stirrup, the horse quickly moved and shifted position. Dad was on the verge of giving up when, by sheer luck, Cousin G. showed up.

"*Epa, tío.* What's wrong? Can't you get on that *potrillito*, pony?" he shouted in a sarcastic voice, knowing quite well that the horse was full grown.

"Come on! Let's see if you can get on that pony," my father, who had a creditable reputation in breaking *mesteños*, mustangs, responded in kind. "*Hay que ser valiente, pero no descortés.* One must be brave, but not discourteous," Dad added, somewhat miffed at Cousin G.'s cockiness.

"There's nothing to it! I'll show that horse a trick or two," countered Cousin G. who, in all fairness, was a pretty good bronco rider. I had witnessed his riding skills myself.

No sooner said than done. Quicker than lightning, he secured his left foot in the stirrup, swung his right leg over the saddle, gripped the reins with his left hand, raised his right hand in the air, and let out a yell. Cousin G. lasted a scant two to three seconds and kerplunk! He landed with a thud smack on top of a sage bush. Cousin J. and I were stupefied. First of all, when Cousin G. landed in the *chamizo*, he disappeared. Sank into the bush! We could not see him. Dad immediately ran toward him, presumably concerned for his well-being. Instead, Dad's reaction surprised me.

"*¡Mira lo que hicites!* Look at what you did to the brush! You squashed it," he said, seemingly getting even with Cousin G. for his sarcastic remark earlier.

Cousin G. looked up at Dad from his self-made nest in the bush. He was dumbfounded at Dad's comment, but he delicately managed to extricate himself without any help from the rest of us. Seeing that he was all in one piece and with no apparent broken bones, everyone had a good laugh, including Dad.

A WALKING STICK

I had an uncle who was a bit cantankerous and at times mean-spirited. He didn't have many good days, or so it seemed. If he did, I hadn't been privy to any of them. Word even within his immediate family was that he had been born in a bad mood. Yet he had a funny side to him, provided one bothered to observe other facets of his character besides his crankiness.

To begin with, he was short, and the things he did to compensate for his diminutive stature were themselves comical. He owned a pickup truck, but to reach the steering wheel and to see through the windshield he stacked at least three cushions (*cojines*) on the driver's seat. He also pushed the seat forward so that his chest was right up against the steering wheel. During the warm months he drove with his right hand on the steering wheel and with his left arm hanging out the window, hugging the door. Some people thought he did these things for self-assurance; others believed it was part of his cockiness. The truth is, he was nearsighted and blinder than a bat. It was not a laughing matter. You had to feel sorry for him.

But another comical side to his persona was his false teeth. He had uppers and lowers, but he hardly ever wore them. He carried his dentures in his right hip pocket and used them only when he ate. Even then the loose-fitting teeth rattled and swam in his mouth when he chewed. He looked like two different people, depending on whether the teeth were in or out. He also smiled so infrequently that when he did he was a changed person.

Even more hilarious than his false teeth was the fact that my uncle was the only man I knew who cupped his penis when he peed. Some men thought he was striking an air of sophistication; others speculated it was because of the shortness of his manhood. Nobody, to my knowledge, ever bothered to find out, fearful they might get the tar beaten out of them. He had one good thing going for him—he had the reputation of being pretty good with his fists. And it was best not to end up being his punching bag or at the receiving end of his blows (moquetes).

I had been spending a few days in Bernalillo with Grandma Cinda; it was something I did from time to time during the summer. Mom found out that my uncle was going to Albuquerque and returning to the ranch the next day or so. She asked him if he could stop for me on the way back to the ranch.

He honked, and Grandma Cinda went out to greet him and exchange a few pleasantries. Grandma informed me that I was to return with him. I was not at all happy about going back with my grumpy uncle, although I looked forward to seeing Mom. I missed her.

I gathered a few of my possessions, gave my grandma a hug, and received her blessing before my uncle and I were on our way. He wasn't very communicative, either. That made the sixty-plus miles (about a two- to three-hour drive) rather long and humdrum. Fifty or sixty years ago ranchers didn't drive very fast, above all on country roads. My uncle was no exception.

The first moment of excitement came about a mile off the highway on the dirt road that led into the Río Puerco Valley. A heavy downpour evidently had preceded us, because there were large pools of water on the side of the road. Now it was barely sprinkling, but the roaring waters of the first of several arroyos we were to cross concerned my uncle. He stopped, got down from the truck, and looked at the huge waves of water rolling and jumping over the road. He weighed the situation carefully, with a predictable reaction. "We have no other recourse but to try to cross," he said without turning his face toward me as he got into the truck. His words, his first since we had left my grandma's house, were more a mechanical pronouncement than an acknowledgment of my company, let alone an expression of genuine concern for my safety. He pumped his chest right up against the steering wheel and gripped it firmly with both hands.

"Hold on! I'm going to gun it," and gun it he did as the truck bounced up and down on top of rocks that had washed down the arroyo but were hidden underneath the water and invisible to the naked eye. By the time we reached the other side of the arroyo, which wasn't too wide, the windshield was splashed with muddy water. My uncle tried to turn on the wipers, but they didn't work. He stopped the truck, stood outside the cab on the running board, and attempted to move them back and forth by hand. His efforts were fruitless, whereupon he let out a palabrota, thinking, no doubt, that I wouldn't understand the big, bad word.

His brow between his eyes turned red. He was furious, so mad, in fact, that he hopped back in the truck and stomped on the gas pedal. Then he pulled the throttle way out. The truck took off, moving at a high rate of speed on the muddy road. I glanced at the speedometer out the corner of one eye. He was going about forty-five miles an hour. He was flying! The junipers to the side of the road were coming at us in bunches—or so it seemed—instead of one by one. I was holding on for dear life.

We reached the village of San Luis, known for its mud called *barrial*. It was like clay, and if it got stuck in the drums, the sticky stuff could stop a vehicle in its tracks before you could say boo. My uncle knew about the mud and therefore was very cautious; he slowed down until we got through the treacherous stretch without a-slippin' and a-slidin' all over the road.

A steady rain continued without stopping. By the time we reached the next village, Cabezón, the road conditions were miserable. But I could tell my uncle was determined to get home if at all possible before the situation worsened. The skies had darkened, and gloom had begun to set upon us. After crossing the Río Puerco south of Cabezón, we went up the Cuesta de Chihuahua, a pretty steep hill, with little trouble, thanks to the slabs of stones on the road that gave us traction.

From here to my house we lacked about three to four miles. The road was not as hazardous as in San Luis or Cabezón, but it was slippery—so slick, in fact, that my uncle was holding onto the steering wheel with both hands. Except for when we crossed the arroyo earlier, I had never seen him use both hands with such a determined look on his face. At times he fought to keep the truck on the road as well as to cope with the muddy windshields.

Every once in a while he'd glance over at me as I bounced around on the front seat trying to hold onto the door handle (we had no seat belts back then). The dashboard was of little help. "Don't be afraid. I'm a good driver.

I own this truck; the truck doesn't own me" were hardly comforting words coming from him.

Just as he uttered the last words he took his eyes off the road, rounded a bend, and bingo! The truck went off the road, right into a deep arroyo! "Now we've had it," he mumbled in disgust, punctuating his exclamatory words with yet another one of his doozies. He climbed down from the truck to survey the situation. He got back in, gunned the motor, spun the tires, and tried to back out, but it was useless. All he could accomplish was to dig the tracks deeper and to make the mud fly high in the air as I looked out the rear window.

"Slide over," he said to me. "Here's what I want you to do. I'm going to try to push the truck from behind. When I holler at you, I want you to step on the accelerator, okay?"

I had never driven before, but I did as he commanded. The next thing I heard was him shouting at me to take my foot off the pedal. "Stop, stop!" he yelled, at which point he stood looking at me with his face full of the mud that had flown right at him when I accelerated and made the tires spin. He was quite a comical sight, but I refrained from laughing.

"Get down. It's no use. We'll have to walk home. We'll have your Grandpa come pull us out with his team of horses. We'll just leave the truck here until we get back," he said, as if he had any other choice. "And make sure your window is rolled up. I don't want the rain to come in."

We took off down the road by foot. The rain continued to come down relentlessly. Neither he nor I had a raincoat. All we had were thin jackets. I walked right behind my uncle. I could tell he was still angry at the turn of events. He kept kicking the ground and splashing mud on his boots. I moved farther back. I didn't want any more mud on my shoes than necessary.

As we continued walking, my uncle spotted what looked like a long stick in the middle of the road. He reached down to pick it up to use as a walking stick, another one of his habits. As soon as he grabbed it, he let out a loud scream, and another palabrota spewed out of his mouth. He quickly slammed the "stick" to the ground. It was a snake!

I burst out laughing. I couldn't contain myself. "What's so funny? I could have gotten bit!" He scowled at me, sporting a rather mystified look on his face. I walked over and picked up the snake with my bare hands. It was a bull snake.

By the time we got home his face was pale as yogurt. I told Mom about the incident, and she laughed. "Serves him right for being such a *mala cacha*, sourpuss. Maybe that'll teach him a lesson." Ironically, Mom's words turned out to be prophetic. From that episode forward, my uncle mellowed. I think the harmless snake embarrassed him as much as it frightened him to death. All the same, I was glad to be home with my mother.

NO HAT ON THE DANCE FLOOR

Dances in my placita were popular and special. They were celebrated several times throughout the year, above all during the summer months, when most secular holidays were observed. If people spoke of a baile, or dance, they invariably employed the word bolote (a roaring dance) or fandango. Both were culturally charged terms that inspired a festive mood.

I attended countless dances with my parents. By being a keen observer I learned that dancers adhered to a particular decorum lest they be looked upon as being disrespectful and uncouth. The rules of good manners applied first and foremost to men. There was a tacit understanding among local residents and guests as to what constituted respectability. For example, a cowboy was not allowed to dance with spurs on; doing so was deemed ungentlemanly and tantamount to being a show-off, a faceto.

But the one thing most people frowned upon, as mentioned in chapter 23, was for a man to saunter into a dance hall and ask a woman or a young lady to dance while he was wearing a hat. Hats on the dance floor were forbidden. The bastonero, or floor manager, saw to that. He also made certain that rambunctious men did not disrupt the dance; he tried to keep matters under control but wasn't always totally successful.

At a community dance that I attended at the Romero Dance Hall with Mom and Dad, the sound of music was in the air and so, too, was the dust from the dirt floor, some of it going out the front door; other dust escaped through the open windows. But people were having a jolly old time. Men came inside between each number to find a partner to dance with.

All of a sudden my mom and I noticed a man who had entered the dance hall wearing a hat. Other people, in particular the women, noticed as well. They murmured among each other. As I looked closer, I realized it was don Flavio, a man who hailed from El Alto, a few miles from my placita. I had seen him once at Grandpa Lolo's house. Looking dapper and rather unconcerned, he asked a young lady not too far from my mother and me to dance. Whether a man was in his best behavior or not, a woman or a young lady dared not refuse or shun (desaigrar) a man's request to dance. To do so was deemed rude.

As soon as don Flavio and his partner got on the floor, the bastonero walked over, tapped him gently on the shoulder, and stopped the couple in its dancing tracks. All eyes were upon them. People wondered what was going to happen. Some villagers knew about the hat etiquette; others were in the dark and wondered what prompted the bastonero to approach don Flavio. A few words were exchanged between him and the floor custodian. Don Flavio shrugged his shoulders but removed his hat. Just as he did, people cracked up laughing. They saw a long streak of black hair that ran down the middle of his head to the nape of his neck. Except for this strand of hair, he was bald as a cue ball. The strange line of hair was the funniest thing I'd ever seen on a man. It resembled the tail of a horse glued to his head; perhaps that's why people chuckled.

Embarrassed by the sudden burst of laughter, he bowed before the young lady, excused himself, and walked out of the dance hall, his face as red as a chile pepper. He was a shy little man, obviously oblivious to the fact that he shouldn't have been wearing a hat. I felt sorry for the gentleman. Not even his suave dancing moves, however brief, spared him embarrassment on the dance floor.

CHOCOLATE, MY FOOT!

Mom and I were on our last bite of lunch when we heard a loud and rapid knock on the door. It sounded urgent. "Quick, go see who it is, hijito!" Mom said.

Without uttering a word I got up from the table and looked through the kitchen screen door. It was Cousin J.

"Hey, come in. What's up? Is something wrong?"

"No. Why do you ask?"

"Because of the way you banged on the door. I thought you were bringing bad news or something."

"No. I bring good news. I came to invite you to go shoot marbles with me. I have a new agate that my father bought me."

"Amáaaaa," I shouted at Mom, who was in the bedroom. "Can I go shoot marbles with Cousin J.?"

"What about your siesta?"

"That's okay. I'm not tired or sleepy."

"Okay. But be back here by suppertime."

As soon as I was given the green light, I got my little tobacco sack of marbles and Cousin J. and I walked down the hill slowly, so my food could settle. When we got to his house he had already drawn a circle with his marbles in it.

"All you need is your shooter. Let's use my marbles today, okay?"

"Okay," I responded nodding my head.

We shot marbles for quite a long time while Aunt Taida went to visit my mother. Cousin J. asked if I wanted a drink of water, which was just as well because my aim was terrible. I couldn't have hit a pumpkin with my shooter if I had wanted to. After we each drank a jumate (dipper) of water, Cousin J. said to me, "Want a piece of chocolate candy?"

"Yeah, sure! Where'd you get it?"

"I found it yesterday in Mom's chest of drawers. I was looking for a handkerchief when I came across it."

He opened a small red and blue box. Sure enough! Wrapped in tinfoil were small chocolate squares. He handed me two, and he took two for himself.

"Boy, I've never tasted chocolate candy this good! Could I have another piece, Cousin J.?"

"Sure. Here. Take one," he said, and I grabbed it and again feigned putting it in my mouth. I was familiar with ex-lax tablets and what they did to your intestines. I had stolen some from Grandma Cinda in Bernalillo once . . . and paid the price. He took an extra piece also. He didn't even wait for the chocolates to melt in his mouth. He chewed and swallowed faster than I could count one, two, and three!

"Let's spin tops," I said to Cousin J. "I'm tired of shooting marbles. I'll go get my top."

"No need to. You can use one of mine."

We spun tops until it was time for me to go home for supper. My aunt was still at our house, so Cousin J. went back with me. Just as we got there, my aunt was leaving. Before she could say anything, Cousin J. asked her, "Mom, could Junie spend the night at our house?"

"That's up to his mom."

"Auntie, could Junie spend the night at my house?"

"Yes, but he has to eat supper first . . . and I want him back here for breakfast."

I hated to leave Mom alone with my little brothers and sister, but staying overnight at Cousin J.'s was not something I got to do very often. That evening he and I played cards with Aunt Taida until we went to bed. She and Uncle Antonio slept in a room next to Cousins J. and G.'s bedroom. He started cutting up. Jumping up and down on the bed was one of his favorite antics, until the springs on the bed started squeaking. That's when my aunt came in and extinguished the wick to the kerosene lamp.

She warned us that it was time to go to sleep. It wasn't long before Cousin J. began complaining that his stomach hurt. He kept holding his tummy. He got progressively worse. I knew he was in trouble—and the reason why.

My aunt fixed Cousin J. some atole (blue corn gruel), which was always good for a bellyache. He gobbled it down. But for some inexplicable reason, the atole made matters worse. He began to complain that he had to go to the bathroom. Although it was already dark, he refused to use the bedpan, the bacín. He preferred to use the outhouse (escusao), but he didn't want to go alone. My aunt and uncle's outhouse was a two holer. I sat next to my cousin to keep him company.

"¡Híjole! I really have the run-dums. This *chisguete* is going to kill me. I think it was those chocolates we ate." I didn't say anything, knowing that his assessment was correct. We made several trips to the outhouse during the night. It was spooky walking and stumbling in the dark, but that was the least of his worries. One of the times we sat in the outhouse, two shiny eyes were staring right at us. As it turned out, it was his dog, without doubt curious about what two little boys were doing there in the middle of the night. Luckily for us, the night beast wasn't a bobcat (*gato montés*).

Somehow we made it through the night, but with hardly any sleep. As soon as I woke up, I went home to join Mom for breakfast. I didn't have to get dressed, since we had slept with our clothes on. Cousin J. seemed to be asleep when I left. He came up to the house later on, but he was still complaining about his incessant trips to the outhouse.

I offered what I perceived to be the perfect solution. On one of our trips to the Bernalillo Mercantile Company, my father had discovered citrate of magnesia. I thought a swig or two of this sweet-tasting so-called medicine would do the trick. I had tasted it on the sly—and I liked it! While Mom was making the beds, Cousin J. took one small swallow, then a big one. "Boy, that's good stuff!" he exclaimed with a smile. "Are you sure this will help?"

Regrettably, the citrate of magnesia instantly had the opposite effect. I followed my cousin when he ran like a deer to use my parents' outhouse. He dashed inside, sat on the toilet seat, slid halfway down, and couldn't get unstuck. He found himself a prisoner of our outhouse for the next hour or so. The whole experience was awful. I was beginning to feel guilty myself.

When I returned to tell Mom about Cousin J., I found Aunt Taida in the kitchen. "Where's your cousin?" she asked, showing little patience.

"He's stuck in the outhouse," I responded meekly.

"You go get him and tell him to get his nalgas in here, right now!" She didn't realize that he literally was stuck and couldn't pull himself up from the unfamiliar cutout hole in our outhouse. I ran back to the outhouse.

Sensing that Cousin J. was in double jeopardy, I tried time and again to get him unstuck, but I couldn't. His efforts, too, were to no avail. By now he was feeling the effects of the lack of sleep and of numerous trips to the outhouse, not to mention numbness due to a lack of circulation. Finally, through a miraculous surge of strength and leverage, I managed to yank him from his predicament.

Cousin J. struggled back to the house. We walked in. Mom and Aunt Taida were at the table. They looked at us with distrust and suspicion. I knew right then and there that something was terribly wrong. You could tell from my aunt's demeanor that she was madder than a hornet.

"Sit down. I want to talk to both of you," she said as she reached with her right hand into her apron pocket. One by one she took out small pieces of tinfoil. "Explain to me what you did with the chocolates that were wrapped in this aluminum."

While Cousin J. timidly explained what happened to the chocolates, I kept looking at Mom for some reaction. She looked like she already knew the whole story. Her face was about ready to crack a smile.

"Do you know why you're sick in your stomach?" my aunt asked as she tossed the little blue box with red letters on the table.

"I thought they were chocolates," responded Cousin J., as if to hide his guilt.

"Chocolates, my foot! What you ate were ex-lax tablets that your father takes when he's constipated!"

"No wonder you have all that chisguete," I said, putting in my two cents. "That explains last night's thunder down under," I added jokingly, causing Mom and my aunt to laugh. As for Cousin J., he didn't think I was a bit funny. He was hurting.

"Come along, *purga* kid," my aunt said, grabbing my cousin's hand. "Let's go home so I can fix you some mint tea."

Laughter has a way of evoking forgiveness. But one thing for sure, Cousin J. never again ate ex-lax tablets. Luckily for me, Mom never found out about my drinking Dad's citrate of magnesia, nor did I ever get the runs.

A BEER EXPLOSION

As a young man in his late twenties and early thirties, my father loved beer. Schlitz and Pabst Blue Ribbon were his favorite commercial brews. On one of Mom and Dad's rare shopping trips to Albuquerque, we ended up at Eddy's Market in Los Candelarias, north of Old Town. Somehow I thought that Eddy, a García himself, was related to us, but that was not the case. How my parents came to know about Eddy's Market is unclear in my mind, but it was there that my father learned from a man how to make home brew. I believe the gentleman was a bartender at the Saguaro Nightclub, located practically next door to Eddy's Market.

After that encounter my father became intrigued with the idea of brewing his own beer and decided to give it a try. He inquired of Eddy if he had the necessary ingredients, consisting of malt, hops, and beer yeast; they were all available at Eddy's Market.

As for the bottles, bottle caps, and a machine to cap the bottles, Dad was directed to the AAA Food Market at the corner of Mountain Road and Broadway. Dad either bought everything there or he went to a place one of the Archuleta sons suggested. At any rate, he bought an assortment of empty bottles—between twenty and thirty. Some were clear glass; others were amber or dark red. By the time we left town, Dad had the whole lot for making and bottling his own beer at the ranch.

He was excited at the prospect of drinking his own homemade beer. Mom was cautious, however. As for me, I was curious more than anything else. "Will he be able to do it? Will he like the taste of his own beer?" I asked myself in silence. These were questions that right away popped into my head. I'm sure Mom had her own queries. As for Dad, he always exuded confidence and self-assurance. He was not a pessimist by any stretch of the imagination. I liked that in him.

It was summer, a propitious time for beer, even though we had no refrigeration to keep it cool. The coolest place was Dad's storage shed next to our home. That's where Dad planned to put the beer. I helped him prepare everything for the big event one early morning.

In addition to the ingredients and the bottle paraphernalia, he needed water, sugar, and a small tin tub, which Mom had in her repertoire of tubs. He set the tin tub on top of the kitchen table along with the ingredients. Dad could not read, and I wasn't much help, so his measurements were imprecise at best. He played everything by ear, using his own intuition, following pretty much the ways of rural Hispanic women in the kitchen. Whenever they were asked for a recipe, their answer, including Mom's, was consistently the same: "A little bit of this and a little bit of that." This could very well have been their motto for cooking or baking.

Dad proceeded to pour into the tin tub what he thought would be enough water to fill up all the bottles. He knew that malt was the most important ingredient and as a result decided to toss in the entire can—about a quart. I believe the malt came from barley, because I recall seeing "bar" on the can, a word I was familiar with because of the Triangle Bar in San Ysidro where Dad stopped periodically (and ritually) on the way back to the ranch. Next Dad put in the hops (I didn't have the vaguest idea about hops except for what my rabbits did) and one or two—possibly more—packets of yeast.

He knew that yeast fermented and turned into natural sugar and how yeast produced the alcohol in beer. Besides, the man from the Saguaro Nightclub evidently had told him that adding extra sugar increased the beer's potency. Dad then poured in close to a five-pound bag of C&H sugar.

When the beer presumably had finished brewing later in the day, it was ready to be bottled. Dad lined up twenty-plus bottles on top of the kitchen table. Mom loaned him a small spout to use. One by one he filled them in the most meticulous sort of way. He was a perfectionist at anything he undertook. After he capped the bottles, he moved them to one side of the table to rest until the next day, when he planned to taste the first bottle of beer. The rest he would store in the shed to keep cool. I regret to say that this final step in his beer-making experience never came to pass.

The following evening, when it wasn't awfully hot, Dad was working in the cornfields while Mom was kneading dough at the kitchen table to make tortillas for supper. I was peeling potatoes for a stew that she was going to fix. Suddenly something went terribly wrong.

Bottles of beer started popping, first one, then another and another! "*¡Santísimo sacramento del altar!*" Mom shouted as the beer splashed against the ceiling. "What in tarnation is happening?" she added. I was speechless and scared. I didn't know what to think. "Quick! Out the door! And get your little brothers," Mom hollered amid the explosion as she picked up Julianita, who was on the floor. We scurried outside as quickly as we could, bumping into one another as we converged at the screen door. We stood outside looking toward the door, waiting for the next bang, but it never came. "Quick! Go get your father. Tell him to get here, pronto!"

She barely uttered the last word before I was on my way, running down the hill as fast as my legs could carry me. It took me no more than five minutes to get to where Dad was working. He saw me running and realized that something was wrong, so he ran toward me. Before he could say a word, I cried out to him, "*Apá, apá,* come quick. *¡Explosión, explosión!*" It was the only word I could utter or think of.

Dad's face turned to panic. He took off like a deer. I had never seen him run that fast. I wasn't even halfway between the cornfields and the house when Dad got there. By the time I reached the house, Mom and Dad were out of sight. I couldn't imagine where they were until I heard them laughing aloud. The laughter was coming from the kitchen. I slowly opened the screen door and peeked inside. They were both sitting on the floor, laughing and laughing.

"Look at the *bate*, mess, you made. And look at all the broken glass on the floor," she said to Dad.

"I didn't do anything. The beer did it all!" my dad exclaimed with a giggle.

Seeing that the situation was not as serious as I had first perceived, I glanced at Dad and asked innocently, "What happened?"

"I don't know. I guess the bag of sugar was too much. The *cantinero* from the Saguaro Nightclub told me that if I wanted the beer to have a real kick, to add plenty of sugar, but he didn't tell me how much. I guess I overdid it."

"Yes, but why did the bottles blow up?" I asked.

"Oh, I suppose it's because the beer was still brewing. The yeast was still acting up. It hadn't settled. Do you understand what I mean?" Dad asked, as though he had the correct answers to my questions.

"Yes and no," I replied.

"Let me put it to you this way. It's like when your Grandpa's cow got bloated and exploded!"

I accepted the analogy much more easily than his scientific explanation. Before we started cleaning up the mess, I asked Dad one last question. "When are you going to brew more beer?"

I had hardly finished asking him when Mom interjected. "No more beer in this house. If you want beer, you can buy it at the liquor store. One explosion in this house is enough! For a moment I thought you were ringing in the New Year," she quipped with a smile.

28

Freedom

A Priceless Commodity

FREEDOM DENOTES DIFFERENT THINGS to different people, given the individual's circumstances and raison d'être. But for someone who lived and experienced freedom in the open terrain of the Land of Enchantment, the true meaning of what comprises freedom can be elusive. "Freedom is roaming unrestrained throughout the terrain like a mustang," I once overheard Grandpa Lolo tell one of his compadres.

A tad romantic, perhaps, but if anyone understood and was eminently qualified to speak on freedom, it was my grandfather. As mentioned earlier, about 1880, at eight years of age, he migrated to the Río Puerco Valley with his parents and a brother and a sister from Algodones, north of Albuquerque, where he was born. In his adopted valley he eventually married, raised a family, and carved out an existence for the better part of his one hundred years on this earth.

For a small boy like me living in the hinterland, his words regarding independence spoke volumes. Grandpa knew the landscape up and down the Río Puerco Valley, above all our village of Ojo del Padre and its environs, like the palm of his hand. What the terrain meant vis-à-vis being free, with the right to enjoy life at will and to the fullest, was second nature for him. The splendor of hills, arroyos, ravines, mesas, volcanic plugs, sagebush, and the plains (el llano), plus the headstrong Río Puerco, which epitomized its own sense of free will, had a profound effect on me during the formative years of my life. To be able to wander hither and thither seemingly unencumbered by an array of prescribed rules that curtailed one's freedom of movement was precious indeed.

Living in the backlands and having an appreciation for freedom of movement and its trappings is something that to a large extent was taken for granted until governmental rules and regulations began to squeeze the life out of the farmer-rancher like a coiled snake strangling its prey.

My paternal grandfather, a man of wisdom and fairness, though un-educated, once reflected on how the government had begun to infringe on the rights of ranchers in ways that he himself did not fully comprehend. "For a long time," he said to me toward the end of his life, "the country-side was available for raising cows, goats, horses—everything. The gov-ernment didn't prohibit us from doing that until it passed a law reducing our grazing rights; then the government showed no mercy. I don't know if what the government did to us was fair or not. Only God can be the judge of that."

Children like me relished life in the open spaces year-round, where people did not delineate the terms of freedom or its lines of demarcation. The landscape and animals, both domestic and those in the wild, defined it for us. Based on what I observed in my parents, grandparents, and other people, I believe there existed an implicit understanding between humans and the flora and fauna. To respect the forces of nature was paramount. After all, whenever a river or an arroyo rumbled with gushing water fol-lowing a torrential downpour, it had a mind of its own, and neither you nor I were apt to change its course. To tamper with or to try to tip the eco-system was tantamount to infringing on nature's self-determination.

Of course, freedom of movement and action for a young boy like me started at home. And though my parents did not set down a list of ironclad rules describing what constituted freedom, they did insist on at least one thing—not to encroach on the rights and possessions of your neighbor, el prójimo.

The essence of independence in the countryside is best symbolized by the rancher and/or farmer's most trusted animal—the horse. In many respects the horse was not only his closest companion and an integral part of the land in his daily work, but his alter ego as well, reminiscent of don Quixote's workhorse, Rocinante. Every rancher and his sons and daughters were proud owners of at least one prized horse that stood out in either roping, cutting cattle, racing, rooster racing, or farm work.

I recall clearly to this day the following incident about Grandpa Lolo and the close bond that existed between him and his horse named Alazán. Grandpa was in his mideighties at the time. The story goes something like this.

My family was now living in Los Ranchos de Alburquerque. My father and I departed for the ranch in Ojo del Padre on a Friday evening in early spring after he got off work. The trip on Dad's truck from our home to the Río Puerco Valley took about two to three hours. By the time we reached our ranch home, dusk had begun to set in. Once we unloaded our belongings and took them inside, Dad went to see Grandpa Lolo, but he wasn't home. (My grandmother was in Albuquerque at the time.)

After searching the modest two-room house, my father looked around the corral, but my grandfather's sorrel horse, his trusted companion, was also nowhere in sight. My father walked down to the Río Puerco, a short distance from our home, to see if Grandpa was watering his horse. He wasn't there either, so Dad went back up the hill to our house. When he reached the top of the hill, he saw in the distance a man on horseback headed home by way of the cornfields. As he got closer my father recognized Grandpa's horse Alazán. My grandfather was not sitting upright, as he normally did, but with his head stooped down, as though he was tired or asleep. My father hollered at him, "*Apá, apá,*" but he didn't hear him. He repeated the words more loudly.

At that moment my grandfather snapped to. "*¿Quién es? ¿Quién habla?* Who is it? Who's there?"

"*Soy yo, apá. ¿Te sientes mal o qué?* It's me, Dad. Do you feel bad or what?"

Grandpa Lolo did not answer. My father noticed that Grandpa did not look directly at him but straight ahead. He recognized that there was something strange, if not wrong, with Grandpa.

Dad walked alongside his horse to the corral. Once my grandfather dismounted, Dad unsaddled and fed the horse, keeping an eye all the time on Grandpa Lolo, who seemed to stumble in the semidarkness. On the way up the hill to the house, Grandpa said to my father, "*Dame la mano, hijo.* Give me your hand, my son."

This was the first indication that Grandpa Lolo's eyesight was failing. Dad helped him into the kitchen and prepared supper. A discussion ensued between them while we ate. Apparently my grandfather's eyes had been failing for quite some time, but he never told Grandma Lale or the rest of the family. By now he lived by himself at the ranch. Everyone else had moved to Albuquerque, a place my grandfather tolerated sparingly because he could not stand the city, La Plaza, for long. His place was in the countryside raising cattle, tending to animals, and farming. He was a man of the rancho, a man wedded to the land through and through.

My grandpa's loyal companion and savior while his eyes failed him was Alazán. The steed took him here and there as he tended to his ranch chores. Despite Grandpa's visual disability, it was his horse that continued to provide him with the freedom of movement that he had enjoyed throughout his life. Alazán knew the trails to and from the house, some of them manmade, others created by animals themselves. Grandpa's present horse, and those of the past, epitomized an inner part of his being.

But what about a rural country lad like me? What sense of freedom or appreciation did I have for the open range that differed from, or was similar to, that of my grandpa? Grandpa Lolo came and went as he pleased until he no longer could function because of his limited vision—overwhelmed by forces beyond his control. Perhaps in many ways, I, like countless other individuals in our valley, mirrored Grandpa's sense of independence amid the mountains, the ravines, and the domestic and wild animals that dotted the landscape.

Here is a list of wildlife (mammals, birds, reptiles, and insects) that once upon a time inhabited the area where I grew up but that are rarely seen nowadays. The Spanish names were those typically used in the Río Puerco Valley.

abejas	bees
arañas	spiders
ardillas	squirrels
avispas	wasps
berrendos	antelope
chapulines	grasshoppers
chicharras	cicadas

chinchontes	mockingbirds
conejitos (conejos)	cottontail rabbits
cornices (codornices)	quail
corpospines (puerco espines)	porcupines
coyotes	coyotes
cuervos	crows
culebras	snakes
garrapatas	ticks
gatos monteses	bobcats
gavilanes	hawks
golondrinas	swallows
gorriones	sparrows
lagartos	lizards
lechuzas	prairie-dog owls
liebres	jackrabbits
liendres	nits
lobos	wolves
moscas	flies
mosquitos	mosquitoes
osos	bears
paisanos	roadrunners
pedorros	black beetles
piojos	lice
ranas	frogs
ratoncitos	mice
ratoneras	bull snakes
ratones voladores	flying bats
santopiés	centipedes
sapos	toads
tecolotes	barn owls
tejones	badgers
tórtolas	turtledoves
tuzas	prairie dogs
venados	deer
víboras	rattlesnakes
zorras	foxes
zorrillos	skunks

In looking back at my childhood at the ranch, I do so with reverence and fulfillment. Being the first offspring in my family, and no doubt spoiled to some extent, by the time I was six or seven years old I was the proud owner of not one but two horses that my father had given me.

Owning two horses at my age was a rarity. One was jet-black, Prieto. Bayo—or Bayito, as Dad liked to call him—looked more like a palomino than a bay horse. He was not fast, but his poise and elegance were precious. His stride evoked pride. Prieto, on the other hand, was less graceful. He was a workhorse, the embodiment of endurance, but his ebony color made him stand out. My horses complemented each other in grace, strength, and temperament.

They were set free in late fall to join other horses in the open range for the winter so they could fatten up after growing thin during the hard work of the summer months. This was a cyclical process and something my father recommended every year. Every spring Cousin J. and I went looking for my horses and his as well. Invariably we found them far from home, at a place called El Cerro de la Yeguas, west of the majestic Cabezón Peak, which loomed over the miles on end of the llano. They were free spirited and running like untamed horses as they mixed in with a herd of mesteños, mustangs, in their natural habitat.

As soon as I spotted them, I called them by name: "Eh, Prieto, Bayito." Bayito would raise his head and tail, ostensibly jubilant and appearing to recognize my voice. But it was Prieto who always warmed up to me much more quickly, happy to see me. Bayito was a bit more skittish and aloof, as if to say, "Who are you?" Coyness was part of his nature.

First my cousin and I cut Prieto from the rest of the herd, and, with a little coaxing, I didn't even have to rope him. Instead, he stood in his tracks, and I simply draped my rope around his neck. I knew from past experience that once Prieto was in my possession, Bayito, his loyal companion, would follow suit. They were like brothers, inseparable indeed.

Summer was here and it was now time for them to become part of the family again, to be ready to help in tending to the newborn calves, branding, watering the livestock, going after the mail in our village, and providing all the other help needed at the ranch. My horses' limited freedom during the hot months meant I regained my own, because they would take me wherever I needed to go, whatever the circumstances. It was a fair trade-off.

But it was not all work and no play either for my horses or me. Seeking pleasure and enjoyment that engaged Prieto and Bayito was also part of ranch life in Ojo del Padre. Horse racing and rooster racing meant competing against rivals from nearby villages on Sundays, considered a day for rest and for having fun, or on holidays like Saint John's Day.

Bayito was not fast enough to win races; therefore, many times I just I rode him to the placita on Sundays to show him off. From my vantage point the admiration people heaped upon him, especially the old ladies and their granddaughters ("¡Oh, mira qué caballo tan bonito! Oh! Look at what a pretty horse!") was as good as winning a couple of races. Competing without an insatiable desire for winning races and the like satisfied me. I think Bayito felt the same way.

Away from the village proper or the daily work at the ranch, I had ample opportunities to enjoy a rather footloose existence without shirking responsibilities. Prieto was particularly sure-footed, so he and I climbed peaks and mesas and explored rock basins, or I looked inside abandoned homes (during daylight hours, of course) that were part of the local lore, rich with stories regarding colorful people who had inhabited them before they died.

I recall my father and paternal grandmother also talking about mysterious Indian dwellings. At one of these sites, a butte overlooking our ranch from which the Indians "spied" on the local population not long before my grandparents settled there in the 1880s, a pile of rocks can still be found today, testimony to the small Indian dwellings that were used as lookout points. Curious, just like most kids seven or eight years old, I dared to visit the site. Little did I know at the time that I was viewing history firsthand rather than reading about it in textbooks.

Other places, like what came to be known as the Guadalupe Ruin(s), were strictly off-limits. This site was situated on top of a butte directly across the Río Puerco from my house. My cousins and I were not to visit it. Time and again, Grandma Lale, more than anyone, warned us never to climb to the top of the butte where Indians had dwelled once upon a time. The bluff purportedly was enchanted. She did not wish for us to become

victims of sorcery or turn into goats; this was a common belief among
the local people.

Fact or fiction, I was petrified at the thought of being bewitched
(*embrujado*) and therefore was never overcome with enough compulsion
to find out if her words of warning were true or not. My sense of right and
wrong told me that there were limits to indulging one's inquisitiveness.
Besides, having heard countless stories of people who had been inflicted
with excruciating pain due to witchery, I was less than eager to disobey my
grandma, fearful that I would end up like those people and have to endure
discomfort for the rest of my life. Hence, I shied away from the mysterious
ruins, even though Prieto, whom I rode on all my exploring ventures,
surely had the power (black was magic!) to ward off evil in places with supernatural tendencies.

Much to my surprise, a few years after my family and I left the ranch for
the city, I learned that archaeologists discovered the "enchanted butte."
Digs ensued and articles appeared in magazines and journals on their findings (e.g., it was an outpost for the Anasazi, the ancient Pueblo peoples),
dispelling the notion of an enchanted mesa. Unbeknownst to my family
and me, an important slice of raw history had existed right in front of us,
right in our own backyard. But the lore of witches in retrospect proved to
be much more alluring.

Prieto and I embarked on numerous adventurous trips. One day
Cousin J. and I rode to the placita to bring back the mail. We did that routinely almost every week. That is how often the postman delivered the
mail, however scarce, to our village. After we picked up the mail, I said to
Cousin J., "Have you heard of the Indian paintings"—which is what we
called them—"in a canyon not far from here?"

"No," he responded.

"What do you say we go see what they're like?" I added.

"Let's go. You lead the way," he answered, and we spurred our horses.

We reached the entrance to the canyon a short distance southwest of our
placita. Little did I know that we would be in for a bit of excitement as well
concern for our safety. As sure-footed as Prieto was, the canyon turned out
to be a challenge for us. There were narrow gaps between the canyon wall
and huge boulders where I had to raise my legs and drape them around the

saddle horn so that Prieto could squeeze his way through. Little by little we maneuvered our way deeper and deeper into the canyon, with no visible exit or place to turn around.

I looked back to see if Cousin J. was still with us and saw that he had a petrified look on his face, his eyes bulging like soup bowls. I tried to show that I wasn't scared—even though I wondered what predicament I had gotten us into. "*Ya mero, ya mero.* We're almost there, we're almost there." I did my best to assure him, even though we were treading new territory. It was the classic case of the blind leading the blind.

All of a sudden one or two swallows flew off the canyon wall and startled Prieto. He tried to spring forward but without success. There was little room to maneuver. Although I hadn't seen the swallows until they took to the air, their mud houses were right above us. "There has to be water nearby," I conjectured. This gave me hope that maybe we were not far from the end of the narrow confinement we were in. Sure enough! Gradually the space between the canyon wall and the huge line of boulders began to widen. We finally found ourselves free from a very scary situation. And Cousin J. and I could breathe a sigh of relief.

"I told you we'd make it," I said somewhat smugly as I turned around and smiled, when out of the blue he hollered, "Look! Look!"

There in front of us was a potpourri of Indian drawings. I pulled the reins on Prieto and stopped. I looked up at the smooth canyon wall and saw magnificent sketches of deer and birds. I couldn't quite discern the other figures, but some resembled people dancing. The drawings looked like they had been made with black and red chalk. I had never seen anything like them before.

Cousin J. and I found what we were in search of, but now the worrisome thought got into my head that maybe these drawings, like the Guadalupe Ruins, also enjoyed supernatural powers. Maybe that's why they were in such a remote and inaccessible location. Quickly, I dispensed with the idea as nothing more than sheer nonsense or a wild scheme gone amok in my brain.

Now the real trick was how to reveal our findings at home without getting into trouble. A reminder about respecting your neighbor's property, which Dad insisted upon, popped into my head. After all, the drawings were on private land; they belonged to the Gonzales family. But the more pressing thing confronting Cousin J. and me at the moment was to return home as quickly as possible. We had tarried long enough.

"¡*Ándale!* Shake a leg!" I said to him. "Mom's going to be worried, and so is my aunt." Mom trusted me on my horseback outings; thus she never concerned herself with my getting in trouble. Rather, she worried more that I might fall off a horse or be swept away by the strong Río Puerco currents. In fact, on our way back we took a shortcut and crossed the river near our house, where the waters were much more serene and less treacherous, but deep.

"¡Hijito! Where have you been? I've been here biting my nails wondering about you."

I proceeded to tell Mom what happened, and she vowed to keep our discovery a secret. Neither she nor I wanted Dad to know, lest he get angry and scold me for trespassing on somebody else's property. Explaining my curiosity would not appease him in the least, either. The Indian drawings were one of the best-kept secrets between my mother and me. My cousin J. also gave his word not to reveal our discovery to anyone.

The day following the canyon episode I decided to give Prieto a rest. I normally rode him and Bayito every other day, but this time he would get two days' rest. I saddled Bayito and headed for El Ojito (old-timers like Grandpa called it El Ojo de Esquipula), which belonged to my father. Grandpa Lolo had given him the property when Dad was a young man (see chapter 12). It was called El Ojito because of a natural spring that oozed plenty of water for livestock at the bottom of the arroyo. By now my grandpa, in an arrangement with the Bureau of Land Management (BLM), had installed a windmill that pumped the water to a tank on the ground level above the arroyo. The spring was only one of two in the region. The other one was in Ojo del Padre, the village.

On the way to El Ojito, a stone's throw from my house, I had to cross La Cañada del Camino, populated, as we've already learned, with a multitude of prairie dog mounds and three or four times as many prairie dogs. I enjoyed galloping at full speed, dodging both the dirt mounds and the little critters, just to remind me of Bayito's agility and finesse. With one misstep Bayito could break a leg by stepping in one of the holes, but I had the utmost confidence in my steed. A mishap of that sort never came to pass.

Soon after our frolicsome moments with the tail-wagging critters, Bayito and I crossed El Aguaje before reaching El Ojito. I watered him and turned him loose while I made sure the water tank was full for the rest of the livestock that came down from El Bordo to quench their thirst. I also had to set out a block of salt for the cows. I fetched it from the little casita that served as a stockroom, located between the corral and the windmill.

For the moment, Bayito wandered off, out of sight, but when I got ready to return home, I ambled to the bottom of the arroyo, where I found him stretched out on the ground. He appeared in distress—kicking and grimacing. It was an ominous and creepy scene unlike anything I had ever seen. I felt helpless and beside myself. All I could think of was to loosen his cinch to relieve whatever pressure or discomfort he felt. I didn't know what else to do. He stopped kicking, and he let out an ugly groan.

I had heard that animals died only at night. So I held out hope. I put my head to his stomach; its rumbling seemed to grow fainter and fainter. Was his death imminent? The answer came soon. His bloated stomach stopped heaving up and down. I sat down and leaned against a small embankment and asked myself, "Why?" I mulled the same question over and over in my head, with no logical answer to comfort me.

As was true with Grandpa and his horse Alazán, Bayito and Prieto had become my loyal and trusted companions on the open range. We were one and the same. They in turn were like twins, inseparable in friendship. The day that Bayito passed away, a part of me died with him. A few days later, my brother Beltrán found Prieto in the Río Puerco's riverbed. "He died from sadness. He missed his cuate," he said, reassuring me of the strong bond between them.

His words sounded a trifle melodramatic, but animals had an unspoken way of communicating among themselves and intuitively sensing whenever something was wrong. Regardless, my horses were gone, and the freedom they symbolized had come to an end.

POSTSCRIPT

Mi caballo bayo

Vengo andando a pie
del Ojo de Esquipula
donde se ve una mula

sin mi caballo bayo.

Pastó quelite
del burro
con un susurro
y tragó agua salitre

mi caballo bayo.

Le dio un torzón
luego un desazón

a mi caballo bayo.

Más lelo que muerto
con un ojo tuerto,
corta su vista mide,
se me despide

mi caballo bayo.

Me cuelgo al seno
las riendas del freno,
trabo en mi cabecilla
los estribos de la silla

de mi caballo bayo.

My Bay Horse*

I'm headed back afoot
from Ojo de Esquipula
where I spot a mule

without my bay horse.

He ate silverlike
poisonous spinach
in secret and drank
saltpeter water

my bay horse did.

He suffered uneasiness
then a discomfort

my bay horse did.

More dazed than dead
with one eye shut,
his sight in short demand,
he bids me farewell

my bay horse does.

I drape the bridle's
reins around my chest
and fasten the stirrups
to the saddle horn

belonging to my bay horse.

....
*   From my book *Tiempos Lejanos: Poetic Images from the Past.*

Atravieso El Aguaje	I cross El Aguaje
con mucho coraje,	in a state of anger
bajo por	and go down
La Cañada Ancha	La Cañada Ancha
caliente como una plancha	where it's hotter than blazes

sin mi caballo bayo.   **without my bay horse**.

Voy viendo en la loma	I begin to discern atop the hill
a mi mamá que se asoma	my mom peeking her head
por la ventana de la cocina	out the kitchen window
que queda en la mera esquina,	from a corner of the house,
contando los pasos lentos	counting the slow steps
que voy dando violentos	I take as I stomp the ground

sin mi caballo bayo.   **minus my bay horse**.

Llego con el subadero	I reach home, saddle blanket
en la tierra arrastrando	dragging on the dirt,
por la cara derramando	as bitter tears of whey drip
lágrimas amargas de suero	and roll down my face
que se resbalan sin aliento	as they cascade breathlessly
por cada látigo y tiento	down each leather strap

sin mi caballo bayo.   **minus my bay horse**.

Sale mamá de la cocina,	Out comes my mom from the kitchen.
aquella cara tan fina,	wearing that delicate face of hers,
me da un cariñoso abrazo,	and gives me an affectionate hug
pues ya adivina el caso	for her anxious heart
en su ansioso pecho	and grieving pain know
mi doloroso despecho	the whole story concerning me

sin mi caballo bayo.   **minus my bay horse**.

29

From Cradle to Grave

IT IS A QUANTUM leap from the joyful sounds of a newborn baby cuddled in a cradle to the wailing of grown-ups at a camposanto, sacred ground, to bid farewell to a loved one who has ventured to a better life. The disparity in time and space may be short or long, but it is not beyond the comprehension of the families affected.

A first birth to a young couple is jam-packed with anticipation, excitement, and cause for jubilation. The death of an older person, on the other hand, evokes sadness, but his or her demise is also grounds for celebration of life, albeit one that rests in the past and not in the future, like that of a child. Yet in both instances a common element—the joy of life—is what brings families, friends, and acquaintances together.

I recall to this day an unexpected visit to my parents' home from the Gonzaleses. They had come to ask Mom and Dad to be the padrinos, godparents, for the latest addition to their family: "We've come as humble but happy friends to ask you to be the godparents of our daughter, who was born ten days ago. We would be so honored if you accepted." (The forty-day period in bed demanded of the mother by a folk healer was evidently no longer in vogue.)

"The honor is ours to cherish. We would love to welcome a new *ahijada*, godchild, into our lives," answered my father, with Mom nodding her head in agreement.

I could tell that my parents were overjoyed. Mom stoked up the fire in the woodstove, brewed a pot of coffee, and served the future compadres coffee and bizcochitos to celebrate the occasion. At the insistence of

Mrs. Gonzales, I was permitted to remain in the kitchen, where the conversation took place—children, as a rule, were not allowed in the presence of visitors. Even so, I wasn't quite clear what being godparents signified or entailed. I knew I had my own padrinos, whom I looked up to and respected, but that was the extent of my knowledge.

In the past, a formal baptismal letter (*carta de bautismo*) was composed—in most cases authored by the local scribe, a friend, or someone in the family who was literate—and hand delivered by the newborn's parents. Now that practice was deemed passé. Asking the prospective baptismal godparents (*padrinos de bautismo*) and future *compadres* (coparents) *viva voce* was becoming a more popular approach to a long-standing tradition among the people in my village.

The change in practice did not lessen the importance of being invited to become godparents. To be asked was indeed a great honor, but acceptance (to my knowledge hardly anyone ever said no) carried an awesome responsibility that could not be taken lightly. I could tell my parents accepted with their eyes open; they were fully cognizant of the expectations of being godparents and the importance of fulfilling the sacramental rites of the Catholic Church.

Of equal significance was the unbreakable and lifelong bond that was established between the godparents, the child, and the child's parents. Should anything dire (e.g., death) happen to the parents of the child, the godparents were then to assume full responsibility for the godchild's well-being and his or her moral and spiritual upbringing.

Also important was for the baby to be anointed with the holy waters of baptism within thirty days after birth, in case he or she fell ill and died in infancy. This time frame fell within the once-a-month visit by the priest from Jémez Springs. My parents and their compadres-to-be knew that the priest would be celebrating Mass in two to three weeks, hence preliminary preparations to baptize the Gonzaleses' daughter on the priest's ensuing visit were agreed upon over coffee and bizcochitos.

Another facet of tradition that had changed in recent times was the naming of the godchild. In years past the godparents had a free hand in selecting the child's Christian name or names (*nombres de pila*), which were kept a secret until the day of the baptismal ceremony. As a courtesy, however, at times the godparents consulted with the parents about their choice of names in case the parents wished to keep a particular name alive in the family lineage.

I was the first grandchild in my family; that's why my maternal grandmother and step-grandfather, who acted as my padrinos, named me after my father. Other times the parents had no strong feelings; consequently the godparents, as mentioned above, had the freedom to name their godchild.

In my parents' case, the Gonzaleses gave them the name to be used at the baptismal font. That was the new practice, and it caused no ill feelings. The honor rested more in becoming godparents than in choosing the name.

But the most important part of the baptismal tradition was to provide the baby with a full set of clothing, called a *canastilla* (layette). For the madrina (godmother) and the child's mother, this was perhaps one of the most exciting features of baptism, aside from the actual rite. The responsibility of dressing the child for the momentous occasion fell solely on the godparents' shoulders, unless they were very poor, but theoretically it was the madrina who took charge of putting the layette together. In fact, the role of the padrino (godfather) throughout the baptismal process was pretty passive—that of a bystander at best.

Canastilla is a word that was quite familiar to me because it had been employed during the baptisms of my younger siblings as well as of my cousins who resided nearby. The term derives from *canasto* (wicker basket), which traditionally was used by the godparents to carry the infant's clothes in on baptismal day. The custom of taking the clothes in a basket was no longer fashionable when I was a small boy. Instead, the clothes, which constituted the layette, were wrapped in the baby's blanket or put in a bag or box and transported by the godparents to the child's home, where the godmother dressed the newborn in private. The main reason for the secrecy was to surprise the infant's parents and grandparents when the godmother emerged from the room where she had dressed the infant. That moment was special for all the parties. However, there were times when the godmother invited her future comadre to assist in dressing the child.

Most godparents were poor and as a result could not afford to fork out money for the layette. And so the godmother took it upon herself to make the baby's clothing from scratch, with the exception of the shoes. The godfather usually bought those at a general store, along with the materials necessary for the layette. If time was not pressing, the godmother even knitted the baby's socks and blanket. Otherwise, it was her mother or mother-in-law who lent a helping hand in preparing the baby wear.

In my parents' case, they bought the materials. My mother was an excellent seamstress. She used a baby girl's pattern she found in one of the catalogs that came through the mail. The ahijada (godchild), dressed in pink (boys wore the traditional blue), would be sporting the latest fashion. Mom made the tiny skirt, the blouse, and the diaper cover. She did not have time to knit the blanket, so she sewed a pink border that looked like silk around a square piece of material, and that served as a baby blanket. The layette was now ready. A barrette and a small baby bracelet completed the godchild's outfit.

When Mom finished everything, she neatly laid the baby's clothes piece by piece on the bed and showed them to my father. They were two happy people. As it turned out, the Gonzales baby was to be my parents' first godchild. Now they were ready for the big event.

That Saturday before the Sunday-morning baptism, my parents went to the placita and paid the priest a courtesy call to inform him of their plans to have the Gonzales child baptized. On Sunday morning they stopped by the Gonzales house for Mom to dress their future godchild. The room where the baby slept was prepared for the occasion. My mother outfitted the baby girl and then stepped into the living room to show off the future ahijada amid ohs and ahs from the parents. "She looks precious!" said the mother, enunciating each word. She was teary eyed.

Halfway through the Mass, the priest made a public announcement regarding the baptism and congratulated both the parents and the coparents. At the end of the Mass, my parents took the child to a small room where the baptismal font had been set up. The proud parents of the baby were also present, along with the paternal and maternal grandparents plus additional members of the child's family. Once the priest asked for the child's name or names, the ceremony was relatively simple. He recited a short prayer appropriate to the solemn occasion, then dipped the tips of his fingers in the holy water and made the sign of the cross on the baby's forehead.

Mom and Dad were now proud godparents. When of age the godchild

would refer to them as "mi padrino Nasario" and "mi madrina Agapita."
For now it was time to stop by the Gonzales house so that my parents
could make a formal presentation of their ahijada to her dutiful parents.
As Mom and Dad walked into what at best could be called the living room,
or sala de recibo, my mother, with her godchild cuddled in her arms, recited the following words. She undoubtedly had learned them from my
maternal grandmother, whose repertoire of folklore seemed endless.

Compadre y comadre,	Compadre and comadre,
aquí está esta flor	here is this flower
que de la iglesia salió	who emerged from the church
con los santos sacramentos	with the blessed sacraments
y l'agua que recibió.	and the water with which it was anointed.

The mother of the child then responded:

Recíbote, prenda mía,	I welcome you, my jewel,
que de la iglesia salites	who emerged from the church
con los santos sacramentos	with blessed sacraments
y l'agua que recibites.	and the water with which you were anointed.

As soon as she uttered the last words, she called out, "¡A comer! ¡A
comer! Let's eat! Let's eat!" As a small boy her words were music to my ears
and signaled the best part of the baptism. I didn't care if we ever went
home! There was food galore at these functions, as well as plenty of kids
my age to play with until my parents loaded my siblings and me on the
horse wagon for our short trek home. (I now had a brand-new baby sister
named Mary Elsie, born in 1945.)

I could tell that Mom was still beaming with pride. Everything had
gone without a hitch, especially the presentation of the layette. Mom was
happy, but she reminded me that the birth of a baby didn't always turn out
to be a joyous event. I asked her, "Why?"

"Look, hijito. Remember how one time you asked me about the ironlike
baby crib in front of the church?"

"Yes, I do."

"And I told you that an *angelito*, a little angel, who died shortly after birth was buried there?"

"I remember."

"Long ago that's where babies were buried, so they'd be closer to God. But now there's no more room near the church, and that is why they're interred in a special section of the cemetery reserved for all the angelitos who are called to heaven by God."

As the horse wagon rounded the butte near our home, Dad sat passively without uttering a word, egging the horses on with an occasional "giddyap" as if to interrupt our conversation.

"You see, hijito, even little babies die, not just old people" were Mom's last words before we walked inside our house.

Ironically, almost three months later a death occurred in our placita. Mom had sent me on a Tuesday morning to check on our mail at the post office. She was eager to receive a canister set I had bought for her through J. C. Penney's catalog with savings I earned working in the Salas family's cornfields, across the river from where we lived. I myself was waiting for an order of Rosebud salve, which I sold every year to family members and friends for a modest profit. It was my first crack at being an entrepreneur, a notion that had sprung out of nowhere, as nearly as I could recall.

But my anticipation of carrying home two packages in my knapsack soon turned to curiosity as my horse rounded a bend and reached the top of a slope beyond El Coruco, known for its allure of witchcraft. I was about a quarter of a mile—an ear's shot—from the village when I heard the mournful sound of bells tolling at the Virgen de Guadalupe Church—the slow double sound of dong, dong, as opposed to the more rapid one of ding-dong, ding-dong. The echo reverberated across the Río Puerco and the sagebrush fields between the church and me. I knew about the sorrowful tolling of bells from Mexican ballads that my mother sang. They could only mean one thing—someone in the village or close by had just died. I was anxious to find out who the person was so I could have more than just the mail to share with my mother.

When I reached the post office—if one could even call it that—I knocked on the screen next door, which was the main entrance to the Salas home.

Out came one of the daughters, who, coincidentally, belonged to the same Salas family for whom I had worked in the cornfields. She was the older of the two daughters, and she ran the post office for the Salas family. After exchanging cordial greetings, I could hardly resist asking her about the church bells before I even inquired about the mail.

"Why are the church bells tolling?" I asked, knowing that the sound was different from the ringing we heard on Sunday mornings when the priest came to celebrate Mass.

"Doña Juanita Sánchez died early this morning," she responded, straight and to the point. "There will be a velorio, religious wake, tonight at her home. Be sure to tell your mom and the rest of the García family."

"I will," I answered and rushed to mount my horse.

"Wait, wait! What about the mail?" she cried. I had totally blocked it out of my head. I was too excited about spreading the news among my family of doña Juanita's death. I had never heard of someone from the placita dying. This was a new experience for me.

Neither the canister set nor the Rosebud salve had arrived, only an official-looking letter for my father from the government. I secured it in my saddlebags, climbed on Prieto, and galloped down the short hill, by-passing the church. I dashed down to the bottom of the Río Puerco, crossed its shallow waters, and headed straight for the home of the Gonzaleses, my parents' new compadres.

I stopped to tell Mrs. Gonzales about doña Juanita, but she already knew. Her husband, having heard the doleful tolling of the bells, had gone across the river to inquire who had passed away. The Gonzaleses were familiar with the tolling of the bells (el doblar de las campanas) and their significance.

By now doña Juanita's only son, José, had undertaken the unenviable assignment of informing people up and down the valley—from Santa Clara to Casa Salazar—of his mother's death. He was the bearer of un-pleasant news, informing relatives, friends, and fellow villagers that one of their own had left this earth and that her departed soul was now in the loving hands of her Tatita Dios.

Since a priest was not in residence, extreme unction or the last rites were usually not bestowed upon the person's deathbed. One of the first people summoned to view and bless the body of the deceased was a local member of the Penitente Brotherhood, whose members served as spiritual leaders in the community.

Following a blessing of the departed and a short prayer, it was customary for a relative to place a mirror under the dead person's nostrils to check for any signs of life and to confirm that the person indeed had expired. Another family member would then rest a cold flatiron on the departed's abdomen to prevent swelling before rigor mortis set in.

I learned the forgoing post obitum tidbits from my own mother and grandmothers, especially after my aunt Cristina on my father's side died and was buried at the Santa Barbara Cemetery in Martíneztown when I was about four years old. That was the first death I experienced and the first funeral I ever attended as a child.

The second death in my family that I recollect plainly to this day was that of my maternal great-grandmother in Bernalillo. I would spend summers with her and my grandma Cinda. I knew her well. I was about five, no more than six, years old when she passed away. She was buried at the local cemetery in Bernalillo. Her name, coincidentally, was also Juanita, just like doña Juanita in my placita. I called my great-grandma, who was totally blind, Mamá Juanita. (My great-grandfather on my father's side, whose name was also Juan, was blind as well.)

As soon as I said good-bye to the Gonzaleses, I spurred Prieto and galloped all the way home. Halfway there, as I rounded the bend near El Coruco, the thought of rattling chains and witches associated with this enchanted place flashed across my mind. Just the idea was chilling enough to raise my hair on end, even though it was daytime, when supposedly only errant sorcerers might be encountered—a prospect that was highly unlikely. The dark nights are what spelled doom and gloom for us kids. By the time I passed the butte next to my grandpa's corral and got home, the white lather oozed from Prieto's ebony neck, which glistened from the hot midday sun.

I dismounted, threw the reins on the ground, and darted inside the kitchen, where Mom was ironing the last batch of clothing from Monday's wash day. "And to what do I owe this remolino, whirlwind?" Mom uttered in a calm sort of way.

"Amá, amá." I spewed the words out, almost out of breath. "Doña Juanita has died! She died this morning," I added as I halfway caught my breath. "There will be a velorio this evening after dark."

"Calm down, calm down, hijito. Doña Juanita was quite old, and people have to die. We are all going to die one of these days. We can't live forever," she said, as if to teach me a lesson about life and death. Her words left me pondering for a split second what they really meant. I then dashed outside to go tell my grandparents, Aunt Taida, and Uncle Antonio.

Like doña Juanita's son, I, too, had become a messenger, but I wasn't the only one. One person told a neighbor, the neighbor told a friend, and so forth. By the end of the day a corps of individuals had notified people in the outlying areas of the death in my placita. The oral means of notification, which had the so-called domino effect, was expeditious.

Given that it was at the height of summer and embalming was unheard of in rural communities like mine, interment of doña Juanita had to take place within twenty-four hours. For that reason, her body could only lie in state that evening, and the burial would be the next morning.

Before long, dusk began to descend on Ojo del Padre and its environs. Soon the Valencia, Armijo, Griego, and Montaño families passed by our house in a parade of horse wagons to attend doña Juanita's wake. Mom and Dad, my four siblings, and I joined the line of wagons soon thereafter.

Before we crossed the Río Puerco, a few flickering lights were already visible in the distance. The kerosene lanterns and lamps reminded us that darkness was setting in. After we arrived we joined the throng of wagons by now present near the church and the oratory, not far from doña Juanita's house. Her small abode facing the Mesa Prieta was slightly north of the village and a stone's throw from the Río Puerco (see map 2, number 6).

My parents, siblings, and I walked over to the home of Sánchez family. We went in the living room (la sala de recibo), and the first thing I saw was doña Juanita on top of a small bed that looked like Grandpa's folding metal cot. She was dressed totally in a black—black dress, black stockings, and black shoes—with her hair combed straight back and tied in what appeared to be a chongo, or braid. She looked even more petite on the small cot than I recalled her to be. Two tall, glowing candles on a small wooden table at the head of the bed made her look even smaller.

A short column of people was waiting to pay their respects and to offer their *pésame*, condolences, to family members. We stood in the receiving line as well. As we waited our turn amid the somber laments and sobs of doña Juanita's relatives, I cast an eye at the old woman. I kept looking at the body. Out of the blue, a woman's voice boomed, "*¡Ay, hermanita!* My dear sister, why did you leave us here all alone? What will we do without you?" The cries and sighs that followed were chilling. The whole scene was creepy. Shivers ran up and down my spine. "Death," I thought to myself, "is dark like the witches' nights I had been told about and am somewhat familiar with." I knew that doña Juanita was not a witch, but her sister's pleas and wailing reminded me of La Llorona, the legendary Wailing Woman.

My parents shook hands with each member of the Sánchez family, offering at the same time their condolences ("*Sentimos muncho la muerte de doña Juanita*"). I followed right behind them. Mom and Dad then proceeded to where the body rested. They knelt and made the sign of the cross. Mom recited a short prayer before they stood up to view the body. All of these actions, I was to learn later as a young boy, constituted tidbits of our culture that people adhered to and practiced in small Hispanic communities like mine.

Apart from the occasional wailing of relatives and close friends, new arrivals (mostly women wearing tápalos, shawls) joined the other mourners who, after paying their respects, were sitting in silence around the room, staring at the floor, waiting until it was time to recite the rosary. The local villager reputed to be one of the best rezadores (prayer leaders) recited tonight's rosary.

Once the rosary was over, a profound silence set in, quiet enough to hear a pin drop, but suddenly as if out of nowhere a beautiful, poignant voice exploded and pierced my eardrums. As I looked toward doña Juanita's body lying in repose, the opaque face of a woman emerged from the semidarkness; she was wearing a black mantilla draped over her head and running down to her shoulders.

Of all people, it was Grandma Lale! I had heard her sing Christmas carols but never alabaos, hymns of praise. Such a ritual in honoring the deceased was traditional. I was awestruck by the razor-sharp quality of

Grandma's voice; it cut through the silence in the room like a sharp ax
slicing the frozen waters of the Río Puerco. As she sang, little by little her
voice became more and more subdued and somber. The alabao spoke volumes in terms of repentance for one's sins. Here are a few of Grandma
Lale's verses as I learned them from her booklet of alabaos shortly after
doña Juanita's death.

Alma pecadora	Sinful Soul
Alma pecadora,	Sinful soul,
mira adónde vas.	look where you're headed.
Vuelve atrás tus pasos,	Retrace your steps,
y no te perderás.	and you shall not get lost.
Llora lo pasado.	Atone the past.
Llora tu pasado,	Atone your past,
mira adónde vas.	look where you're headed.
Vuelve otra vez tus pasos,	Retrace your steps once again,
y no te perderás.	and you shall not get lost.
Llora lo pasado.	Atone the past.
Si mi Dios te llama	If God beckons you
al dulce reposo,	to His sweet rest,
confiesa cada pecado	confess each sin
y no seas descuidado.	with care and diligence.
Llora lo pasado.	Atone the past.
Llora tu pasado,	Atone your past,
mira adónde vas.	look where you're headed.
Vuelve atrás tus pasos,	Retrace your steps once again,
y no te perderás.	and you shall not get lost.

A few new arrivals made their presence known after the praying and
singing ended. They came from the outlying areas, including Casa Salazar,
several miles southeast of Ojo del Padre. Most of the people present, however, were from the local village or nearby enclaves. Most of them brought

all kinds of foods for people to eat after reciting the rosary and singing alabaos. It was customary—a cultural tradition—for residents to bring *charolas de comida*, pans full of different foods, pastelitos (fruit pies), bread, and tortillas to religious wakes.

I could see the kitchen not far from where we were seated. A group of women, three to four at least, were setting the table and inviting people to eat. *"Pasen, pasen a comer.* Come in, come in to eat," said one of the women.

Only the elderly men remained inside with the women and the young children. The rest of the men were outside, huddled around a bonfire, but the fire was more for show than anything else. The night was cool but hardly chilly. Gathering with their backs to the fire, listening to its crackling sound and sharing a joke or two, was traditional among the men. This was particularly true if the deceased was a male and a friend to boot. Recalling the good times and accentuating the positive were more important than recounting the person's misdeeds or shortcomings. It was a time to forgive and forget.

One by one the men filed into the kitchen to eat. Their boisterous nature suddenly broke the silence in the living room. It was time to celebrate the life of doña Juanita. And what better way than by consuming the potluck dishes the neighbors had prepared for guests of the Sánchez family! By the time friends, relatives, neighbors, and children finished eating, it was well into the night and time to head home for a good rest before returning the next day for the interment. Most of the people from far away stayed with friends or acquaintances in the village. Others, like us, who lived a short distance from the placita returned home.

In the meantime, the village carpenter had scrounged up enough pine lumber to build the coffin. Once it was ready, a group of local women, more than likely intimate friends of doña Juanita, covered the entire coffin with white muslin. Black crosses were cut from a coarse material and sewn onto the muslin on both sides of the coffin. The wooden lid also had a cross on it.

The day of doña Juanita's death, three or four men had visited the local cemetery, which was located on a hillside about a quarter of a mile west of the village, with the Mesa Prieta in full view to the east. Once they chose the burial site, with the blessings of the family, of course, they prepared to

Hand-crafted headstone, Ojo del Padre (Guadalupe) Cemetery, date unknown.
Photo taken in 2004.

dig the grave. To do so they took with them a pickax, a shovel, and a bucket
with a short rope attached to it. After they dug the grave, they covered the
burial site with a heavy canvas. They put rocks around the edges of the
canvas to protect the grave in case it rained overnight.

On the morning of the funeral, the body was placed in the open coffin
and taken to the church for mourners to view for the last time. Members of
the Penitente Brotherhood then recited a few prayers—only the priest could
celebrate Mass—before the funeral procession proceeded to the cemetery.
A cadre of pallbearers, three on each side, with two backups if needed, carried the coffin on their shoulders, making intermittent stops along the way.
Called descansos, these were resting places that allowed the pallbearers in
particular to rest and women to say a short prayer. Following each rest, the
men lifted the coffin onto to their shoulders and walked another short distance before coming to a descanso once again. The Penitentes, followed by
family members and the other the mourners, walked behind the men with
the coffin until the cortege reached the cemetery.

Once they reached the grave site, the coffin was placed next to the grave, and the Penitentes uttered a short prayer and blessed the departed person. Several men then looped a couple of ropes underneath the coffin, one toward the head and another at the foot, before slowly lowering it into the grave. Without exception, one at a time every adult, including my parents, walked up with a fistful (*un puño*) of dirt and tossed it into the grave, uttering the words, "*Que en paz descanse*. May she rest in peace."

I asked Mom as we walked back to the placita why people tossed dirt on top of the coffin. "Look, hijito. It's because we are taught that 'we are dirt, and to dirt we shall return.'"

"Do you mean that when I die I will turn to dirt?"

"Yes, that's right."

"And does that also mean that if it rains and water gets into the grave I will turn to mud?"

"That's enough questions for now. Let's go pay our last respects to the Sánchez family." So we stopped by their house along with other people before going home.

As per tradition, a yearlong mourning period for the family members began immediately. In the interim, periodic visits to the cemetery by the family, coupled with their praying at the church, signaled that the deceased was still on their minds and not forgotten. A year later a special Mass was celebrated in honor of the deceased.

A longer period of mourning was not unusual if the person who died happened to be a husband married to a young wife who had no aspirations of remarrying. Black clothing became part of her attire, in some cases for the rest of her life.

Whether one's journey on this earth is destined to be long or short is something we as Homo sapiens cannot determine. Fate is in the hands of Providence. We have no control over the number of years we are to enjoy from birth until that fateful day when the lights of life are shut off forever.

30

Hoe, Heaven, and Hell

NO HAND FARM TOOL among rural farmers in the Río Puerco Valley was more important and symbolic of their hard work for survival and the kinship they fostered with the land than the hoe. In colonial times this outwardly self-effacing implement was called an *azada*, lighter than the *azadón*, another hoe that enjoyed a certain popularity during that era.

During my childhood, we called the hoe a "cavador," literally, a "male digger." It was utilized for digging furrows through which to direct irrigation water to the planted fields from the acequia, the ditch system that was in place before the 1940s. What's more, the hoe was used to remove debris from arroyos and thus ensure that water ran freely following a rainfall, since arroyos—in addition to man-made dams—provided water for the ditches.

My father and other farmers also used the hoe for several other farm duties. Among these were breaking up and cultivating the dirt, piling it around plants (e.g., corn), and weeding. In addition, the cavador was used in small garden plots adjacent to the houses, where the husband or wife planted vegetables and herbs, like mint, that did not find their way into the big fields.

Away from the planted fields, the hoe was a handy and reliable agricultural implement. Once a year, when people mud plastered their homes or the local church, the hoe undoubtedly was the most ubiquitous tool. It certainly qualified as the most versatile implement in the farmer's repertoire of agricultural tools, outdoing the shovel, pitchfork, and pickax. The hoe of course was helpful in mixing mud for making adobes.

The inimitable hoe was forever inseparable from the farmer. With a file in his hip pocket, ready to sharpen the blade whenever it turned dull, he carried the hoe on his shoulder, prepared even to fend off a coiling rattlesnake that dared to hiss or strike at him on a hot summer day. I was taught that rattlers, like other reptiles or wild animals, were critical to our ecosystem and therefore should be treated, not as foes, but as friends—unless they posed a danger to your safety. Grandpa Lolo in particular was a firm believer in respecting God's creatures and not deliberately doing them harm.

In my family, both immediate and extended, the hoe symbolized success and survival on the ranch. But more importantly, the hoe in the planted fields helped bring us our daily bread—*"el pan de cada día,"* as proclaimed by my mother. The hoe created heaven in the arid desert.

We did not live in splendor; far from it. Nonetheless, although it may sound like a cliché, my parents never once failed to put food on the table. Our contact with nature and practice of living off the land were the crowning glory of our existence. And through it all, the hoe, like a good neighbor, stood tall and loyal. If only this unobtrusive friend of the farmer could have uttered a few words, I dare say they would have been poetic. It was hardly a prosaic implement.

The following bilingual poem, which I wrote a few years ago, perhaps captures the spirit of what the hoe meant to me as a small boy.*

El Cavador	The Hoe
Todo sembrador	Every sower
reclama su buen cavador.	boasts his good hoe.
Lo carga	He carries it
al hombro izquierdo	on his left shoulder
o al hombro derecho	or on his right one
con gran provecho.	with great aplomb.
Con su cavador	With his hoe
escarda,	he hoes,

---

*   From *Tiempos Lejanos: Poetic Images from the Past.*

escarba,	he digs
riega	he irrigates
y hace zoquete.[*]	and he mixes mud.
Con su cavador	With his hoe
defiende su querencia	he defends his homing instinct
y honor.	and his honor.
Con su cavador	With his hoe
le mocha la cabeza	he chops off
a las víboras	the heads of snakes
que se arrastran	that slither
por la tierra	on the ground
o que andan	or walk
de pie.	on foot.

But the day would come when the hoe no longer served its purpose, and it wasn't because it was being replaced by modern machinery. On the contrary, Mother Nature had a hand in its demise as well as in our future. Droughts, according to Grandpa Lolo, a sagacious old-timer who knew the Río Puerco Valley like no other farmer, loomed ominously on the horizon. He also based his dire prediction on a wealth of information, dating back decades, he had stored away in his head. He had gleaned the data from the Spanish editions of *The Old Farmer's Almanac*, a publication he read and followed religiously year in and year out, above all during the planting season. His reading comprehension in Spanish was rudimentary at best, as nearly as I could tell (he had taught himself to read), but he assimilated what he read and took the information to heart.

By all accounts, and from what I remember of conversations at the dinner table, his pessimism regarding the imminent lack of rain began to take form in the 1930s, when the makeshift dam on the upper Río Puerco a few miles north of our village, which supplied water to the ditch system for valley inhabitants, gave way during a torrential downpour. This episode

....
[*]   Nahuatl term meaning mud.

marked the end of local ranchers and farmers utilizing an elaborate irrigation system that had been in place for decades, plus—ironically—it signaled
the beginning of sustained perennial droughts that left the irrigating system high and dry and farmers praying for rain. Sole reliance on dry farming (de temporal) eventually was to discourage and doom every rancher
and farmer in the Río Puerco Valley.

As the benevolent skies quit crackling with thunder and rain became
more and more scarce, the frazzled crops teetered between growing and
wilting. My grandparents even paraded the Holy Child of Atocha and my
grandmother's Nuestro Señor de Esquipula through the scorched fields,
begging for rain. But as the old folk saying goes, "When God turns a deaf
ear even the santos, religious images, are helpless." And so it was with
farmers here and there who sooner or later were unable to eke out a respectable living by tilling the soil and living off the fragile land they had
come to love.

I recall those dreadful and unforgiving days as though they were yesterday. Even the hoe in our capable hands seemed reluctant to weed the
pitiful-looking plants. The weeds hugging the plants seemed to squeeze
out what little life they had left in them. Only the repulsive gray and
brown worms gnawing at the delicate plant roots thrived beneath the dry
brown soil.

By the beginning of the 1940s, with more children around the breakfast
table to feed and Dad's manual labor job with the government in jeopardy,
he and Mom, like countless Río Puercoans, began to take stock of their
tenuous existence. Because they were at the mercy of dry farming, with the
people having no desire to rebuild the dam (the government refused to
lend a helping hand) and the heavens ostensibly dried up, living off the
land became a veritable hell. The heat waves coming from the once-verdant
cornfields seemed to be bidding us good-bye. Even the once benevolent
Mother Nature appeared to issue her own ominous admonishments: "It's
time to leave. Get out while you can. I can help you no longer."

And leave we did, in Dad's old clunker of a car. We packed our meager
possessions in the late summer of 1945 and left for a place unfamiliar to us
called Martíneztown in Albuquerque. There my father, uneducated and
without any technical skills to speak of, would try to find work to feed a

family of seven, with three more siblings to come later. Our future looked as much in doubt and as bleak as the parched and waterless fields we left behind in my much-loved Río Puerco Valley.

But Mom, my beloved and incomparable Muse, who was always an inspiration to the whole family, stood ready to face the unknown challenges that faced us. Her reassuring voice calmed the waters of despair and anxiety. My father was no less optimistic, albeit more reserved in his pronouncements. He invoked his favorite dicho, folk saying: "*No hay mal que por bien no venga*. Every cloud has a silver lining." He never once thought of the dicho as negative.

Both Mom and Dad epitomized hope. What more could my siblings and I ask for under the circumstances? Whether my parents' confidence panned out or not, only time would tell. For the moment, our future hung very much in the balance. It was a scary feeling. That in essence added to the real hell facing us in a new and unfamiliar environment, far removed from my childhood deeply rooted in Ojo del Padre. Our lives were surely destined to change, for better or for worse.

31

One Final Glimpse

FROM TIME TO TIME I return to my childhood home and my village of Ojo del Padre in the Río Puerco Valley. Today my placita is a ghost town. Once I'm there, the life of yesteryear comes alive. I see, I listen, and I hear, but it is my sixth sense of deep feeling that provides me with the sounds that once were audible but are no longer. I hear the wise voices of our elders, children playing, horses whinnying, cows lowing, sheep bleating, coyotes howling at the moon, rattlesnakes hissing, birds singing their sweet music, plus the noisy cicadas' melodic sounds. The inimitable rushing waters of the Río Puerco provide the overall background to the forgoing sonata.

On a breezy day I can even hear the melodies of tree leaves playing their wind-surfing tunes down at the riverbed. The colorful hills, arroyos, mesas, and ravines play their own music in silence, while the volcanic peaks stand tall as ever as if to remind me of their majestic presence, imposing beauty, and eruptions eons ago. All that is gone now, and I can't help but wonder about and ponder their silence. Destiny, a mystery in and of itself, has a mind of its own.

Nostalgia could set in, because we as Homo sapiens are susceptible to melancholia, but my sixth sense of sensibility keeps it in check. My childhood is replete with joyful memories too precious to be overshadowed by sadness; there is much to rekindle and bring back to life. To ignore that period of my being would be like putting it under lock and key and therefore suggest that my early days in my beloved Río Puerco Valley were humdrum and lackluster. In essence, to entertain such a notion is to declare cultural bankruptcy, which I refuse to do.

335

There are those who claim that you can't relive your past. I beg to differ.
One can reexperience the happier times of yore—*melioribus annis*, as
Virgil would say—if glee, love, and laughter formed part of your everyday
life. Absence of these attributes implies a bogus past lost in a sea of insig-
nificant, inane, and unhappy times.

Happiness is what engenders goodwill, and goodwill in turn leads to a
healthy outlook on life. That is what I recollect about my early, innocent
years in the Río Puerco Valley. That is what I continue to relish to this day.
Perhaps it is nothing profound, intellectual, or even philosophical, but to
me it is something real, robust, and an inner part of my persona.

Maybe those are the reasons I still visit my old village and what little
remains of my crumbling casita. For me it is of utmost importance to remember a joyful time gone by and to express a quiet appreciation for my
parents' affection and good counsel, above all my mother's, whose kindness to this day shines like the morning star. She was always ready to welcome a new dawn (*el alba*), another tomorrow, and the day after, until that
fateful day came, while she was still a young mother, when she failed to see
the sunrise over the eastern horizon one more time.

When I was a kid I had no conception of time. It was not only elusive
but indefinable as well. Only three things seemed to matter: eating, playing, and sleeping. Anything and everything else in between was fluid;
whatever happened came and went, leaving me with no sense of substance
or concern.

Time is never retrievable. Once past, it's gone forever, like a puff of
smoke into the heavens. But what can be recovered for posterity are one's
remembrances of yesteryear. Every tidbit of information can be likened to
tiny grains of salt that add flavor to one's favorite foods, such as posole at
Christmastime.

A while back I visited my valley. As happens always, the sounds of nature
came back to entertain me, to soothe my soul, and to make my heart happy.
Remembered voices resonated as joyful memories enveloped me, slowly filling the pores of my being. I felt at ease. I sensed an epiphany.

As I departed and reached the top of El Aguaje, which I had traversed
hundreds of times as a small boy, I paused, looked back, and cast a fleeting
glance at my forlorn little adobe house beyond La Cañada del Camino,

Los Cerros Cuates (Twin Peaks).
A painting of the peaks is featured on the 2012 New Mexico Centennial Stamp,
issued by the U.S. Postal Service. The author grew up one-half mile from the peaks.
Photo taken in 2014.

once populated with prairie dogs. As I glanced down at the scorched earth, in the stillness of the moment I reflected and wondered if this glimpse at my casita would be my last. I dared to ask my Tatita Dios, for only He knows. After all, what did I have to lose? Suddenly, He whispered in my ear, "It's a secret I cannot divulge."

The day will come, for we are all mortals, when I cast—and catch—one final glimpse of my beloved valley, thus closing the final chapter to my childhood in the countryside.

Bibliography

Books Authored or Edited by Nasario García
Related to the Río Puerco Valley

Abuelitos: Stories of the Río Puerco Valley. Albuquerque: University of New Mexico Press (in cooperation with the Historical Society of New Mexico), 1992.

Bernalillo: Yesterday's Sunshine—Today's Shadows. Albuquerque, NM: Rio Grande Books, 2014.

Bolitas de Oro: Poems of My Marble-Playing Days. Albuquerque: University of New Mexico Press, 2010.

Brujerías: Stories of Witchcraft and the Supernatural in the American Southwest and Beyond. Lubbock: Texas Tech University Press, 2007.

Chistes: Hispanic Humor of Northern New Mexico and Southern Colorado. Santa Fe: Museum of New Mexico Press, 2004.

Comadres: Hispanic Women of the Río Puerco Valley. Albuquerque: University of New Mexico Press, 1997.

Fe y tragedias: Faith and Tragedies in Hispanic Villages of New Mexico. Albuquerque, NM: Rio Grande Books, 2010.

Grandma Lale's Tamales: A Christmas Story / Los tamales de Abuelita Lale: Un cuento navideño. Albuquerque, NM: Rio Grande Books, 2014.

Grandma's Santo on Its Head: Stories of Days Gone By in Hispanic Villages of New Mexico / El santo patas arriba de mi abuelita: Cuentos de días gloriosos en pueblitos hispanos de Nuevo México. Albuquerque: University of New Mexico Press, 2013.

Grandpa Lolo and Trampa: A Story of Surprise and Mystery / Abuelito Lolo y Trampa: Un cuento de sorpresa y misterio. Albuquerque, NM: Rio Grande Books, 2014.

Grandpa Lolo's Navajo Saddle Blanket: La tilma de abuelito Lolo. Albuquerque: University of New Mexico Press, 2012.

Más antes: Hispanic Folklore of the Río Puerco Valley. Santa Fe: Museum of New Mexico Press, 1997.

Rattling Chains and Other Stories for Children / Ruido de cadenas y otros cuentos para niños. Houston, TX: Arte Público Press, 2009.

Recuerdos de los Viejitos: Tales of the Río Puerco. Albuquerque: University of New Mexico Press (in cooperation with the Historical Society of New Mexico), 1987.

Tata: A Voice from the Río Puerco. Albuquerque: University of New Mexico Press (in cooperation with the Historical Society of New Mexico), 1994.

The Naked Rainbow and Other Stories / El arco iris desnudo y otros cuentos. Albuquerque: University of New Mexico Press, 2009.

The Talking Lizard: New Mexico's Magic and Mystery. Albuquerque, NM: Rio Grande Books, 2014.

Tiempos Lejanos: Poetic Images from the Past. Albuquerque: University of New Mexico Press, 2004.